# The Principles of Multimedia Journalism

In this much-needed examination of the principles of multimedia journalism, experienced journalists Richard Koci Hernandez and Jeremy Rue systemize the characteristics of the new, often experimental storyforms that appear on today's digital news platforms. By identifying a classification of digital news packages and introducing a new vocabulary for how content is packaged and presented, the authors give students and professionals alike a way to talk about and understand the importance of story design in an era of convergence storytelling.

Online, all forms of media are on the table: audio, video, images, graphics, and text are available to journalists at any type of media company as components with which to tell a story. This book provides insider instruction on how to package and interweave the different media forms together into an effective narrative structure. Featuring interviews with some of the most exceptional storytellers and innovators of our time, including Web and interactive producers at *The New York Times*, NPR, the Marshall Project, the *Guardian*, National Film Board of Canada, and The Verge, this exciting and timely new book analyzes examples of innovative stories that leverage technology in unexpected ways to create entirely new experiences online that both engage and inform.

**Richard Koci Hernandez** is an Assistant Professor of New Media at the University of California at Berkeley Graduate School of Journalism and a National Emmy Award–winning multimedia producer. His work for the *Mercury News* earned him two Pulitzer Prize nominations. In 2003, he was the recipient of the James K. Batten Knight Ridder Excellence Award.

**Jeremy Rue** is a Lecturer of New Media at the University of California at Berkeley Graduate School of Journalism. He was formerly a multimedia instructor for the Knight Digital Media Center at UC Berkeley, where he taught new media storytelling workshops. He is a former print reporter, photojournalist, and Web developer. In 2007, he was the recipient of the Dorothea Lange Fellowship for his photo documentary work on migrant farmworkers in California's Central Valley.

# The Principles of Multimedia Journalism

## Packaging Digital News

Richard Koci Hernandez and
Jeremy Rue

R Routledge
Taylor & Francis Group

NEW YORK AND LONDON

First published 2016
by Routledge
711 Third Avenue, New York, NY 10017

and by Routledge
2 Park Square, Milton Park, Abingdon, Oxon OX14 4RN

*Routledge is an imprint of the Taylor & Francis Group, an informa business*

*Library of Congress Cataloging-in-Publication Data*
The principles of multimedia journalism : packaging digital news /
    Richard Koci Hernandez and Jeremy Rue.
        pages cm
    Includes bibliographical references and index.
  1. Journalism.   2. Online journalism.   3. Interactive multimedia.   4. Journalism—Case
studies.   5. Online journalism—Case studies.   6. Interactive multimedia—Case
Studies.   I. Rue, Jeremy, editor.   II. Title.
    PN4775.H368 2015
    070.4—dc23
    2015004457

ISBN: 978-0-415-73815-6 (hbk)
ISBN: 978-0-415-73816-3 (pbk)
ISBN: 978-1-315-81756-9 (ebk)

Typeset in Warnock Pro
by Apex CoVantage, LLC


Printed and bound in the United States of America by Publishers Graphics, LLC on sustainably sourced paper.

For Grabs

And to our wives, Christina and Denise, and to our daughters,
Sophia and Ellie

# Contents

# Figures

# Preface

This book is a great journey. It guides readers in a world of contemporary multimedia storytelling, letting them dive into its history and evolution and explore the diversity of its forms. It also winks at the future—at all the possibilities still unfolding. It invites students in journalism schools as well as journalists in newsrooms to play a role in understanding the nature of digital news.

I've been lucky to follow Hernandez and Rue closely while they were embarking on this journey. We identified a whole new world, naming digital "creatures" encountered during our explorations. Chapter after chapter, through numerous case studies, interviews, insightful analysis of platforms, devices, and user experience—this book gives the reader the knowledge and the tools necessary to understand the present (and to get a glimpse at the future) of multimedia storytelling and its defining of in-depth news digital packages.

Digital packages, or multimedia packages, are these new entities in news that have lately been described by some as "Snowfallen" stories for their ostentatious use of technology; but they are also much more. They allow journalists to tell a story using the tools that fit it the best. They tell a story in a more complete way or, even better, in many different ways. They tell a story that is read, watched, and heard all at once, and as such they can become more deeply affecting.

When I first came to UC Berkeley as visiting scholar of the Graduate School of Journalism, I had been a science writer for both online and printed magazines for nearly eight years. I'm a biology major and my experience with multimedia was limited to creating photo slideshows (not with my own pics, of course), embedding photos or videos in online stories, or using Word-Press to edit articles.

Honestly, I don't remember if I had known anything about the *New York Times*'s "Snow Fall" story before arriving here. If I did, I must have completely forgotten about it, because I can clearly recall, instead, rushing to Google to figure out what was this amazing project everybody was talking about. When I heard the term "digital news packages" I didn't actually know what they were. It was during my first week at the university in the fall of 2013, the aforementioned "Snow Fall" was a year old, and Paul Grabowicz, a senior lecturer and director of the New Media Program, gave students a lecture they wouldn't forget: He showed them how different media fit different stories and fulfilled certain purposes and platforms better than others. It might sound obvious and naive, but this exercise helps journalists to answer the most important question asked today in every newsroom around the world: "How do we want to tell this story?"

In another class four months after that experience, I learned how to design news packages myself, how to put together a team to make one, and how to actually write enough code to construct one from the ground up. At the end of that class I was in love with this form of storytelling. I looked forward to learning more about how they are made and why they are made.

So when Richard and Jeremy asked me to help them with the book, I didn't hesitate. It was the best thing I could have ever done. Because of that decision I had the chance to interview and listen to interviews of the best in the field, to explore the scope of good practices, and to learn about weak and strong points of these subjects.

From the beginning of my work on this book, I focused in particular on developing a "taxonomy" of news packages. My interest began with the word "taxonomy" itself. I have an Italian degree in biology (the equivalent of a BA plus one year of master's work) and I've been a science journalist for several years. So I was very attracted by the idea of exploring how this biological concept could be adapted to such a different field.

The starting point of my research was once again Paul Grabowicz. He, in fact, had already been working on developing a classification of multimedia packages. I had studied his work during our spring class and used it to look at different kinds of packages and elements. The more I studied it the less I could find my way through this jungle of projects I was entering. The projects were extremely diverse. Grabowicz's taxonomy—focusing on both the narrative structure and the individual media elements driving each package—didn't help me to univocally sort them. Some projects could be grouped into more than one category and some defied classification. It could be due to the fast-paced evolution and nature of experimentation used inside newsrooms all over the world. Everything that was being created was rapidly being challenged and changed, and even projects that weren't considered a news package were now being studied in this new light.

In order to better understand these fascinating forms of storytelling, I had to develop a brand-new classification and taxonomy. I began with the only one I knew, the Linnaean one. It didn't take me long to realize I couldn't apply a biological concept based on evolution and genetics and other natural forces to something as artificial as news packages. It forced me, though, to follow a certain *modus operandi.* I first built up a large database of packages, which as of writing this book counts around 1,000 entries. Once I had my "samples," I then deconstructed them by their main elements and structures, and we eventually developed a triangle model, which is described in the third chapter of this book.

In this process I had the chance to go through and analyze hundreds of projects. This gave me an opportunity to define which structures—not just the elements—work better to reach specific goals. I've learned, for example, that a linear narrative is the best choice when you want to tell a story from beginning to end, even if you want to integrate it with non-textual elements that take some weight off of the narrative. A topic-page-like display helps the user to easily navigate through and enjoy huge amounts of information. And a cinematic project with video and audio elements makes the audience feel like they are "experiencing" a story. I also began investigating the impact on the user and trying to find what works best on different platforms/devices. The results of these two aspects, though, are ever-changing because of the rapid evolution of users' consumption modes and habits.

In the past two years I've also witnessed how news packages are becoming more common inside both classrooms and newsrooms. This is why I think this book can be really useful in both environments. The body of knowledge that Hernandez and Rue have put together is an invaluable starting point for new but well-grounded experiments. This book gives journalists and media professionals background information (how we came to be where we are now), guidelines (where do I begin building multimedia packages?), and insights (why should I do one thing instead of something else?).

I think this text and the classification in it can spark fruitful discussions about good practices, story impact, and better measurements of success.

Personally, I also can't wait for this taxonomy to be challenged, both in theory and with packages that don't fit in any of our categories. I think, in fact, that the digital journalism panorama will change again as it has changed during the past decades. It is continuously evolving. Society, knowledge, and, consequentially, technology evolve too, creating new tools and forms. This means consumer habits will change as well.

I have to say that because of this book and everything I've learned during my time at UC Berkeley, I feel that what is facing us now and what is coming next are very exciting! I'm prepared to face it. And I think that those who read this book and embrace its journey will feel the same way.

Caterina Visco
UC Berkeley Graduate School of Journalism,
Visiting Scholar and Researcher
Berkeley, CA, January 2015

# Acknowledgments

We would like to express our sincere gratitude to everybody who saw us through the creation of this book, allowed us to quote their remarks, and offered their precious time for interviews: Kainaz Amaria, Mike Bostock, Brian Boyer, Carrie Ching, Jarrard Cole, Gabriel Dance, Loc Dao, Scott DeMuesy, Andrew DeVigal, Steve Duenes, Nicholas Dynan, Matthew Ericson, Leah Gentry, Seth Gitner, Aly Hurt, Emily Juden, Paul Grabowicz, Wesley Grubbs, Jonathan Harris, Jesse Hicks, Simon Jacobs, Jonathan Jarvis, Nick Jones, Andrew Kueneman, Wes Lindamood, Eric Maierson, Geri Migielicz, Jacky Myint, Avni S. Nijhawan, Janet Northen, Francesca Panetta, Nora Paul, Sabrina Shankman, Brian Storm, Corey Takahashi, Joshua Topolsky, Joe Weiss, Erica C. Wetter, Adam Westbrook, Josh Williams, and our colleagues and students at the Graduate School of Journalism at the University of California, Berkeley. We are especially grateful to Caterina Visco, who provided support, talked things over, read, wrote, offered comments, and assisted us in meeting our deadline.

# 1

# Introduction to Digital News Packages

A new medium is never an addition to an old one, nor does it leave the old one in peace. It never ceases to oppress the older media until it finds new shapes and positions for them.[1]

When we set out to write this book a year ago, our ideas about digital news were different than they are today. Throughout the process of writing, we felt like we were chasing a train we would never catch. Every time we thought we unearthed some truth about digital storytelling, a new storyform would emerge, throwing our models into disarray. In some ways, this could be seen as a reflection of the tumultuous and rapidly changing pace journalism has endured for years, or that endured by any industry bound to technology for that matter.

What we do know is that the foundations of a good news story are eternal. All good stories are important and interesting. They have to engage audiences. But how a story is told can change depending on the device from which it's consumed. So, this led us to ask, what are the ingredients for telling a good news story? At its core, this book is about how stories are adapted for the Web, particularly how different media forms come together as a package. The device a person uses to consume news—whether it is a television, newspaper, laptop, smartphone, even a wristwatch or some other medium—affects the way a story is told. It molds the techniques used for telling that story: the words a writer chooses, the voice and tone, the presentation and design. To some extent, the device even affects the very types of stories told in that medium.

This book goes beyond traditional mediums like television, newspapers, and radio. Entirely new forms are emerging and creating new rules—new formulas—about how to design stories. Everything is on the table now. Most journalistic start-ups don't think in terms of a singular medium. They incorporate it all: text, videos, podcasts, data visualizations, interactive elements, participatory or social media, and other novel forms, all within the same rubric of news. The challenge in this type of journalism is how these respective media forms fit together within a single news presentation, or even within a single news organization. How do videos coincide with text, graphics, and photos in a cohesive manner? When do these elements stand alone in a digital medium, and when do they appear together?

Each media form of journalism dictates a different approach to storytelling. Shooting a video requires different ways of thinking than writing text. Not only do the mechanics differ, but so do the intentions of the media form. A still photograph, for example, is a moment frozen in time, contemplative and emotive. Its format not only differs from video—which is constantly in motion—but its ability for reflection affects people in a different manner. Both can be equally powerful in their own way; one isn't better than another. Rather, understanding the nature of each media form and the role it plays in affecting the audience begins a process of understanding the nature of digital communication itself.

What's more is that these media forms are evolving from their former counterparts. Photographs are no longer devices of preserving memory but forms of communication. (One only needs to look at Snapchat to see how images are used like words to communicate rather than only documenting events.) Data journalists, programmers, entrepreneurs, and technologists are bringing different media forms to the craft of journalism. They are helping to reimagine the very nature of journalistic purpose and the role of news to go beyond one-way publishing paradigms. The traditional mode of reporting was to research, report, then produce content. Technology of the Web allows stories to be iterative or dynamic, changing even after they've been published. Some forms allow for consumers of news to play an active role in defining the content, as occurred when the *New York Times* published an interactive graphic illustrating public sentiment on the election of President Barack Obama.[2] Visitors to the story page, published on the night of his 2008 election, were asked to submit words describing their mood. After thousands of responses, what resulted was an entirely crowdsourced color-coded visual word-graphic of public sentiment—Obama supporters describing their elation and John McCain supporters expressing concern. The more traditional method for a newspaper to include reaction from the public on such a story would have been to quote a variety of individuals in text. Technology allows journalists to break the traditional mold of a story and realize possibilities for innumerable ways to capture and convey news.

This decade, the Internet has taken over as the dominant form of news consumption in most journalistic media industries.[3] If the medium of the Web is to truly dictate the format of the story, we must begin to understand the *mode of consumption* of the digital devices. How are people consuming information on the Web? What devices are they using? What is their level of attention? NPR's guidebook *Sound Reporting: The NPR Guide to Audio Journalism and Production* describes how to write a script for a distracted listener who might be driving.[4] So how should content be designed for an equally distracted PC user when they have a dozen browser tabs open, e-mail or Facebook notification alerts vying for attention, and hyperlinks in stories that invite interruption from any cohesive narrative? What is even more disconcerting is the rate at which entire new platforms of news consumption are proliferating. Mobile devices are changing the way people consume content and vary considerably from a traditional computer device like a desktop or laptop. One Canadian news chain, Postmedia, describes mobile consumption as "snacking" on content throughout the day, while tablets are more akin to the leisurely magazine experience.[5]

As the Internet evolved and the proliferation of "digital first" content became the norm, new storyforms began to take shape. Blogging, a mode of expression often associated with opining amateurs, suddenly became a common form for covering topical news in many vertical niches. Publishing frequency tended to be more rapid and the length of copy, or "posts," was shorter, the tone much more conversational. Blogging seemed to be a precursor to many digital-native text publications like *Huffington Post*, Talking Points Memo, Vox, and Buzzfeed.

With a rapid accessibility to professional-grade recording technologies like video cameras and audio recorders—sometimes embedded directly in computers or phones—journalists of all disciplines began experimenting with mediums outside their expertise. Print news reporters were being given video cameras. Newspapers across the country launched podcasts. Multimedia journalism seemed to reach a fever pitch at the rise of the frenzied economic recession in 2008. Due to retrenchment, many news organizations scrambled for new ways of building readership and doing more with less. This made multimedia journalism an appealing endeavor. Now journalists of all ilk could take part in all mediums of journalism. Multimedia journalism was very much a "spaghetti-on-the-wall" approach—try everything to see what sticks. It was an experiment, and it also evoked negative reactions by some reporters who were being asked to gather content outside their medium of expertise. At journalism training workshops during this period at Berkeley's Knight Digital Media Center—an organization devoted to retooling mid-career reporters with multimedia principles—anecdotes abounded of newspaper editors requiring reporters to shoot video, even if the subject matter was mundane. It was an effort to capture a piece of the highly coveted TV advertising market. What was lost on many at the time was an understanding of how mediums like video differed from text. Some print-turned-video journalists had even chalked up online video as a nonstarter. Yet at the same time, YouTube was seeing jaw-dropping growth in the hundreds of millions of site visitors and sold to Google for $1.6 billion. Why did raw, unedited video appeal to people online? The unpolished genuineness, campy subject matter, and compact length made these clips instantly shareable—and more importantly, relatable. However, experiments in online video by news organizations, particularly newspapers, borrowed heavily from traditional broadcast conventions. Could that style work online? In computer jargon, the term "shovelware" is used to describe software ported over to different computer platforms or mediums with little consideration of adapting it to that medium. This term has been applied to news organizations during the early days of the Web to describe taking legacy content and "shoveling" it online.

Harvard business professor Clayton Christensen described a similar process as when businesses struggle to adapt to new technologies, calling it the "innovator's dilemma" in his seminal 1997 book of the same name.[6] In the face of disruptive technologies, large successful corporations often failed to adapt and lost market dominance. Christensen describes how companies view emerging technologies as not worth the investment during the nascent stages, until it was too late. Also, adapting to untested experiments too soon often resulted in companies competing with themselves. This might sound familiar to many in the news industry experiencing the tumultuous disruptions of the last decade. Christensen wrote this book in 1997 and the focus was not on the Internet or the publishing industry, yet its lessons seem eerily prescient. The innovator's dilemma transcends the economic implications Christensen describes—it's a descriptor for all forms of disruptive innovation.

Disruption relating to the state of the media is not new; it predates the Internet and digital platforms. It is well documented and understood by many institutions. This book is not intended to be a look back at the problems of early Web journalism, but rather a look forward to identifying what a news story of the future looks like. The journalism industry now has several years of collective experiments where we can derive some common understanding about online presentation. This book begins the process of classifying methods of online storytelling into a taxonomy of story types. We base these on case studies and interviews with authors, producers, and thinkers about innovations in storytelling.

The primary challenge we found with classifying the future of news is one of broadness. Given the paradigm-shifting nature of digital publishing, existential questions like "what is news?" become apparent. When one considers user-generated content, social media, or even emerging forms of journalism completely separate from the computer—sensor journalism, wearable devices like glasses or watches—it becomes onerous, if not impossible, to codify all of the many different ways news is changing.

We decided to narrow our focus in this book to looking at some ways *in-depth story packages* are evolving online. By in-depth, we mean the digital equivalent to what is commonly described as longform stories in journalism. (However, even "longform" is a misnomer because length is not always equivalent to depth and analysis in this case—in fact, longer stories are often antithetical to many types of digital consumption.) To better understand the type of stories tackled in this book, it might be easier to describe what this book doesn't cover: daily news or breaking news stories. Although there is intense interest in how the unit of a daily news article is evolving in the digital space, there are too many logistical factors that need to be considered, which don't always align with the best use of the medium. Some media forms like video are very time consuming and expensive to produce for news organizations that aren't native to it, like newspapers. Other times, innovation is hampered by the skillset of staffers within a news organization. Many of the experiments referred to in this book utilized specialists like programmers, photographers, designers, or visual journalists. In order to best appreciate what news can be, we attempt to look beyond logistical obstacles present in many newsrooms—not that they aren't important or don't have deep relevance to the evolving nature of news. We hope that by classifying examples of news that are done well—we think—it will be aspirational or minimally thought-provoking.

## ▶ PICKING THE RIGHT MEDIA FOR THE STORY

To fully understand multimedia storytelling, we must first look at the individual forms of journalism and follow a process of identifying their key characteristics, and more importantly each media form's strengths and weaknesses. Because journalism industries have been traditionally defined—and thus separated—by their medium, it's easy to fall into a trap of assuming one media form is generally better than another. Television, or video, has a power to tell certain types of stories more effectively than text, but the opposite is also true.

Understanding the strengths and weaknesses of each media form is an essential step (described more fully in chapter 9). During newsroom training workshops by the Knight Digital Media Center (KDMC) in 2008–2009, many newspaper reporters described how they were required to take video cameras on every story they went out on, regardless of whether the story lent itself to video. What resulted was lots of awful video of events like city council meetings, which few readers watched on the Web. Yet on occasion a video of compelling subject matter would unexpectedly be a hit and garner thousands—or even millions—of views. One such event occurred in 2011, when a photographer for the *Columbus Dispatch* shot a quick video of a then-homeless man named Ted Williams standing next to traffic demonstrating his radio announcer–like voice. Williams, later described as the "man with a golden voice," was catapulted to fame when the video went viral.[7] (Interestingly, it was an unauthorized re-poster of the video to YouTube that caused the video to go viral. The *Columbus Dispatch* attempted to remove it from YouTube.[8] After outcry, they later re-posted it under their own account.) The power of other mediums like photojournalism hark back to key events in history, such as the Vietnam War and the role it played to evoke emotion in the public and to aid in swaying public opinion on the growing crisis.

A single story can also be composed of multiple media forms on the Web. Part of this process is deconstructing a story into its parts and then evaluating how each segment should best be told. This sets up a foundation for packaging multimedia stories. This process also forces journalists to reconsider the very notion of what a story is and what it's trying to convey. More importantly, storytellers must think critically about each media form independently and discern why they might use one over another. It also places the story as the primary device that leads this decision, rather than a more arbitrary reason like tradition or availability of expertise. It precludes a journalist from simply defaulting to any single medium based on habit or expertise. "The story will tell you how it wants to be told" is an aphorism we often cite in the classes we teach. The Internet converges all tools for story creation and in some ways levels the playing field for media organizations.

## ▶ THE TAXONOMY OF AN ONLINE NEWS PACKAGE

At its core, this book is about organizing in-depth feature stories into a taxonomical classification. The term "news package" is still not very common in the Web industry. (Some broadcast news veterans use a similar "package" term to describe story segments.) Mindy McAdams, a journalism professor at the University of Florida, wrote the seminal 2005 book *Flash Journalism: How to Create Multimedia News Packages*, which was among the first to formalize news packages and the notions of unifying multimedia into cohesive story packages.[9] We felt the term "news package" better described the types of stories we wanted to classify than more generic terms like "interactives" or "features." These news packages—formerly called "spreads"[10] in newspaper parlance—are feature stories, which typically go more in-depth on a topic; think the Sunday edition of your local paper. They tend to consist of multiple different pieces of media in order to express multifaceted stories through an organized layout, such as a video paired with text, or an interactive graphic. In the days of news spreads, this was usually presented in a double-truck—two conjoined newspaper pages—with graphics, text, and photos. With the advent of the Web, suddenly journalists are awash with a multitude of new mediums and dimensions to organize and tell stories: video, photos, graphics, data charts, and others. Even technologies that break out of the confines of the screen, like location tracking or real-time interaction from the audience, may need to be considered when designing a story package. While length is not a prerequisite, most of the news packages described in this book tend to be more involved. Sometimes there is a narrative; other times it's simply giving a more comprehensive look at an issue or topic.

The impetus for classifying these stories into a taxonomy really began with Senior Lecturer Paul Grabowicz at the UC Berkeley Graduate School of Journalism (J-School), who began classifying multimedia examples into categories on a school-related training website in 2013.[11] Since the late 1990s, Grabowicz has taught multimedia classes at the Berkeley J-School, whose lessons included deconstructing story ideas, reporting them in multiple media forms, then building websites to showcase these stories. Later, in the 2000–2010 decade, Adobe Flash (back then Macromedia Flash) was used to package these presentations in a more cohesive manner.

During the time period of Flash's peak popularity, the news industry saw a surge of multimedia news packages, given the ease with which many digitally inclined journalists could learn Flash. Because of the way Flash worked, it had two significant effects on news: First it forced many journalists to consider the notion of combining multiple mediums like video, graphics, and photos into a single, often interactive, presentation. But Flash also had a secondary effect on story presentation. Because of its design, Flash stories were confined to a single frame or box-like area, which was then embedded on a webpage, as opposed to being a part of the web page itself. Flash is described as a "browser plug-in" run by a third-party company, meaning it's separate from native HTML content that comprises most of the text and pictures seen on the Web. This constraint resulted in most multimedia becoming an ancillary component to stories rather than the central body of a story. Regina McCombs, formerly of the Poynter Institute, described this as the Christmas tree effect (she attributes it to a colleague of hers when she worked at the *Minneapolis Star Tribune*), where multimedia would be hung off of a text story like ornaments on a tree.[12]

In 2007, Apple released its first iPhone, which did not run Flash. A few years later former CEO Steve Jobs outlined the problems with Flash, essentially declaring it a dead technology when it came to mobile.[13] While Flash was a great tool for multimedia, most Web consumers only recognized it in the form of distracting advertisements, which not only caused design annoyances when using the Web but also caused major usability issues as it was the root of many slowly loading web pages.

The lack of Flash on iPhones changed multimedia storytelling in very dramatic ways. It was a worrying time for developers and journalists who invested heavily in learning the technology. But as Flash was being phased out on the Web, advancements in other technologies like HTML5 and JavaScript were quickly taking its place. As multimedia journalists, producers, and other newsroom technologists transitioned to HTML5, multimedia elements began to take center stage in stories, often being embedded directly in the content of a story or in some cases becoming the central component of the story itself.[14] Many news organizations have seen an influx of multimedia presentations since then. Data visualization—and its sibling data journalism—saw a resurgence in form of interactive charts, graphs, and other novel displays of quantitative information. Organizations supporting data journalism, like the National Institute for Computer-Assisted Reporting (NICAR), founded in 1989, are experiencing record attendance at recent conferences.[15] Other new presentation forms emerged, like using scrolling on a web page as a mechanism of advancing a story narrative. Design conventions like parallax, background videos, curtain effects, and autoplaying sounds or videos also gave rise to entirely new immersive presentations on the Web that are akin to a cinematic movie experience.

We worked with Grabowicz to begin the intricate task of classifying some of these new Web presentations into various archetypes, generically described as a taxonomy. It was a tricky process, as we often found examples of story packages that didn't subscribe to any single classification. In the process of drafting this book, we crossed paths with a visiting scholar at the Berkeley J-School, a science writer and biology major from Rome named Caterina Visco. Visco was intrigued by this notion of a "taxonomy" of news stories, particularly as it related to her background in biology. A true biological taxonomical classification follows a detailed process of first identifying shared characteristics of stories and grouping them by rank, rather than starting with the end categorization. In working with Visco, we first began by analyzing an exhaustive database of online news packages put together by *Matter*,[16] along with other databases we collected in our research, and checking off key characteristics of each story. We identified which stories had maps, which had video or audio, which presented a linear narrative versus multiple sections that allowed a user to jump around the story out of order. Visco tagged each entry, and what ultimately emerged was a triangle diagram, which generally describes three primary characteristics that can encompass all online news packages.

At the top of the triangle is the Continuous category, which describes news packages that are the most straightforward, traditional forms of news presentation. Examples could include a text story with some photos or videos, or conversely a longer video piece with a few complementary elements, like text or photos, or a long video piece separated into chapters. Continuous stories characteristically have one central medium driving the story and a few ancillary components. Often the central story is narrative rather than strictly informational, and the package takes a more linear path to presenting the subject matter.

On the left corner is the Comprehensive category. News packages in this category are structured with multiple elements—videos, photos, or text stories—typically organized in sections. These tend to be story packages that cover a topic and tend to be more informational, covering multiple facets of a story rather than following a linear narrative path. In most cases, a user can consume the information in any order, choosing to view different parts of the story at different times, although most of these news packages organize content minimally in some type of order of preference. These stories range from exhaustively in-depth stories on a topic, for example a news package on climate change, or more simply two or three related pieces of journalism packaged together but not intended to be consumed with as much continuity.

On the right corner is the Immersive category. These stories typically create a more cinematic immersive experience. They place users in an environment where they can explore—sometimes along a predefined path, other times on their own. Sometimes these stories use multiple mediums that are more intertwined and not as separate as seen in the Comprehensive category. These are often interactive games or presentations, which take up the full screen and break out of the standard template of a news website. Some are often described as interactive documentaries because of the nature of the story topics and the presentation style.

We conceived this diagram to also allow for stories to be placed inside the triangle. This allows for a granular approach to quantifying how much of each category influences a particular news package. In some iterations, our triangle resembled a Venn diagram, where a news package could be seen placed among intersections and comprising two or more elements.

The triangle diagram solves several problems we encountered in creating a multimedia taxonomy: The first was having a way to place stories on a grid where they can express multiple characteristics at varying degrees. But it also allows us to create boundaries for stories. In the case of a Continuous-Immersive, the Continuous part of the experience would probably follow along a more linear path using a central medium as the vehicle through the story. One example could be a choose-your-own-adventure style of interactive documentary, where the user is immersed in an environment but adheres to a mostly structured path.

Later in the book, we delve a little deeper into the triangle diagram, which is simply another step in the classification process of story elements. The triangle diagram alone is not designed as a tool to be used for picking how to tell a story. Rather, it is designed to better understand existing presentations and where they might align quantitatively. One can glean the different stories, which are placed at different areas of the triangle, and better understand the characteristics that lend themselves to different presentational styles. Which stories most often appear as Continuous, Immersive, or Comprehensives, and when do the intersections make most sense? What is the intent of the story: to inform, evoke an emotional reaction, or incite policy change in the public interest? If differing storytelling styles can elicit different reactions from viewers, it is important to understand which styles of presentation work best for achieving a story's intended purpose. The process we are presenting in this book is a fairly analytical approach to a subjective matter. Nearly all of the stories we use as examples and case studies didn't go through this level of systematic scrutiny. Most were designed and built on experience and intuition, which can mean a lot for veteran designers. However, it helps to begin to codify this process in a more systematic way, and thus to really understand approaches to storytelling on the Web. It is meant to be not restrictive but a basis for inspiration.

## ▶ DECONSTRUCTING NEW FORMS OF JOURNALISM

In this book, we also spend time deconstructing some new media types increasingly found in journalistic stories. Until this point, we've described the media forms as video, audio, photography, text, and graphics. But while researching this book we found many innovative components of online storytelling, some of which are intrinsic to a digital presentation. For example, an interactive video that requires the user to click on different portions of the display as the video is playing might require a whole different set of rules than traditional lean-back videos found on television and the Web.

We also increasingly saw an influx of new video types, like kinetic typography (motion graphics where text animates around the screen), animation, collages, and vox pops, where videos can exist in a grid to illustrate a swath of public sentiment on an issue.

While motion graphics videos are not necessarily revolutionary forms—and have existed in some form over the years—they were rarely utilized on television, especially in the context of news. Something about the culture and characteristics of the Web led to a rebirth of these media types existing in stand-alone forms. There are enough examples that we can begin to draw conclusions about their power in conveying certain types of news stories. With kinetic typography, text zooms across the video frame synchronized with narration. Each word and its trajectory of motion adds a punching emphasis to the narrative cadence, depending on how its motion is visually depicted; a word that moves in slowly can convey different meaning than one that falls into frame from above with a crunching thud. Operative words are emphasized not only by the inflection in a narrator's voice but also visually on the screen. These combined stimuli create a very impactful and attention-grabbing video. We see these styles used mostly as explainer videos, as depicted in "The Crisis of Credit Visualized" by Jonathan Jarvis.[17] Through use of moving text and graphics, this film explained the financial collapse of 2008, a very complex and arcane subject for most people. Other examples include the University of North Carolina, Chapel Hill's "Powering a Nation,"[18] which served as an introductory component that helped people to visualize a sense of motion and scale of the energy problems that lay ahead. The video served as a precursor to the rest of the reporting project; its essence: Almost everything in your daily life can be traced back to energy usage.

Animation has recently become a useful tool for many video journalists. Working with an animator, Carrie Ching of the Center for Investigative Reporting produced a series of videos on subject matter that would be prohibitively difficult to depict on camera. One such award-winning piece was titled "In Jennifer's Room,"[19] about the sexual abuse of an intellectually disabled patient at a clinic in Sonoma, California. The animation was a way to provide visual empathy for the viewer without using the actual subject (and possibly subjecting her to further humiliation). An animator made drawings, and through the use of sounds and narration, the viewer was shown the bruises on Jennifer's body, which led investigators to inquire as to the cause of her injuries.

Animation was also used in a similar fashion in the piece "Haiti's Scape-goats" by Caroline Dijckmeester-Bins.[20] In this piece, about the devastating 2010 earthquake in Haiti, many religious Haitians claimed the natural disaster was an act from God to punish Haiti for homosexuality. Sometime after the quake, many religious leaders shifted blame to the Haitian gay community, resulting in a stark increase in violence against gays and lesbians. Dijckmeester-Bins traveled to Haiti and interviewed several individuals from the gay community there who live anonymously and in fear for their lives. She used animation as a vehicle for illustrating anecdotes told by the subjects. Animation provided a mechanism that aided in two ways: maintaining anonymity to the subjects, but also allowing for the retelling of past events where a camera was not present.

## ▶ STRUCTURE OF THIS BOOK

In chapter 2, we examine the evolution of digital news packages, from the advent of personal computers in the 1980s to today's more modern browsers. A look at history in context allows us to understand how things came to be and to better identify the foundations of various storyforms that are popular today. Lessons from these past decades also teach us strategies moving forward.

In chapter 3, we cover the process of developing our taxonomy. Through iteration, we achieved a form that we think helps us better understand different forms of news. We hope our model presents a framework for additional study into codifying news packages.

In chapters 4–7, we dissect examples through case studies of six different news packages that journey around the corners of our taxonomical triangle diagram. We start in chapter 4 with a traditional form: Continuous, using an example from Vox Media's technology news site, *The Verge*. Since their launch in 2011, they have made early forays into longform digital journalism and given particular attention to integrating multimedia throughout their stories. In chapter 5, we dissect a project by an NPR show called "Planet Money Makes a T-shirt." In collaboration with NPR's News Apps and Multimedia teams, they produced a Comprehensive package that looks at the process of making a T-shirt in the global economy. In chapter 6, we cover a series of interactive documentaries by the National Film Board of Canada's (NFB) Interactive studio. The NFB is known for wowing audiences with powerful immersive Web interactive pieces that are forging new forms of storytelling. We decided to cover an evolution of several packages by NFB that show how their form has developed over time in the digital space.

In chapter 7, we cover the three "intersections" of our triangle diagram. These are instances when news packages fall within two taxonomical categories and demonstrate two different characteristics. We cover the *New York Times*'s "Snow Fall" story (Continuous-Comprehensive), the *Guardian*'s "Firestorm" (Continuous-Immersive), and *National Geographic*'s "The '80s" (Immersive-Comprehensive). Each of these projects exemplifies a particular mode of storytelling that is characteristic of these sections of our taxonomy.

In chapter 8, we discuss how "mode of consumption" affects content. More specifically, how different devices lend themselves to different ways of telling stories. We introduce terms like "lean-forward," "lean-back," and "stand-up," which cover a range of device types. The way a person consumes media should affect the design and types of stories told within that medium.

In chapter 9, we cover the new digital workflow for creating news packages. This now consists of a process of deconstructing/reconstructing a story, then packaging it into a cohesive format. This chapter also includes new ways of developing collaborative physical environments, which are important to creative development as well as the production process. This also aids in facilitating the new roles in newsrooms that are vital to the process, such as programmers, graphic designers, and visual journalists.

Finally, in chapter 10, we offer a few parting thoughts based on our research into this book. The numerous interviews, newsroom visits, and project analyses have given us some insights into how different news organizations are tackling digital longform. We provide some conclusions based on these examples.

## ▶ NOTES

1   McLuhan, Marshall. *Understanding Media: The Extensions of Man*, critical ed., ed. W. Terrence Gordon. Corte Madera, CA: Gingko, 2003, 237.

2   Dance, Gabriel, Andrew Kueneman, and Aron Pilhofer. "What One Word Describes Your Current State of Mind? ELECTION DAY 08." *New York Times*.

November 3, 2009. Accessed January 2015. http://www.nytimes.com/interactive/2008/11/04/us/politics/20081104_ELECTION_WORDTRAIN

3 "State of the News Media 2014." Pew Research Centers Journalism Project. March 25, 2014. Accessed October 1, 2014. http://stateofthemedia.org/

4 Kern, Jonathan. *Sound Reporting: The NPR Guide to Audio Journalism and Production*. Chicago: University of Chicago Press, 2008, 6.

5 Ingram, Mathew. "The Postmedia Chain Is Trying to Rethink Not Just How People Read Its Content but Where and When." Gigaom. May 20, 2014. Accessed January 2015. https://gigaom.com/2014/05/20/the-postmedia-chain-is-trying-to-rethink-not-just-how-people-read-its-content-but-where-and-when/

6 Christensen, Clayton M. *The Innovator's Dilemma: When New Technologies Cause Great Firms to Fail*. Boston, MA: Harvard Business School Press, 1997.

7 "Ted Williams: A Homeless Man with a Golden Voice." YouTube. January 7, 2011. Accessed January 2015. http://www.youtube.com/watch?v=iv-F5JnnGo0

8 Matyszczyk, Chris. "When YouTube Sensation Ted Williams Was Removed from YouTube." CNET. January 10, 2011. Accessed January 2015. http://www.cnet.com/news/when-youtube-sensation-ted-williams-was-removed-from-youtube/

9 McAdams, Mindy. *Flash Journalism: How to Create Multimedia News Packages*. Amsterdam: Focal Press, 2005.

10 "Newspaper Jargon." New York News Publishers Association. Accessed January 23, 2015. http://www.nynpa.com/docs/nie/niematerials/NewspaperJargon.pdf

11 Grabowicz, Paul. "Taxonomy of Digital Story Packages." KDMC Berkeley. April 28, 2013. Accessed January 23, 2015. http://multimedia.journalism.berkeley.edu/tutorials/taxonomy-digital-story-packages/

12 McCombs, Regina. "How Far Have We Come in Creating a New, Multimedia Style for Online Journalism?" Lecture, International Symposium on Online Journalism, Austin, TX, April 19, 2003. https://online.journalism.utexas.edu/2003/transcripts/d1p3.pdf

13 Jobs, Steve. "Thoughts on Flash." Apple.com. April 2010. Accessed January 23, 2015. http://www.apple.com/hotnews/thoughts-on-flash/

14 Williams, Josh (*New York Times* multimedia producer), interview with the authors, August 2014.

15 "Conference Blog." IRE. June 25, 2014. Accessed January 2015. http://www.ire.org/blog/ire-conference-blog/2014/06/25/welcome-2014-ire-conference/

16  Johnson, Bobbie. "Snowfallen: Just Because You Can, It Doesn't Mean You Should." *Matter*. July 16, 2013. Accessed January 23, 2015. https://medium.com/@bobbie/snowfallen-66b9060333ad

17  Jarvis, Jonathan. "The Crisis of Credit Visualized." Crisis of Credit. January 20, 2011. Accessed January 2015. http://crisisofcredit.com/

18  UNC, Chapel Hill. "Powering a Nation: An Introduction." Vimeo. November 16, 2009. Accessed January 2015. http://vimeo.com/7648216

19  Ching, Carrie, and Ryan Gabrielson. "In Jennifer's Room." California Watch. November 29, 2012. Accessed January 2015. http://californiawatch.org/public-safety/video-jennifers-room-18695

20  Dijckmeester-Bins, Caroline. "Haiti's Scapegoats." Vimeo. February 20, 2012. Accessed January 23, 2015. http://vimeo.com/37122552

# 2

# The Evolution of the Digital News Package

Everything is the way it is because it got that way.
—D'Arcy Wentworth Thompson, *On Growth and Form*

*Richard Koci Hernandez is an assistant professor at UC Berkeley's Graduate School of Journalism teaching new media. He is a 15-year veteran multimedia journalist for the* San Jose Mercury News. *In this chapter, he shares a firsthand account of his early experiences with digital journalism and a history of multimedia storytelling through the eyes of a photojournalist.*

## ▶ AN UNCERTAIN PATH TO MULTIMEDIA

One afternoon in 1999, as I pulled my company car into the parking lot of the *San Jose Mercury News*, I was met by security guards who greeted me playfully, yet forcibly, to inform me they would be removing the film cameras from my trunk and replacing them with the latest technology at the time: Canon EOS D2000, one of the first usable professional digital cameras. I had dug my heels in the sand recently during a staff meeting, declaring exaggeratedly, "The only way I'll switch from film to digital is by force." So the staged presence of security guards by the top brass was a bit of playful payback for my stubbornness.

Swapping film for pixels, I was suddenly ushered into the digital age. Little did I know the rest of my career trajectory hinged on what had happened that day. We were on the verge of the new millennium. It wasn't only the journalistic tools that were about to change—it was also the journalist. In time, I would be the first photographer to hold a newsroom position at the *Mercury News* with the word "multimedia" in my title. It was a dizzying time to work at the "*Merc.*" I had started in 1991 as a photo intern. A few years later the digital skunk works dubbed Mercury Center by then executive editor Bob Ingle were in full swing. In hindsight, Ingle would be seen as one of the early digital media revolutionaries. By 1995, the *Merc* became the first news site in the nation to migrate to the Web.[1]

But, despite being in the heart of this commotion—a tech boom under way in the Silicon Valley—I didn't immediately recognize the introduction of the World Wide Web as anything other than another vehicle for delivering news, no different than newsprint. Lost on me was the interactive and immersive potential of this medium. As a content producer, I couldn't imagine anything beyond adding a hyperlink to a story or having a user just click the "next" button to advance a gallery of photos. I didn't see the true potential of digital for more expansive and engaging storytelling.

But at some point during those formative years of digital journalism my opinion began to shift. Online journalism pioneers like Leah Gentry of the *Orange County Register* began to challenge the "shovelware" approach of newspapers, TV, and radio. It was common practice then to take stories that were designed for legacy platforms and shovel them onto the Web—often with few, if any, changes to adapt them to the medium. Gentry was one of the early advocates for new forms of storytelling. In the 2002 book *Journalism Online* by Mike Ward, Gentry was quoted in an interview as saying, "You need to look at the medium you're working in and ask 'What are the strengths of this medium and how can I use those strengths to help me tell my story?' So you work with the medium instead of against the medium."[2]

Gentry, along with other early digital champions like Ingle, envisioned a new breed of journalist, equipped with new gear and a new mindset that would allow reporting and producing of content in all sorts of novel ways, not merely for print. Ingle was the first editor to refer to his staff as multimedia reporters.

My photography assignments at the time took me inside fledgling media companies like Netscape, Yahoo, and Google. I began to realize I was at ground zero of something revolutionary. My photos of the offices of these start-ups often reflected the silliness of a culture, such as playground-sized slides instead of stairs, a replica of the Golden Gate Bridge made out of Coke cans in a corner office, beanbags for chairs, foosball tables, Nerf guns, free snacks, and Star Wars action figures lining cubicle walls. But the photos also revealed serious work was at play in the cubicles of Silicon Valley. Things were changing fast, big ideas were in the air, and I wanted somehow to be part of the excitement. But how?

In the late 1990s, bandwidth expanded on the Web and the newshole shrunk (the amount of space available for content in the print newspaper). I found myself, along with my fellow photographers, glued to computer screens surfing the Internet in the photo department. Together we witnessed a new form of digital storytelling emerge: audio slideshows. Photojournalists from the *New York Times, Washington Post*, and MSNBC, among many others, were experimenting with mixing still images with sound. Recorded voices of subjects in photographs, and sometimes the voice of the photographer explaining the image, brought these images to life. There was a rawness and power to what I saw pulsing through a dial-up modem into my 13-inch computer screen.

Inherent in these new presentation forms was a level of control that I as the user had over the story. I was able to experience the narrative at my own pace—pausing and playing and returning to it on-demand. There also was a depth to the essays: an immersive quality that had a strong emotional pull. In the slideshows I felt transported into the scene, where I experienced the emotions of the characters whose photos I saw and whose voices I heard. And for the photographer there was the appeal of not having to limit oneself to a single image on a page; we could publish as many images as we deemed necessary to tell the story. In print newspapers, a photographer getting less than four photographs published from an assignment was standard. But with a smaller newshole, the average had begun to shrink to only a single image per story—a frustrating reality, if you're a photographer whose primary means to tell a story was images. At the same time, the Web was expanding as a seemingly wide-open canvas: an enticing force for a photographer whose voice was increasingly diminished in print.

One story that struck me was a Web project called "Bosnia: Uncertain Paths to Peace," published in 1996 by the *New York Times* (at that time with a paltry 70,000 online subscribers). The interactive photo essay was produced by French photojournalist Gilles Peress in collaboration with Fred Ritchin, a professor at the Tisch School of the Arts and former *New York Times* photo editor. Ritchin described the project on his blog:

> Nominated in 1997 for the Pulitzer Prize in public service by the *Times* and then immediately rejected because it was not on paper, "Bosnia: Uncertain Paths to Peace"—about an attempt to create peace after four years of horrific slaughter—used hypertext and photography to try and immerse the reader/viewer in the Bosnian post-war experience. We were, in effect, attempting to make the reader into both a collaborator and co-author (I called this approach "hyperphotography" in my book, "After Photography"). That is what this site tried to do: to explore the limits of journalism, and to expand the conversation. We need many more such experiments, and even more paths to peace.[3]

In photos, text, and several 360-degree interactive panoramas, Peress documented the last weeks of the bloody siege of Sarajevo. He added his own voice to the story with audio snippets embedded throughout the package in which he commented on his photographs or reconstructed experiences he had at the scene. A large portion of the multimedia presentation consisted of documenting the exodus of Serbs from the suburbs where the siege had been mounted. This multimedia photographic chronicle left me stunned. I will never forget feeling like I was floating in the package's 360-degree panoramic photograph—created with a technology called QuickTime Virtual Reality (or

**FIGURE 2.1 Open graves of the Ilidza Graveyard. "Bosnia: Uncertain Paths to Peace,"** *New York Times,* **1996**

QTVR), which was only a few years old at the time. With the open graves of the Ilidza Graveyard seemingly just beneath my feet, I could look anywhere in this 360 image, navigating a virtual reality scene with my mouse. There was an overwhelming sense that the slightest misstep with the mouse would send me plunging to the bottom of one of the six-foot-deep open graves.

As I "moved" through this package I learned via audio and text that the graveyard shown in the 360-degree photo was where the Serbs had been exhuming their dead. Serbs have a strong connection to the land where their dead lie. Knowing that the land was going to become part of Bosnia, they concluded their dead could not rest in peace in this graveyard, and thus they began the process of exhuming loved ones. The interactive photo was a haunting experience that I felt could not be equaled in newsprint. The Web presentation had captivated me like never before. The package also was immense—more than 100 photographs—and expansive: maps, chronologies, a glossary, even a list of further reading material. It took me several hours and multiple viewings to take it all in. Also memorable was how the design defied traditional newspaper design conventions of the time, with a discordant layout that mixed photos in a collage-like fashion.

As we walk through the maze of improvised alleyways, trenches, behind giant hanging screens made of a patchwork of tarpaulin and colorful blankets shielding the passers-by from the eyes that kill, past the slits that seem like modernist gargoyles of a world where every angle has been computed by the centimeter, we are visiting the "sniper's world."

Audio (623k): Photographer's Comments
The Real and Virtual Worlds Around Sarajevo's Sniper

INDEX|GRID      CONTEXT|FORUMS          TO SUBURBS      PREVIOUS|MORE|NEXT

**FIGURE 2.2** "Bosnia: Uncertain Paths to Peace," *New York Times*, 1996

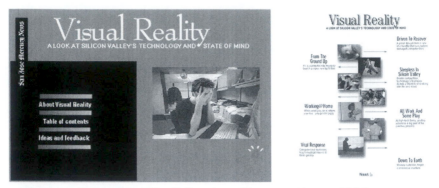

**FIGURE 2.3** "Visual Reality," *San Jose Mercury News*, 1996

Everything about this digital news package was new to me, and I had a profound foreshadowing of things to come in the world of storytelling. My photographs were published to the Web for the first time in 1996 in an online gallery called "Visual Reality," produced by *Mercury Center* photo editor Scott DeMuesy. But it wasn't until I experienced the *New York Times* Bosnia project that I was able to grasp the potential of this emerging platform.

This wave of excitement over multimedia storytelling helped form my career trajectory. In the years that followed, I transitioned into a full-time multimedia journalist—a great leap from that fateful day in the parking lot of the *Merc*, when I traded in my beloved film camera for a digital device. From that point on, a digital-first mantra dictate not only the form of my storytelling but also the tools I used to report those stories.

## ▶ ORIGINS OF THE DIGITAL NEWS PACKAGE

Every story has a beginning, and anything worth exploring has an origin. But what exactly is this digital storytelling process, which now defines not only my career but increasingly my profession? Buried beneath the glamor of all of the current new forms of online presentation—scrolling parallax, inter-active data graphics, or choose-your-own-adventure-style navigation—is a story about the origins of multimedia journalism. Exploring the evolution of online journalism presentation from its first forays helps one gain insight into the current structure and application of multimedia presentation and design.

## ▶ DIGGING UP THE PAST

Somewhere in the world buried on a hard drive is an artifact that has yet to be uncovered, dusted off and studied, set in a glass case on display in a museum. A holy grail for us: the very first digital journalism multimedia news package.

The problem is that hard drives don't really fossilize—their components can only spin, whirl, and deliver information so many times before they break. It's no wonder that our first attempts at producing multimedia on the World Wide Web left nominal physical tracks.

In 1994 we assumed our digital breadcrumbs (URLs) would be easy to find years later. It's disheartening to find most of them devoured by the very technology that promised to archive them. The promise of the Internet as the ultimate digital shoebox didn't materialize until the formation of the Internet Archive in 1996, a nonprofit organization that indexed and saved the world's websites. Despite the Internet Archive's aim to keep digital-born materials from disappearing into the past, little if anything exists of journalism's first multimedia forays using the "Wayback Machine." It would take two more years, until the first Google index—which collected 26 million web pages[4]—before digital new packages began to surface. Even after this exhaustive crawl, there continues to exists a black hole between 1994 and 1995.

It has been well established that this digital decay and obsolescence is attributed to "link rot": the process by which hyperlinks point to web pages, servers, or other resources that have become permanently unavailable. Consequently, visual evidence for the first package remains extremely dicey. What to do? Leave them unearthed and move on?

It becomes apparent after a deep dive that as journalists, we failed to record our own history as it pertains to digital news packages. Just as the chroniclers of the "first draft of history" continue to debate who actually came up with that phrase (was it really *Washington Post* publisher Philip L. Graham, or a 1943 book review in *New Republic*?[5]), we too failed to properly record our own beginning.

One of the earliest pioneers in the production of digital news packages, Brian Storm, founder and executive producer of the award-winning multimedia production studio MediaStorm, had this to say in reference to the history of multimedia journalism: "In the 90s there was a historical, seismic shift happening in online storytelling. Everybody wanted to do it, to work at it, be involved. So, to stop and write about it really never occurred to me. And as far as I know, no one else did either. I guess it's that time for some of us."[6]

This is an attempt at that first rough draft as witnessed firsthand through the eyes of a photojournalist. I must readily confess my photographic bias to the following evolution. Despite my personal history and visual proclivities, it's hard not to see my own profession as playing a critical role in the evolution process.

## ▶ THE FIRST *ROUGH* DRAFT

It's imperative at this stage that we define exactly what we are trying to unearth: the digital news package (DNP). At its core, it's commonly referred to as an in-depth feature story. While it's still not a universal term in the online journalism community, we felt DNP better describes the types of stories we wanted to explore than more generic terms like "interactives" or "features." These packages—formerly called a spread in newspaper jargon—are feature stories that typically go more in-depth on a topic, like the Sunday edition of your local paper. Online, they tend to consist of multiple pieces of media in order to express multifaceted stories through an organized layout, such as a video paired with text, or interactive graphics. During the mid-twentieth century, the golden age of the news spread, content was usually presented in a double-truck—two conjoined pages—with graphics, text, and photos.

Today, that same content reveals itself in various online forms. While length is not a prerequisite, most of the news packages described in this text tend to be more involved. Sometimes there is a narrative, other times it's simply giving a more comprehensive look at an issue or topic.

The choices made in the early days shape the function and structure of today's storytelling. Of course, evolution alone cannot explain every maturation of the digital news package, but without considering its origins we cannot follow the story to its current chapter. Certainly there are more chapters to be written beyond this text, but this can serve as the first rough draft of the story.

▶ **THE *WAY* WAYBACK MACHINE**

From royal decrees carved in stone to ink on parchment to mechanical type, tracing the evolution of digital news packages is anything but simple. The genesis of DNPs cannot be found in the HTML code that created the World Wide Web; it is farther back in the history of visual design itself. Given the dynamic visual nature of its presentation, and its extension from both photojournalism and graphic design, the DNP's evolution exhibits many parallels to the history of newspaper design—rooted at the intersection of both communication and art. Any medium, especially one with roots in the Internet, develops a complicated and dynamic set of prehistorical relationships. We will start at the beginning, with an overview of the significant early influences, then expand to a more detailed exploration.

The journey into the history of the digital news package will take us through the first pictograph in 10,000 BC to its current state, certainly a vast timetable—we will traverse at lighting speed to get us to today's DNP.

▶ **PRE-DIGITAL STORY FORMS**

From the moment we swipe through our Instagram feed in the morning until we scroll through the final paragraph of a *New York Times* story on our tablet reader at night, we can see how the marriage of words and pictures is deeply woven into our modern lives. Words and pictures—the basic building blocks of the DNP—have been intertwined as far back as 3100 BC, when humans drew imagery to communicate and inversely used words to paint images in the mind's eye.

Surprising as it may seem, immersive storytelling existed well before the invention of the computer. Its origins can be traced back from stone-carved figures of Egyptian religious rituals to the participatory dramas of the Greeks. This is all to say that the modern digital storyteller has more in common with early ancient storytellers than credit is given. An apt testament to this form of graphic-design-as-communication can be seen in what is regarded as the oldest artifact known to combine words and pictures: the Blau Monument. The monument, an early Sumerian shale stone with etched writing and carved relief figures, is widely believed by archeologists to be a recorded land transaction. The carved figures represent the individuals involved in the deal.[7] The stone's text lists commodities and other un-deciphered information. The assumption, according to historians, is that these items were exchanged for land. The Egyptians proved an enduring and profound relationship between words and pictures. It is actually the work of the ancient Egyptians that has come to embody the true origin of what we now refer to as visual communication design and one of the earliest precursors of the DNP. Modern producers of digital news packages may owe much to the graphic forms of early Egyptians, whose work was created on a strict grid system with well-balanced, harmonious, and minimalistic principles. It's important to note that the primitive layout design of the Egyptians eventually made its way in a more refined form—as it still had thousands of years to evolve—onto the pages of manuscripts in the medieval period well before the development of the printing press.

Participatory mythology rituals, reenacted by the Egyptians, played a vital role in the history of visual design. A collection of ancient Egyptian religious texts called the "Pyramid texts" dating from 2800 to 2400 BC are the oldest known religious texts in the world[8] and contain dramatic reenactments in the form of religious rituals as performed by an entire community. While the exact ceremonial process remains unknown, historians believe that the rituals were private affairs among priests combined with public ceremonies. Ritual reenactment of myths was a common element of all preliterate societies, according to American mythologist Joseph Campbell in his influential work *A Hero with a Thousand Faces*.[9] Carolyn Handler Miller, in her *Digital Storytelling*, puts forth the idea that these ritual reenactments are "a far more intriguing model of pre-digital interactivity than that of the old campfire stories"[10] and have a great deal more in common with current modes of digital storytelling. As Miller states, the early ritual-based reenactments "involve the use of avatars; they are a form of role-play; participants interact with each other and work towards accomplishing a particular goal; and they play out scenes that can be highly dramatic and even have life and death significance."[11] For the Greeks these early forms of participatory storytelling evolved into classic theatre.

Hundreds of years later a highly complex, nonlinear, "multi-navigable" form of storytelling can also be seen in a medieval manuscript called the *Glossa Ordinaria*. The book is an extensively annotated Bible printed circa 1841. It contains complex commentary both in the margins and within the text itself. Modern scholars puzzle over how the *Glossa Ordinaria* was actually read, but Russell Sage College professor and author Dr. David Salomon uses the idea of the hyperlink to explain the nonlinear processes of reading the manuscript.

This early form of hyperlinked reading "empowers the reader with freedom of choice, the freedom to explore the text at hand,"[12] thus conferring upon this ancient text a central characteristic of modern hypertext theory.

As you can see, even this hyper-lapse history tour reveals deep-seated strands of the participatory and interactive nature in our storytelling DNA. It appears that our ancestors were predisposed to creating "lean-forward" storytelling experiences. Lean-forward are stories that require active participation, or at the very least, a minimal presence or companionship with the storyteller—be it stunned silence or uproarious laughter. A live audience helped shape the story. Douglas Adams, best known as the author of *The Hitchhiker's Guide to the Galaxy*, proclaimed "interactivity" as a common trait to storytelling. In a 1999 article in the *Sunday Times*, Adams wrote, "all entertainment was interactive: theatre, music sport—the performers and audience were together, and even a respectfully silent audience exerted a powerful shaping presence on the unfolding of whatever drama they were there for."[13] While many of our traditional forms of storytelling remain solidly in place, emerging technologies of the time, like the printing press, cinema, and television, ushered in the great "lean-back" or passive engagement style. The masses traded campfire songs for pre-recorded music on the radio and theatre-in-the-round for dark rooms with large tubs of popcorn in their laps. We became listeners, viewers, and at worst, couch potatoes.

## ▶ A MODERN MARRIAGE: PICTURES, WORDS, AND SOUND

In order to properly connect the digital news package to a more modern online presentation (such as the aforementioned *New York Times*'s DNP, "Bosnia: Uncertain Paths to Peace"), we have to continue our cursory historic traipse and explore its next closest predecessor, the newspaper.

The advent of the printing press saw the production of books from the mid-fifteenth century until the late eighteenth century as printing evolved into a master art form. Printers would take inspiration from their design ancestors and form an early remix-like movement, refining the classic elements of layout. What emerged from this primitive mashup are some of the common design elements of today—justified columns, margins, white space, mathematical proportions, and aesthetic guidelines governing the relationships between elements of lines, points, surfaces, and solids.

The modern presentation of newspaper layout developed slowly as American publishers appropriated the "newspaper" tradition from their European counterparts in the early eighteenth century. The American newspaper—both editorially and in design—was highly influenced by periods of politicization and commercialization. The newspaper as we know it today (although certainly not in appearance) was forged alongside advertising during the Industrial Revolution in order to sustain and promote mass consumption in a burgeoning consumer society. When newspapers appeared on the scene in early modern Europe in the 1600s and 1700s, it wasn't common for news printers to combine images and words. The design tendencies of early newspapers were focused solely on typography rather than images. It's no wonder the *New York Times* earned the nickname "The Gray Lady," referring to its tendency to present more columns of typography than graphics.

Images played no major role in newspapers until the 1850s, when publications like *Frank Leslie's Illustrated Newspaper* found engravings to be the perfect novelty to attract readers' attention. Today we might view this as an ancient form of click-bait—an eye-catching element to encourage people to read on.

Illustrations also had a very practical use in newspaper design: to provide a much needed visual break in the flow of text. Image reproductions of the time served as handmaiden to the almighty word. A definitive boundary was created and a separate and arguably unequal relationship emerged between words and images. Illustrations were most often framed with overly decorative, unnecessarily ornate, and fluffy borders to indicate an ideological estrangement—a scarlet letter of design to distinguish them from the printed word. Illustrations often involved portraiture and scenic depictions of newsworthy events.

Printing at the time was a technical challenge requiring that several drawings be combined into a single continuous image (think of it as early Photoshopping). These panoramic scenes often spanned the length of a two-page center spread and thus the double-truck or news spread layout was born. These multi-image spreads would eventually serve as the foundational design motif for the golden age of the photographic essay layout in early-twentieth-century American magazines like *Life* and *Look*. It is the tradition of the photographic essay, whose origin I discuss later in the chapter, that form the basic building blocks of the DNP as it emerges in the late 1990s.

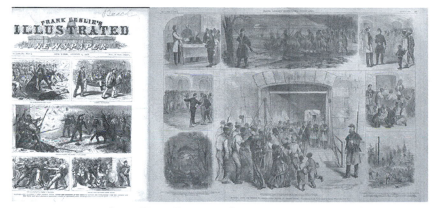

**FIGURE 2.4** *Frank Leslie's Illustrated Newspaper*, 1850s photos

Despite their perceived inferiority to text, the use of illustrations during this pre-photographic period provided a firm foundation of visual design before the introduction of halftone printing.

On March 4, 1880, the *Daily Graphic* in New York published the first known full-tonal-range photograph in a newspaper via the halftone process. This new technique allowed images to be printed with a process that simulated continuous tone imagery through using printed dots of varied size and space, thus generating a gradient-like effect.

While the halftone process removed a technological hurdle and made publishing photographs easier, photos in newspapers remained quite rare. Halftone photographs also suffered the same fate as illustrations, being relegated to enhancing text articles rather than taking center stage as a primary media form of communication. However, the tide began to shift with publications like the monthly magazine *Street Life* in London in 1876. Instead of images acting as a supplement to the text, photographer and publisher John Thomson pioneered the use of photographs as the predominant media form for communication, successfully combining photography with the printed word.[14] Pictures were beginning to be defined on equal footing with text content. Thomson's photographic approach to documenting the lives of everyday street people in London is also credited with establishing social documentary photography as a form of photojournalism and laid the groundwork for the newspaper photojournalist as a profession.

By the early twentieth century, photographs had slowly begun to push illustrations aside as the de facto medium to represent life in its most visually "truthful" state. Photographs had moved from an exception to the norm. Photojournalism as a profession emerged in the 1930s, ushering in a golden age of documentary photography lasting through the 1960s. A convergence of several technological developments—smaller cameras, film on rolls, improved optics, flashbulbs—coupled with economic changes in the news environment like advertising, increased competition, and the emergence of modernist design principles led to visual shifts in print layout from newspapers. The world was changing and so was the presentation of news.

Photographs of this time became increasingly emotive and episodic, moving from merely politicians shaking hands, smiling, and looking into the camera (known as "grip-n-grin" in industry parlance) to a more day-in-the-life, naturalistic vérité style. Smaller cameras like the Leica, introduced in 1925, helped the photographer disappear into the background in order to document a more authentic style of photograph, which was often difficult with the weight and intimidation of previous larger cameras like the Speed Graphic. This new photographic freedom combined with the emergence of a pictorial press, most notably *LIFE* magazine (established in 1936 by magazine magnate Henry Luce), propelled photography to a legitimate presentation form to convey newsworthy events. Luce's goal was to "harness the mainstream of optical consciousness of our time,"[15] thus ushering in an era of visual innovation in the form of the photographic essay. So triumphant a means of communication was the camera at the time that Librarian of Congress and poet Archibald MacLeish, in a telegram to Henry Luce on June 29, 1936, said, "The great revolutions of journalism are not revolutions in public opinion, but revolutions in the way in which public opinion is formed. The greatest of these, a revolution greater even than the revolution of the printing press . . . is the camera."[16]

Printed in the inaugural issue of the groundbreaking *LIFE* magazine was the work of 32-year-old photographer Margaret Bourke-White. Her cover story for the issue is considered the first true photographic essay printed in America. Bourke-White's assignment was to photograph the chain of dams in the Columbia River basin in northern Montana. There, Bourke-White would photograph the construction of the world's largest earth-filled dam, and the resulting image would became the first cover of *LIFE* magazine. But it would be the images she produced of the laborers and inhabitants surrounding the Montana boom town that would make the most impact. Bourke-White recalls, in her 1963 autobiography, *Portrait of Myself*:

> It was a pinpoint in the long, lonely stretches of northern Montana so primitive and so wild that the whole ramshackle town seemed to carry the flavor of the boisterous Gold Rush days. It was stuffed to the seams with construction men, engineers, welders, quack doctors, barmaids, fancy ladies and, as one of my photographs illustrated, the only idle bedsprings in New Deal were the broken ones. People lived in trailers, huts, coops anything they could find and at night they hung over the Bar X bar.[17]

Bourke-White's stark, revealing, and emotional images of the inhabitants of this boom town laid the foundations of what we know today as the photographic essay. It's important to note that Bourke-White's images were presented not in the hodgepodge, haphazard fashion typical of photo layouts of the time, but through a thoughtful collaboration between photographer and editor, with particular attention paid to image sequencing and layout. Bourke-White's photographs of daily life were carefully crafted as a series of images with the express intent to tell a story and evoke emotion. So moving was her photographic portrayal that the editors themselves were taken by surprise and devoted a bit of the opening pages of the inaugural November 23, 1936, issue to Bourke-White's backstory:

> If any charter subscriber is surprised by what turned out to be the first story in this first issue of LIFE, he is not nearly so surprised as [we] were. Photographer Margaret Bourke-White had been dispatched to the Northwest to photograph the multimillion dollar projects of the Columbia River Basin. What the editors expected were construction pictures as only Bourke-White can take them. What the editors got was a human document of American frontier life which, to them at least, was a revelation.

What the editors did not grasp at the time was the fact that they crafted the first true photographic essay. Maitland Edey, editor at *LIFE* from 1945 to 1956, wrote, "More modest efforts had been attempted in European picture magazines, but no editor previously had tried to master a large subject with a comprehensive take by a single photographer, using enough pictures to tell an ambitious several-threaded story."[18]

The form acquired an official title in March 1937 when Luce himself stated that the written essay was no longer "a vital means of communication. But what is vital is the *photographic essay*."[19] The editors of the magazine were so committed to this form of visual communication that the term "the photographic essay" appeared in the table of contents for the first time toward the middle of 1937. The form became a common vernacular in the structure of the magazine, expanding the photographic territory on the printed pages of *LIFE* and other magazines, thus extending photography's reach in a modernist society. This new photographic freedom combined with less laborious printing methods ushered in a golden age for printed visual storytelling for the next thirty years.

## ▶ FROM STILLS TO MOVING IMAGES

As photography rooted itself in society with the help of *LIFE* magazine, another technological development would bring profound change, moving us further from a print-dominated culture to a world influenced by moving pictures coupled with sound recordings. Although moving images in the form of early cinema have their roots as far back as the 1890s, it wasn't until the introduction of sound recordings married to moving images in the early 1930s that a truly new hybrid medium was born. For the first time in history, verbal and visual mediums were paired, and one of the most influential technological developments of visual culture was born: television.

Canadian philosopher of communication theory Marshall McLuhan, in his most widely known work, *Understanding Media: The Extensions of Man* (published in 1964), coined the phrase "the medium is the message," inferring that content cannot be easily separated from form. McLuhan noted, "The personal and social consequences of any medium—that is, of any extension of ourselves—result from the new scale that is introduced into our affairs by each extension of ourselves, or by any new technology."[20] This newly formed symbiotic relationship of image and sound would prove to be an unbreakable bond and bear a close resemblance to a DNP before the advent of the computer.

## ▶ REINVENTING THE WHEEL

In 1965, four years before the Advanced Research Projects Agency Network (ARPANET) carried its first packets of information across computer networks in what would later become the Internet, the Eastman Kodak

Company was busy inventing a new form of pre-computer-based multimedia presentation. This photographic presentation tool would give photojournalists their first experience in sequencing multimedia stories and helped shape early narrative presentation forms of the DNP.

The Carousel, first patented in 1965, was a round tray that held several 35mm photographic slides and allowed a room full of friends and relatives to time travel and view vacations and other important photographic memories on a large screen in the comfort of the family living room. If this sounds nostalgic, it should. This description was also a popular reference by the TV series *Mad Men*, a show based in the 1960s about a group of advertising executives who try to come up with innovative sales pitches for products. In one episode, the series' main character, Don Draper, comes up with the name Carousel, in place of the Kodak executives' original name for it, the Wheel. "This device isn't a spaceship, it's a time machine. It goes backwards, and forwards. . . . It takes us to a place where we ache to go again. It's not called the wheel, it's called The Carousel. It lets us travel the way a child travels—around and around, and back home again, to a place where we know we are loved."[21]

These pre-digital slide show presentations became a mainstay for professional photographers, particularly during conferences held by the National Press Photographers Association (NPPA). In hushed and darkened hotel ballrooms all across the country, multiple larger-than-life images were projected simultaneously from multiple carousels, accompanied by music and narration emanating from an electronic tape deck. The images and photographer's narration were perfectly timed to musical scores and slide transitions; it was emotional and cinematic. Hundreds of attendees filled rooms to standing-room-only capacity as the award-winning work of the nation's most celebrated photojournalists was presented to rapt audiences. Audio slideshows became the standard convention for presenting an extended body of photographic work. Slideshows with audio were highly anticipated, and photographers from the NPPA turned these projections into a niche art form.

Reflecting on these pre-digital multimedia presentations, Geri Migielicz, formerly the director of photography at the *San Jose Mercury News*, said,

> As a profession we've been making slide shows since Kodak invented the projector. I remember the one I put together in 1990 when the

Mercury News won the Pulitzer Prize for news reporting on the Loma Prieta earthquake. We didn't call it multimedia, but the photo department at the Merc was always cranking out audio slideshows on a dual-projector system. It was my first professional foray into multimedia and I got poet Francisco X Alarcon to read one of his magnificent poems about the earthquake into a cassette tape recorder in the living room of the house where I lived. I used this recording of his recitation and some music as a backdrop for a couple hundred slides. I recorded Francisco's poem with a mic I bought at RadioShack and plugged it into the dual cassette audio recorder of my home stereo. There was no such thing as Garageband at the time. I then added an instrumental track from a vinyl or CD. Then I sequenced photographs from the Mercury News' coverage using a multi-projector dissolve unit. The presentation combined prose, poetry and music to showcase photojournalism. It had a power all of its own. The photographs, simultaneously experienced with voices from the rubble, transported me (and I hoped viewers) to another level of visual experience. This felt like a new form that moved beyond the photo story in print. I presented it at conferences all over the county, but few people saw it because it wasn't published, there was no World Wide Web, at the time, you had to be in the room to see it. Really, it was another form of storytelling. These shows had pace, timing, mood and they had flow. They were pretty sophisticated presentations. So if you think about it, as a profession, we've been projecting images on our own private cave walls before we could share them with the world on the internet.[22]

Soon, Migielicz's dream of transporting viewers to the rubble of the Loma Prieta quake and sharing these presentations with a wider audience would manifest itself in another set of technological developments in the rise of visual culture, the computer and the World Wide Web.

## ▶ BITS AND BYTES

The origins of computers can be traced back as early as the 1940s, but their availability and popularity didn't reach prominence until the development of the personal computer in the 1970–1980s. During this time, the news media was beginning to experiment and invest heavily in publishing platforms beyond ink on paper. From the late 1970s to the mid-1980s the industry explored delivery system mashups in hopes of bridging the telephone

and the television into a new platform to deliver news into homes. Companies like Knight Ridder, CBS, NBC, and the Times Mirror Company began
to see the transformative power of the digital delivery of news. Gerald M.
Levin, the former chairman and CEO of Time Warner, explains his early
motivations to create a new platform: "After we started HBO, I kept thinking about ways of delivering news into the home . . . because I was taken by
Life Magazine and pictures," said Levin in an interview with Nieman Lab's
special report titled "Riptide," about the historical collision between journalism and technology. "I asked one of the engineers at Manhattan Cable,
if there was a way you can get a news wire into the home? Let's get pictures
into the home because . . . 'To see life; to see the world,' that's what Henry
Luce said about Life."[23] What emerged from Levin's drive for interactivity was a short-lived project called Time Teletext. The process itself was a
means of sending pages of text and simple graphics to the television screen.

A more notable early venture by the industry was a service offered by Knight
Ridder and AT&T in the early 1980s called Viewtron. Despite being named
by *PCWorld* magazine as one of the biggest project failures in information
technology (IT) history,[24] the service—which provided interactive content

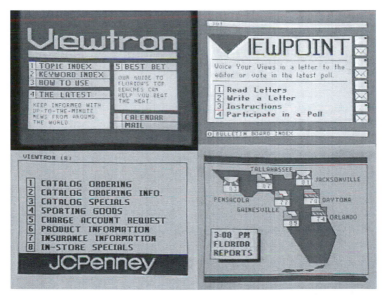

**FIGURE 2.5 Viewtron, by Knight Ridder and AT&T, 1983–1986. Four
photos by Philip Bump, reproduced via Creative Commons license
CC-BY-SA.1.0**

on a television, using modems to send data in both directions—was eerily similar to what would emerge more than a decade later as the World Wide Web. The service offered e-commerce, chat, news, and games.

Viewtron ended in late 1985 when Knight Ridder decided to abandon the service and concentrate on its core—the newspaper. Early analytics had revealed that 80 percent of Viewtron users were spending most of their time using the service's e-mail, message boards, and educational areas, rather than consuming news content. This proved a losing proposition for Knight Ridder as it was spending 80 percent of its budget to create news content. The education editor for Viewtron at the time, Rita Haugh Oates, put it this way: "That's when KR [Knight Ridder] executives decided that this was NOT a news medium and they wanted to continue to be a news company."[25] Despite the industry's explorations at the cutting edge, their experiments came too early. According to Philip Meyer, director of news and circulation research for Knight Ridder, in an interview with Poynter about remembering Viewtron, "Timing is everything! Our vision was ahead of the technology. The ways we found to add value to news and advertising through electronic distribution were, however, right on target and anticipated much of what the Internet does today."[26] After incurring significant economic losses, Knight Ridder turned off the interactive services, and a period of disinvestment in interactive technology was felt industry-wide. Capable multimedia platforms would only later emerge in the form of the personal computer and desktop publishing.

## ▶ DIGITAL PAGINATION AND DESKTOP PUBLISHING

The proliferation of the desktop computers in newsrooms across the country had a significant impact on the production process of news content. Newsrooms moved from analog- to digital-based operations. Newsrooms went from the hammering clatter of typewriters to the soft clicks of plastic keyboards. The pagination process moved from physically pasting up paper layouts on a large composing table to page-layout software like QuarkXPress and later Adobe InDesign. Computers in the newsroom allowed writers to enter copy via a terminal and editors to call up and rapidly edit those stories on-screen. Once the story was edited, it was saved and accessed instantaneously, along with any corresponding photos and graphics, by a page designer, who would then manipulate the assets into a complex page layout using WYSIWYG (what you see is what you get) software. All of this was made possible by the PC's more user-friendly graphical interfaces popularized in the 1980s by the Apple Macintosh computer.

The rise of the PC and desktop publishing software not only gave way to a more simplified page design workflow; it spawned more tools for graphic designers and photographers to create content faster, just as the value of immediacy would dominate in the coming era of the World Wide Web. The addition of detailed charts, diagrams, graphic explainers, and maps became a catalyst for informational graphics in newsrooms. Later, these would make their way online in the form of early digital news packages. Desktop publishing software spawned a modular design revolution, spurred in part by *USA Today*. Jennifer George-Palilonis described *USA Today*'s goal this way in her 2006 book, *A Practical Guide to Graphics Reporting*: "Its editorial mission was simple: cater to the time-starved reader with tightly edited story packages in an entertaining and easy-to-read format."[27] What resulted were shorter stories and a plethora of color graphics in place of the more common longform, text-driven packages. Printed newspapers, largely influenced by *USA Today*, were taking on a more visual appearance that would eventually makes its way online.

Another major change worthy of mention during the years preceding the Web came in the form of digitizing and editing photographs. Gone were the days of darkrooms and theatrical hand gestures to "dodge" and "burn" areas of an image. Dodging and burning are techniques used during the printing process of photographs to manipulate the exposure by blocking the light from an enlarger (which looked like a large projector pointed downward), often by using one's hands or special tools. Enhancing a photograph's exposure, color, and sharpness—aspects that once took years of practice and skill, and often hours of work in the darkroom—could now be completed with a few clicks of the mouse using Photoshop.

It's clear that the arrival of desktop publishing and the introduction of software, like QuarkXPress and Photoshop, ushered in a new generation of graphic designers and photojournalists with an unprecedented level of production prowess. This all-encompassing electronic/digital workflow left the industry with designers, photographers, and reporters poised and prepared for experimenting with new storyforms as the impending shift toward online content loomed.

## ▶ THE WORLD WIDE WEB

While the invention and introduction of PCs is critical to our DNP evolution, it was the emergence of the Internet and the Web that would offer newspapers a platform to create new digitized and interactive multimedia forms.

In 1989, Tim Berners-Lee created the critical ingredients of the Web, paving the way for online digital storytelling. Then in late 1992 the National Center for Supercomputing Applications (NCSA) at the University of Illinois at Urbana-Champaign released the first graphical Web browser, Mosaic. The browser was co-written by Marc Andreessen, who, a year later, would help launch a refined version dubbed Netscape Navigator. Netscape's success from the mid-1990s until its eventual demise in 2002 gave people an easy portal in which to view content on the Web.

In 1994, author Gary Wolfe described the revolutionary nature of the Mosaic Web browser and its power to transform information consumption in an article in *Wired* magazine:

> When it comes to smashing a paradigm, pleasure is not the most important thing. It is the only thing. If this sounds wrong, consider Mosaic. Mosaic is the celebrated graphical "browser" that allows users to travel through the world of electronic information using a point-and-click interface. Mosaic's charming appearance encourages users to load their own documents onto the Net, including color photos, sound bites, video clips, and hypertext "links" to other documents. By following the links—click, and the linked document appears—you can travel through the online world along paths of whim and intuition. Mosaic is not the most direct way to find online information. Nor is it the most powerful. It is merely the most pleasurable way, and in the 18 months since it was released, Mosaic has incited a rush of excitement and commercial energy unprecedented in the history of the Net.[28]

While several newspapers were feverishly scrambling to gain traction online and before "surfing the Internet" became a common phrase across the country, early pioneers like Brian Storm, then a graduate student at the University of Missouri; Andrew DeVigal, then a producer at Chicagotribune.com; and people at the Mercury Center—among many others—were hard at work creating the first online forms of digital storytelling.

# ▶ THE COMING STORM

In 1993 Brian Storm was assigned to cover the effects of a recent flood on local farmers as a staff photographer for the *Columbia Missourian*—a community newspaper staffed by students at the Missouri School of Journalism. After spending more than eight hours in the field making photographs, Storm headed back to the office to develop his film. After printing some of the images, he sequenced several of them into a full-page photo essay layout that visualized the effects of the severe weather on the local farming community. Excitedly, Storm presented his layout to his editor, saying, "I think we've got real insight into what's happening with the flood and its effects." The editor responded, "This is great, but we can only run one picture with a two-line caption, that's what we have room for." According to Storm, that's the day he "swore off newspapers."[29]

Frustrated by leaving so much of his photo essay unpublished and feeling "terribly denied in that moment," Storm was about to discover an alternate passion and outlet for his photojournalism. He recalled with detail the moment his college roommate inserted something called a CD-ROM (compact disc read-only memory) into a Macintosh computer. "I didn't know anything about computers or any of that stuff at the time," said Storm. As the screen went black, words appeared on the screen suggesting that the viewers prepare themselves for a 30-minute experience. Intrigued, with eyes wide open and attention glued to the screen, Storm was presented with a stunning black-and-white portrait of a couple accompanied by a deep voice emanating from the tiny speaker. "Let me introduce you to my parents," it said. Forty seconds later, after more photographs slowly faded on the screen, a haunting piano score began as a very romantic image of a couple engaged in a tender kiss filled the screen. The voice providing the narration to this impactful CD-ROM experience, entitled, "I Photograph to Remember," was produced by renowned photojournalist Pedro Meyer. The 30-minute multimedia presentation was a stunningly personal family memoir about the death of Meyer's parents. Produced in 1991 by Meyer and Bob Stein of the Voyager Company, it is widely considered the first photo-driven multimedia CD-ROM presentation to wed nearly 100 documentary photographs with sound.[30]

While viewing this new media benchmark, Storm immediately realized he was experiencing uncharted territory. Computers were normally used to crunch numbers and edit text-driven documents, not transmit emotional audiovisual content. Storm was being presented with a complex and deep emotional experience via a computer, and he remembers, "That was an extremely impressionable moment, having just been denied a voice at the paper and seeing the potential in this CD-ROM, my mind was blown and I remember thinking to myself, this is it! This has the depth, like a real photo essay, but it has context and narrative sound, it was just beautiful!" The next day, Storm sought out a professor at the University of Missouri, where he was enrolled as a graduate student, and inquired about how he could learn to create CD-ROMs. According to Storm, a few weeks later, he received a piece of software called the Apple Media Kit from his professor's contact at Apple computers. "I had some pretty amazing experiences with that software. I would spend fifteen to twenty hours trying to write some code to make it do what I wanted, like fade an image. Finally, I'd compile the code and it was like my first magical experiences in the darkroom when I dropped a print into the developer and an image magically appeared. . . . I was hooked in that moment. I thought to myself, this is incredibly empowering and it can take me in all kinds of new directions." Storm would go on to help produce four CD-ROMs for the University of Missouri's prestigious Pictures of the Year (POY) competition. Storm's next steps, along with others in the industry, would have a profound and lasting impact on the evolution of the DNP.

## ▶ THE FULL IMPACT OF THE CD-ROM

While digital storytelling would soon find a new ecosystem on the Web, the impact of early CD-ROM presentations—despite their relatively short-lived lifespan—can still be felt today. It is important to step back and examine the influence these compact discs would have on the presentation of digital news packages on the Web before continuing to the next evolutionary phase of early pioneers like Brian Storm.

In a 2001 blog post marking the twentieth anniversary of the first public viewing of "I Photograph to Remember," Bob Stein, founder of the Voyager Company, described its impact: "When Pedro Meyer first showed I Photograph to Remember at the Seybold Digital World Conference in Beverly Hills in 1991 . . . you could hear a pin drop in that Hollywood Conference hall. As people walked out at the end there was an unusual hush in the room . . . business wasn't returning immediately to normal. People were processing something new. No longer simply a productivity tool or game engine, the computer going forward would be at the center of the most deeply personal experiences of our lives." Stein would end the post by noting, "A few months ago a famous Silicon Valley CEO said to me: 'Remember when you presented Pedro Meyer's I Photograph to Remember for the first time? That was really a turning point for all of us. It really changed our understanding of what computing could be about.'"[31] The power and enduring quality of Meyer's work and that of others at the time, like Rick Smolan (a former *TIME, LIFE*, and *National Geographic* photographer), who produced another early and influential CD-ROM "From Alice to Ocean," lies in their sophisticated and cinematic fusion of multimedia components.

While Meyer's work would follow a classic linear structure in a photojournalistic tradition seen in magazines like *LIFE*, Smolan's work on "From Alice to Ocean" and his subsequent project, "Passage to Vietnam," would take the medium a step further by offering a nonlinear structure via multiple entry points and alternate story paths. In creating "From Alice to Ocean," based on his images for a *National Geographic* assignment that documented Robyn Davidson's 1,700-mile trek across the Australian outback, Smolan and his team used the most innovative software to date, Macromedia's Director. The software allowed users the ability to link text, graphics, images, video, sound, and animation on a time line–based interface. The software used a movie metaphor, with the user as the "director" of the experience. In a 1993 *New York Times* article titled, "Technology: The Tools of a New Art Form," Smolan said, "When we put the interactive CD together it gave us an incredible feeling of freedom, because we were able to give people many different paths through the story."[32] Smolan was one of the first photojournalists to venture into the unexplored digital narrative structure of nonlinear, documentary-based presentations. In reference to his use of interactivity as part of his CD-ROM experience, Smolan was cited in a 1997 article by Charles Williams, "Historical Photographs and Multimedia Storytelling," as saying, "We gave people the opportunity to listen to Robyn or interrupt her—to have a conversation with her. There are multiple paths through the same story. Readers can follow their own lines of curiosity."[33]

In broad terms, what's interesting about Meyer and Smolan's CD-ROM packages is not only the control a user would have over the experience, but also the lineage these compact-disc-driven packages owe to the projector-based audio slideshows mentioned earlier in the chapter. It's enough to note that both of these influential CD-ROMs were created by photographers, but there are other striking similarities. For instance, the fading of images on screens,

**FIGURE 2.6** "From Alice to Ocean: Alone across the Outback," 1992

both computer and projector, and the ability to start the narrative on any particular photo in the slide tray (Carousel) or click any particular image on the computer screen are common characteristics of both analog and digital presentation formats similar in nature to projector-based audio slideshows.

In recalling the early years of his career in an interview with the authors, Brian Storm would also make the observation, "Everything is built on top of other ideas. There isn't anything about what was happening at the time that hasn't been done before. I think from a storytelling perspective, there were people doing these epic multi-tray slide presentations, trying to sync music to photos and documentary filmmakers had been doing that forever, but what Pedro did on that CD-ROM, that was the magical moment, an evolution."[34]

In contrast, Meyer's project resembles a single-projector-based presentation with the photographer narrating the work, while Smolan's resembles a more complicated multi-projector presentation with several narrators, lots of buttons, graphics, maps, and video snippets. The path forged by photographers in darkened conference rooms using Kodak slide projectors to computer screens in poorly lit college dorm rooms was complete.

During this time before the introduction of the Web, these discs became a hot commodity. Their popularity would only last about five years, and they spawned several influential games and educational titles for the entertainment industry, like *Myst* and *The Oregon Trail*. The news industry also recognized the potential benefit in packaging content into CD-ROMs.

In late 1993, *USA Today* released what it called a dynamic time capsule in the form of a CD-ROM: "USA Today, The '90s, Volume I." The packaging inside the plastic jewel case promised a multimedia treatment of key stories and topics, including full-color pictures, graphics, maps, and sound clips bringing the news to life. Users of the disc would also have a fully indexed and cross-referenced database giving them access to more than 100,000 *USA Today* stories from January 1990 through August 1992.

In that same year an industry-wide group of magazine editors was brought together in the basement of the Time-Life Building in New York to determine the feasibility of digital delivery of content via CD-ROMs. Among the elite group was *National Geographic* director of photography Thomas R. Kennedy, who would describe this development effort, dubbed Open Project, as a rapid prototyping-like session, using all the most cutting-edge digital tools at the time to create a magazine and CD-ROM in one week. While participating in the project, Kennedy says he quickly became aware of how valuable sound could be as an extension of still photography. Furthermore, he said, "Instead of depending solely on captions to explicate the photograph, we could hear from the subjects themselves or listen to natural sound from the situation as it was being recorded. It also occurred to us that someday soon we could be mixing photography and audio with video to tell richer, more complete stories in the service of journalism."[35]

Within five years, Kennedy would leave *National Geographic* and lead multimedia efforts at the *Washington Post*. Kennedy and others extended the lessons they learned from their foray into CD-ROMs and further increased their influence on photojournalists, designers, and early producers of the next major shift to *online* news narratives.

In hindsight, the prevailing lesson from these early digital experiences seems to be one of distinction. The realization was that combining multiple media experiences into a single, self-contained multimedia package like a CD-ROM is to acknowledge the creation of a completely new technological storytelling platform. A new storytelling form demanded a new attention to production values, structure, and presentation. Early devices, like the videotex service Viewtron from Knight Ridder, or the TimesFax newspaper service from the *New York Times*, relied on existing infrastructure like television or phone lines and were essentially different ways of distributing existing news forms. However, it was the compact disc in conjunction with the personal computer that made a clear divergence from traditional media like the television or the telephone. What the CD-ROM—and eventually the Web—proved was that there could be a merging of distinct media types (photos, words, audio, video, graphics) into a single digital presentation. It was different than information delivery; it was something entirely new: a cinematic and *interactive* package. This was the birth of multimedia journalism. The evolution up to this point shows that users and disseminators of information have the unique capacity to create and manage multiple forms of self-expression.

While the content creators of compact disc were finding creative ways to link and package multimedia narratives together, almost simultaneously the Web emerged. It became apparent in 1994 with the launch of Netscape Navigator that the Web would become a more flexible environment for creation and distribution of multimedia content. Although the compact disc's time in the spotlight was about to end, its glow would remain.

This brings us back to Storm and his seemingly clairvoyant personal journey. From his personal frustrations when a newspaper failed to appreciate the depth of his photography, Storm discovered a new outlet in CD-ROMs. Now, a new discovery—the distribution power of the Web.

> During an annual Pictures of the Year (POY) conference in Washington, DC, where the world's greatest photojournalists gather for presentations, Storm had an epiphany: "It was one of the most important days of my life," explains Storm. "I saw photojournalist Anthony Suau present 80 pictures from his portfolio—just amazing pictures—and at the end somebody asked him how many photos were published and he said *one*. . . . This guy is an incredible photographer and I'm never going to be as good as he is. There is no reason for me to be a photographer with the likes of him around. I knew right then and there that I needed to stop trying to be a photographer. I needed to stop, and instead focus one hundred percent on helping guys like this get their work published."[36]

After leaving the conference and making his way back to Missouri, Storm conceived the idea for a new kind of media company. He called it Media-Storm. "That was the company I was going to run. I was going to help photographers put these kinds of projects together because many of them didn't know how, but I did. That was the day I put the camera down. I knew I was never going to shoot again." Storm would instead focus his passion on publishing, and his timing couldn't be better. Within weeks of returning to the University of Missouri, Storm described a meeting that ultimately changed the course of his career:

> A buddy of mine came into the media lab at Mizzou—which was really just three Macintoshes—but it's the place I would spend countless hours. He came by with a floppy disk with a piece of software on it, so we loaded it up. It was Mosaic. The first web browser I'd ever seen in my life. And he [Storm's friend] says, "alright man, we are sitting on a computer in Champaign Illinois right now." I was like, "what are you talking about? No we're not, we're in the Mizzou lab." He says, no, we are actually reading files off a computer that is in Illinois and we're in Missouri. I was like, wow, that's amazing! I sat there for a minute and I swear to you, it was probably at least a minute that I sat there with my mouth open at what he was showing me and I finally said one word to him . . . distribution! I knew this was going to change distribution.

Storm was adamant that the role of his production company would be to leverage digital forms to surpass the restrictive nature of newsprint and television. The boundaries of the Web were endless, and its distribution could reach far beyond the geographic restrictions of traditional media.

> What I had seen happening was that we had photographers like Suau who were showing 80 of his best images to a bunch of photographers. He was preaching to the choir! The only people who had access to his work were the people who happen to be at that particular photo conference. I felt the same way about the work I was doing with the CD-ROMs. I spent ten months producing a Pictures of the Year CD-ROM that we pressed a thousand copies of and guess who got those? Photographers. I was preaching to the choir, so when the Web came, bam! It was crystal clear to me that we should switch to the Web even though there were incredible limitations in bandwidth at the time . . . but I just felt like the Web was going to uncork distribution.

Storm wasn't the only one to see the Web's potential as a tool for multimedia storytelling. The Microsoft Corporation out of Redmond, Washington, was preparing to form an online news service called MSN—originally the Microsoft Network—and plucked Storm from his studies at Mizzou and made him employee number 11. Storm recalls the early days in Redmond: "I got there in July of 1995. I'll never forget showing up at Microsoft and not even having a computer for about four days. There was no mandate, no philosophy about what our online approach should be. MSN was just like, GO!" Microsoft named Storm, then 24, director of multimedia in charge of packaging photos, video, and audio, leveraging his unique presentation styles gleaned from the hushed photo conferences and his experiences producing computer-based CD-ROM interactives. Within a year, MSN partnered with NBC News and became MSNBC.com. During Storm's tenure at MSNBC, from 1995 to 2002, he created and launched two influential digital news packages: "The Week in Pictures" and "Picture Stories," which were audiovisual photojournalistic slideshows. "People loved it," said Storm. "People kept telling me they hadn't seen work like this before, I said 'I know, I've seen it at conferences, but no one is publishing it.'" The Web gave these visual stories reach, with 25 million unique readers a month, doubling to 50 million by 2001. Storm's influence continued to spread as he presented his ideas on the impact of new media on photojournalism, and, more importantly, he shared his workflow and presentation style for multimedia packages at dozens of conferences around the world.

At this juncture let's take a look at how some media organizations innovated during this period in order to shape digital storytelling.

## ▶ MERCURY CENTER

Notable digital news packages from Mercury Center:

> "Dark Alliance"—produced in 1996, became one of the first "viral" DNPs, and the first to publish an extensive library of sources

> "United States of America vs Microsoft, Virtual Courtroom," 1999—early immersive experience

Most online news access between 1992 and 1994 was not in a Web browser but rather took place on Internet portals such as CompuServe, America

**FIGURE 2.7** "Dark Alliance," *San Jose Mercury News*, 1996

**FIGURE 2.8** "United States of America vs Microsoft," *San Jose Mercury News*, 1999

Online, and Prodigy. Using a portal, you didn't launch a browser and type in a Web address like www.MercuryNews.com; instead you would log on to the Internet via software stored on a compact disc provided by a company such as America Online (AOL) in order to access the *Mercury News* online edition. It wasn't until the mass adoption of Netscape Navigator after its launch in 1994 that news companies left portals behind and ventured onto the Web. The first among them was the Mercury Center of Knight Ridder's *San Jose Mercury News*, commonly referred to as Merc Center.

The Merc Center was named by its founder, editor Bob Ingle, who described his thought process behind the name "Center" in a company memo: "It's not perfect, but it does convey nicely the concept: that the newspaper is at the center of information and communication in the community."[37] With the *Mercury News* no longer bound to its portal service, AOL, Mercury Center continued its legacy of "firsts" and was among the first recorded news sites to break news on the Web, the first to offer its entire digital archive on the Web, and the first to unwittingly create the Internet's first "viral" news story, with a controversial digital news package called "Dark Alliance."

Geri Migielicz, the director of photography at the time, recalled some of the barriers facing the early days of Web publication:

> The best thing about the Mercury News was that it was a place that wanted to break new ground—a mantra was to not be satisfied with doing what everybody else was doing. How could we make a story unique to our readership? In Valley-speak, how do we innovate and iterate? The Web offered the possibilities of sequencing images without the space constraints of print. Telling a story in pictures was a dance with the difficult geometry of newsprint. Photographs are mostly horizontal and the page is vertical, and there were a finite number of ways of displaying a photo story on a news page. . . . With Merc Center, we latched on to the idea that we could offer experiential content on the web and take risks we couldn't do with print. We knew we wanted to run with ideas, but Merc Center proceeded with a toddling walk when it came to photojournalism.[38]

Almost immediately, the staff of Mercury Center gained a newsroom reputation as insular and even secretive, often discouraging the main newsroom from engaging and contributing to the site. Migielicz took the first opportunity to seed Mercury Center with someone from the newsroom. Migielicz tapped one of the newsroom's most talented photo editors, Scott DeMuesy. "DeMuesy loved technology, second only to photojournalism," said Migielicz. "I thought it would be great for photography if we made a commitment to the digital platform [Merc Center] and in doing so had the bonus of getting our very own mole inserted into the heart of the operation."

DeMuesy initiated some of the first online multimedia efforts for Merc Center and the industry at large. "Things for me really started to get exciting when I received beta copy of Adobe PageMill . . . being a visual person I wanted a WYSIWYG (what you see is what you get) program that would help me design pages. I really thought this would become the 'QuarkXpress' of the web and everyone would eventually use it. Well, I was wrong. Turns out PageMill just put too much extraneous code into the documents. I spent most of my time cleaning up the HTML PageMill created."[39] DeMuesy would immediately experience more frustrations of being "first."

As DeMeusy's creativity was ready to run wild with multimedia presentation ideas, the Web itself seemed to be holding him back. Noting the snail's pace of Internet load times, he recalls having to warn viewers that a gallery of photographs might be too large for the Internet speeds at the time (30–40 kilobytes per photo, which by today's standards would be the file size of a site's logo). "The biggest problem with the gallery was that it could not be easily updated. So, there were long periods the same photos stayed on the page, and we actually had to warn people how many images were on the page," stated DeMeusy in an e-mail interview.

Another early disappointment seemed to be lack of audience, as he realized one evening when the site went down and no one complained during the newspaper's annual Thanksgiving day special section.

> This was a project that included a lot of [Web] pages and photos. I spent hours and hours after work trying to get it just right. It was to debut Thanksgiving day 1995 and the link to the online version was published on the front page of the newspaper. The first thing I did Thanksgiving morning was fire up my modem, type in the URL and nothing appeared! So I hauled ass to the Merc and had a security guard let me in to Merc Center so I could post the site. It was at that moment I realized that Merc Center wasn't a high priority to the newspaper: I thought we would get some complaints that the site wasn't up, we didn't.[40]

As the photo editors would realize, being at the cutting edge included plenty of frustration and setbacks. All early multimedia content suffered the same fate at the whim of slow modem connection speeds. The computers the audience had, though revolutionary at the time, were limiting and lacking capabilities of software. While the work of early online content producers was certainly slow to load by today's standards—and their designs, in hindsight, seemed simple and primitive—it was not for lack of expertise. All nascent environments are inherently limiting in nature, and the Web was no different. The infrastructure was still in a 1.0 version. An apt description of DNPs of the time could be characterized this way, "CLICK, *WAIT* . . . REVEAL."

"We couldn't guarantee quality—or actually guarantee anything at all," remarked Migielicz. "And there were few rewards for doing content for the Web. We still had to feed the beast [the newspaper] and make sure our best efforts worked in print, as well. With our early experiments, I knew the potential to break new ground in visual storytelling was perhaps limitless, but that the technology of the time was clearly a barrier. If we created it—could anyone load it and view it? It was one hurdle that we were about a decade ahead of as far as Merc Center and Knight Ridder was concerned."[41]

Despite some growing pains and technological impediments, the answer to the question, "Was anybody out there?" was answered with a resounding "yes" two years later. Although it made its way onto the Web without the strong visual presence desired by the photo staff, Merc Center's reputation was growing—so much so that in 1996 *Editor & Publisher*, the trade magazine of the newspaper industry, named the site the nation's best newspaper on the Web.[42]

Before the word "viral" was used to describe the rapid and wide spread of a story, Merc Center, for better or worse, became an overnight sensation with the publication of an online news package called "Dark Alliance." The series, written by the *Merc*'s investigative reporter, Gary Webb, charged that the US-backed Nicaraguan contras were funded with profits from an inner-city crack trade. The package was printed in typical newspaper fashion, over a series of days with a large amount of the newshole devoted to the story, photos, and maps. These "special" reports have long since been a staple of the print product, but the publication of the "Dark Alliance" series on the *Merc*'s fledgling website was new territory. The Web permitted Merc Center to experiment with seemingly unlimited space and dabble with other technologies unfamiliar to a newsroom at the time, like audio and graphic animation.

In a 2011 article written for the *Columbia Journalism Review*, "The Newspaper That Almost Seized the Future," writer Michael Shapiro described the initial reaction to the series: "The response was electric; the story became the subject of talk radio, and of every conspiracy theorist who believed that the government was secretly behind the crack trade. 'You don't have to be the *New York Times* or the *Washington Post* to bust a national story anymore,' Webb said. Traffic boomed."[43]

Although the reporting for the series was wrought with controversy, mainly accusations that Webb and the *Merc* had overreached in their reporting of the story, there remains a significant contribution by the online series to the evolution of the digital news package. It's certainly true that the aforementioned viral nature of the story—how quickly and widely it spread—is worth mention; so too was the way the online news package was presented. There's no doubt that the story spread because of its publication on the Internet. But the nature of how it was published can serve as an example of how news organizations were structuring and presenting multimedia content during the Web 1.0 era.

The "Dark Alliance" website launched with a clean, minimal, text-driven presentation. Beyond the obvious blue-colored hyperlinks was a sidebar positioned on the left of the page that contained what the *Merc* would call a library. Included in the library were more than 30 documents: court transcripts, agency memos, letters by public officials, audio recordings from wiretaps and hearings, an animated map of the cocaine pipeline through Central America to Los Angeles, bios of the central figures in the story, links to outside resources, and even a discussion board where readers could give their opinions. The stories themselves were separated into three parts: day one, day two, and day three. Once a user clicked inside a story, additional information would appear as links to photos, maps, and audio positioned next to the text on the right-hand side of the page. The entire package was presented in a continuous vertical layout. "Dark Alliance" was the first

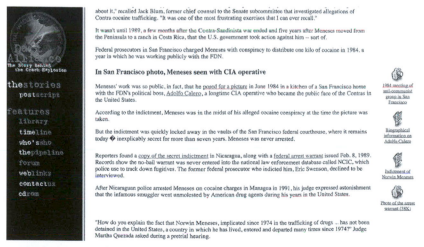

**FIGURE 2.9** "Dark Alliance," *San Jose Mercury News*, 1996

recorded digital news package to deliver such a rich collection of primary sources to the public. Many newsrooms around the country took note of the series for more than its controversial reporting and recognized a new era in online storytelling.

The Internet had arrived.

## ▶ *CHICAGO TRIBUNE ONLINE*

Notable digital news packages from *Chicago Tribune* included these early nonlinear packages:

"Code Blue: Survival in the Sky," 1996

"The Babies Grow Up," 1996

"Chicago: The Convention Capitol Tour Guide," 1996

"Jordan's Journey," 1999

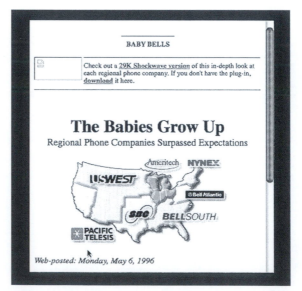

**FIGURE 2.10 "The Babies Grow Up,"** *Chicago Tribune Online***, 1996**

While the DNP was still in its infancy and experiencing growing pains, the *Chicago Tribune* was charging forward into the future, creating a new breed of journalist. Leah Gentry, a former editor at the *Orange County Register*, launched the online version of the *Tribune* in March 1996. She became industry famous for a set of guidelines that she called *Leah's Rules*:

1. All the regular rules of journalism apply. Reporting and editing must be solid. Facts must be checked and rechecked.

2. If you're going to use the week's gizmo it has to help advance the telling of the story in a meaningful way.

3. No instant publishing. Everybody has his or her finger on the press, but nobody is allowed to post a page that hasn't gone through the editing process.

4. Reporters need to think of the medium while reporting. In addition to story information, they must gather or assign information for animated or still graphics, video, and audio.

   **The main rule:** What we're doing is journalism, not stupid technology tricks.[44]

The *Tribune*'s online efforts were unique from the outset in that its reporters were dedicated exclusively to the online version. Most other newspapers at the time had their staff doing double-duty working for both the print and online editions.

Initially relegated to a small hallway-like room on the fifth floor of the *Tribune* building, Andrew DeVigal, then a 27-year-old graphic designer and online producer, recalled, "People called it the dorm room because all of a sudden a bunch of young kids were gathered in a very small space."[45] With almost two dozen staffers assigned to the operation and clear "rules" from Gentry, they would set the standard for early nonlinear DNPs.

During an interview with the authors, DeVigal, now the Chair of Journalism Innovation and Civic Engagement at the University of Oregon's School of Journalism and Communication, recalled some of the early thinking that took place in the dorm room: "We were asking ourselves, how do we pause a piece of media and allow people to engage with it, to be more thoughtful and have control of their own pacing through the story? To a lot of storytellers that idea was sacrilegious. They say, 'I don't want anybody to stop my experience,—grumble grumble—I put together this experience and this is the way it's meant to be.' And while that might be true from a storyteller's perspective, maybe not so for the user." The team at the *Tribune* was on the hunt for authentic interaction. "We were looking beyond press, play or the next and previous buttons of an audio slideshow. To me it becomes interactive when you are purposefully inquiring about a piece of information or a piece of data with the ability to control that experience. Perhaps another way to look at this is that it was an early way to personalize the user's experience through that data. So that's where I think interactive graphics plays an interesting role."[46] One of the earliest examples comes from DeVigal himself. Posted in May 1996, "The Babies Grow Up" interactive feature was produced in Macromedia Director and published using a pre-Flash plug-in called Shockwave. The project mapped the regional phone company's coverage and charted their revenue over ten years. In an online post DeVigal recounted that "in those days, all of these early web pages were hand-built without a content-management system."[47] Instruction on the site advised viewers to drag their mouse "pointer" over regions of the map to identify the telecommunications company's coverage. When clicking on a desired region on the map, the user would be presented with more information on the firm.

"Most graphic journalists have the ability to see things in a very interactive way, a nonlinear approach."[48] The secret to DeVigal's statement and the area in which the *Tribune* would excel lies in the word *nonlinear*. The dedicated staff of the *Tribune* went on to set the early standard for nonlinear story packages. Instead of a single narrative, stories were broken up into component parts, which included a main narrative and then links to the other sections of a story. Gentry described their nonlinear process as deconstructing and reconstructing a story in a 1999 study for the Poynter Institute by Carole Rich titled "Newswriting for the Web." This process included specific steps:

- ▶ **Deconstruct**—Divide your story into its component pieces. Look for similarities and relationships between the pieces, and group together segments that are similar.

- ▶ **Reconstruct**—Use a storyboard to create a diagram that lays out the relationships between the groupings and how the nonlinear story can be organized.

▶ **Micro-element**—Determine the main linear story line—what happened and must be told.

▶ **Macro elements**—Define other more contextual elements of the story that readers can choose to read or not. If there is a cast of characters in a story, these elements could be the different viewpoints of each character.[49]

The online packages that the *Tribune* produced showed a clear distinction between the print edition and online. In Christopher Harper's book *And That's the Way It Will Be: News and Information in a Digital World*, DeVigal named the main differences in platforms: "immediacy, interaction and multimedia."[50]

While many of the nonlinear projects they pioneered are lost to link rot, a few descriptions still remain. A 1996 package, "Chicago: The Convention Capitol Tour Guide," explored in tremendous detail the history of political conventions in Chicago and was part of the *Tribune*'s coverage of the 1996 Democratic convention. The online edition capitalized on the *immediacy* factor mentioned by DeVigal by updating stories throughout the day. *Interactivity* was implemented via an online poll, and *multimedia* features allowed users to listen to speeches, watch videos of delegates, and view the entire convention floor in a 360-degree panorama. There was more: In the spirit of nonlinear presentation, there was a historical tour of some of the previous political conventions in Chicago, starting with the one that nominated Abraham Lincoln in 1860. "The idea was to take people on a tour that was a virtual museum," said Darnell Little, the reporter who conceived the project.[51] In a further breakdown of the project, used by Paul Grabowicz, senior lecturer and Bloomberg Chair in Journalism at the University of California at Berkeley, during his new media courses, Grabowicz detailed the stages of the project. The story had three parallel streams:

▶ a tour through six conventions;

▶ a behind-the-scenes look at what was happening in Chicago at the time;

▶ story archives and political cartoons from the time.

The reporter storyboarded each story in a process called "layering" the story:

▶    an opening page that was based on an anecdote, which had a headline, a digital photograph, and text of usually less than 500 words;

▶    a second page that was the nut graph, explaining the main points of the story;

▶    finally, links to additional pages that guided the reader through the various aspects of the story.[52]

Most importantly, a reader could chart their own course through the stories, moving between the different streams or narratives. For example, the user could be reading about the 1860 convention and want to know what was happening in Chicago at that time. So they could click on the link to the "behind the scenes" section. From there they could click on the story archives to get more background information. Then they could go on to the next convention or instead skip ahead to some other convention.

These early *Tribune* efforts were a clear example that new methods of telling stories and presenting information were being firmly welded together on the Web. Most notably, the *Tribune*, MSNBC.com, and Merc Center proved that creating multimedia content presented fewer boundaries than legacy platforms.

While some organizations were licking their wounds from early failures, others were careening forward. The National Newspaper Association (NNA) reported that 175 newspapers had made their way online by April 1996.[53] It was a time of frenzied activity for multimedia experimentation. Online content producers were presented with multiple avenues as they made their way to the Web. Some early practitioners went beyond a shovelware approach (simply duplicating print content online) to enhance their coverage with additional information, as was done in "Dark Alliance," or to create entirely new content using interactive tools, as the *Chicago Tribune Online* did in "The Babies Grow Up."

## ▶ OTHER NOTABLE DIGITAL NEWS PACKAGES

**Greatest Hits**

"Virtual Voyager," 1995–1998—HoustonChronicle.com

"North Carolina Discoveries," 1996—Nando.net

"Black Hawk Down," 1997—Philly Online

### The *Houston Chronicle*

The still primitive digital culture was shaping up to be the electronic equivalent of the Wild West. One of the most interesting enterprises was conducted at the *Houston Chronicle*. Taking a page from the *Chicago Tribune*,
the *Chronicle* began to send its reporters into the field with digital cameras
and high-quality audio recorders to provide multimedia content for the site.
What resulted was one of the paper's most popular and most innovative multimedia features, according to a 1997 *Los Angeles Times* article, "Newspapers
Take Different Paths to Online Publishing."[54] Dubbed Virtual Voyager, the
online-only project's aim was to take advantage of the Web's ability to create
an immersive experience with users. The scope and ingenuity of Voyager's
presentations marked it as one of the most innovative DNP efforts of the time.

Stories ranged from Australia to China and even points along the famed
Route 66—sometimes with a camera mounted in the backseat of a car—and
the Voyager team took readers as close to these locations as it could without them actually being there. From the Grand Canyon, they provided
360-degree photos, logs, maps, diaries, and audio and video segments.
A detailed examination of Voyager's explorations are presented in Pablo J.
Boczkowski's 2004 book, *Digitizing the News*, where he writes that the project accounted for approximately one-fourth of the site's traffic in 1996. That
year, it was named Best Interactive Feature by the Newspaper Association of
America in their first ever digital media awards competition.

Providing a rare and privileged glimpse into the complex authoring
practices of Voyager, Boczkowski reflects on the editorial distinctions
between working online and working in print by observing an unmis-
takable change in the workflow of early online storytellers. Boczkowski

wrote that content creators now had the burden of deciding "to choose whether to use text, still images, video, audio, computer animation, and 360-degree photographs to tell either the whole story or parts of it, instead of having those choices constrained by the delivery vehicle."[55] Furthermore citing a noticeable mixing of print workflows with that of broadcast, radio, and information systems work, Boczkowski recognized a major shift that would take hold in the thought process of digital story-tellers. The presentation of the DNP was altering and so was the mindset of the creator.

### The *Raleigh News & Observer* (nando.net)

It was becoming blindingly clear that the production of multimedia pack-ages required new skills and more hands-on time to produce than the traditional print edition. This was especially apparent at the *Raleigh News & Observer*, commonly nicknamed the "*N&O.*" They were among those giving the Internet a fresh voice with the site Nando.net ("N and O"). In a 1995 *American Journalism Review* (*AJR*) article titled "The Digitized Newsroom," writer Philip Moeller detailed the *N&O*'s approach to reshaping journalism, depicting a published digital news package, "North Carolina Discoveries," as a massive team effort. The special report, focused on state topics, utilized all available media platforms for publication—an unprecedented move. While *N&O* staffers gathered multiple media in the form of pictures and audio, local TV stations in partnership with the *N&O* gathered video. The final product, a 16-week series, was published to Nando.net, the newspaper, and radio and television stations. The *N&O* was breaking an early stereotype of a multimedia reporter as a one-man band, exemplifying how multimedia was a team sport. In the *AJR* article, *N&O* reporter Julie Ann Powers points out that their project required broadcast skills that were unfamiliar to tradi-tional print reporters. "From the very beginning of the process [the report-ing] is different," she said. "I had to think in terms of sound and motion as well as whether it would support a full length story in the paper." Sound, which is not a factor for print stories, proved a major new concern, she says, as did the need to compensate for the lack of visual elements in radio stories and, to some extent, print stories. She needed to pose questions that would elicit answers in a form suitable for recording, she explains, whereas her traditional interview style was much more conversational.[56] Suddenly newspapers were doing the kinds of things for which they had no template. As the reinvention of traditional news forms and workflows were being reinvented for the online world, the packages themselves began to slowly mature.

The *Philadelphia Inquirer*

On November 17, 1997, four years after two US Black Hawk helicopters were shot down by RPGs in Mogadishu, Somalia, the *Philadelphia Inquirer* began a 29-part print serialization of the events titled "Black Hawk Down." During the fateful operation, some of the wounded survivors were able to evacuate, but others remained near the crash sites and were isolated. An urban battle ensued throughout the night. The saga was reported by the *Philadelphia Inquirer*'s Mark Bowden based on interviews with the men who fought in Mogadishu.

In a 2000 Nieman Foundation Report, titled "Narrative Journalism Goes Multimedia," Bowden would recall the process of creating the online version:

> At the time, it seemed like a fairly simple task. In those early meetings I remember seeing Philly Online's editor, Jennifer Musser, at the table quietly taking notes, and assumed she had a simple job—mounting the text of the series on the Inquirer's Web site. To the extent I thought about it at all, I thought the Web site would give readers who picked up the series in midstream an opportunity to go back and catch up on the earlier installments, which would be particularly beneficial because the story was such a long, dramatic narrative. I figured it meant we would just display the text of the story each day online, along with the rest of the paper's offerings. That was when Jennifer stopped by my desk to ask me what sort of research material and documentation I had for the project. I had been working on it for years at that point, and had piles of audiotapes, notes, documents, radio transcripts, photos, etc.[57]

Musser's next question would become the first step toward creating a landmark DNP, whose approach and presentation methods would be replicated for years to come. "Could you bring them in?" she asked. Bowden did and Jennifer, along with the online team—designer Ches Wajda, photo editor John Williams, and programmer Ranjit Bhatnagar of Philly Online, the *Inquirer*'s official website—packaged the contents into a vanguard of online story presentation. The package featured the full text of the series along with photographs, video and audiotape snippets of the battle, interviews with key participants, maps, graphics, and documents. As you scroll down the page of each chapter, related multimedia content is integrated within the context of the story; readers can click on a variety of links to view maps, audio interviews, or Pentagon video of the raid. By today's presentation standards, the website might seem primitive: a single HTML page, devoid of any photos or video elements, serves as a landing page or an aptly titled "Table of Contents." The text stories are in a column on the right, each linking to the 29 separate chapters, while the multimedia elements—video, audio, maps, and graphics—are hung on the left and at the bottom of the page. Once clicked, each chapter is anchored by the text with occasional thumbnail-sized images, maps, and video and audio clips embedded in the text. What made the presentation different was that, for the first time, related multimedia content was not presented in a separate location or disconnected from the narrative text. But more importantly, embedded within the narrative of the text were links to the relevant multimedia material. For instance, if a reader wondered what was in Staff Sergeant Matt Eversmann's head as he slid down the rope into battle, all they had to do was click on the hyperlink embedded next to Bowden's text description and listen to an audio clip of Eversmann explaining the situation. Bowden summed up the early excitement of the "Black Hawk Down" package and the Web's storytelling potential: "On the Web site, the story

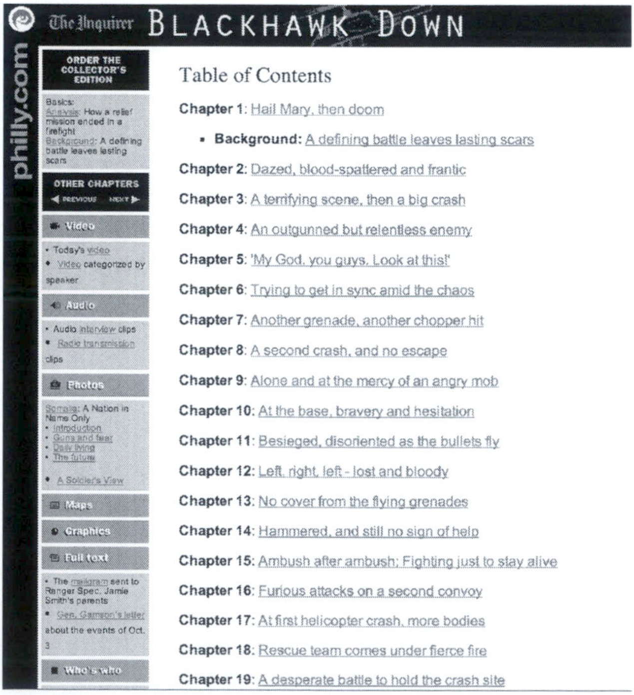

**FIGURE 2.11 "Black Hawk Down,"** *Philadelphia Inquirer,* **1997**

became part illustrated book, part documentary film, part radio program. It was all these things and more, because it allowed readers (who at times became viewers) to explore the story and its source material in any way they chose."

Ten years after the package was published, it was turned into a novel and later adapted into an Academy Award–winning film. Bowden recalled his initial reactions to the online package:

> It blew me away. When I started in the newspaper business, I learned to work on a typewriter with carbon paper, paste pot and scissors. Jennifer's creation combined text, video, audio, documents, maps, illustrations, and a sprawling Q&A feature into something that was more than an amazing presentation—it was a glimpse of journalism's future. It demonstrated the clear superiority of the Internet over the printing press. In the case of Black Hawk Down, apart from all the multimedia razzle-dazzle, it opened up a global dialogue with readers, including men who had fought in the battle. They corrected my mistakes, pointed me to better information, and offered to be interviewed, allowing me to improve greatly on the story before it was published as a book in 1999. Mine may have been, thanks to Jennifer, the first book that ever benefited from this new journalistic tool. In a sense, the story was edited by the entire world.[58]

While the *Inquirer*'s "Black Hawk Down" project was produced during the Web 1.0 design period—with less attention paid to traditional layout methods, owing more to the limitations of the Web and less to the creative intentions of the designer—it is, however, the earliest example of some of the most extensive and significant uses of the features of hyperlinking, interactivity, and multimedia.

In 1997, presentation forms were in various stages of experimentation, but innovative and creative structures were being set into motion by these early multimedia producers.

## ▶ FLASH FORWARD

The year 1997 was a big year for the digital news package: not only was there a notable maturing of the form, but a tsunami of animation and interactive possibilities made their way into the hands of multimedia producers with the release of a software program called FutureSplash Animator. Initially used by MSN and Disney to bring more animated content to their websites, it was acquired by Macromedia and transformed into a popular multimedia tool named Flash.

It would take several more years before a wide adoption of Flash-based websites made their way to the Internet, but the seed was planted. Though there were early adopters of Flash in the news industry for sure, a true era of "Flash Journalism" wouldn't come until 2005 with the release of a "ridiculously simple storytelling" software tool known as Soundslides.

What made the various versions of Flash distinct were their ability to truly package multimedia elements into a single "container" in the form of an SWF file format. It's evident that online producers were already creating provocative news packages on the Web without the need for Flash by linking separate web pages together, like "Dark Alliance." Without the use of Flash, packages consisted of a single web page that served as an entry point to the narrative and then merely hyperlinked to additional pages with related media. In some cases pop-up windows were utilized. As the industry realized the infinite amount of online space, some of these special packages became bloated with multimedia content, such as the 29-part "Black Hawk Down" series. With most users still limited to slow connection speeds, file size of images and videos became an issue. Flash promised larger images, complex animations, sound, and video at a fraction of the size, significantly shortening download wait times. Furthermore, graphic designers who were desperate to bring their design expertise to the Web recognized Flash as a powerful tool to unleash their creativity. Thanks to the Flash interface, designers had precise control of the position of all media elements within the Flash Integrated Development Environment (IDE). Flash offered a harmonious and singular interactive experience on the Web not seen since the CD-ROM.

Flash forward to 2005. A stark reality faced the newspaper industry. As the print product fell on hard economic times, newspapers retrenched, reducing newsrooms with severe cuts and layoffs. It was a tumultuous time for newsrooms across the country. Despite the economic climate, presses kept running and online producers kept posting. This time marked a significant transitional period as the new medium—still young and unprofitable—was shifting, in most cases from an experimental skunk works to a more elaborate operation. This period, marred by an economic downturn, also saw Flash mature, bringing with it more feature-rich tools like streaming audio and video. Users no longer had to wait for an entire video file to download before watching. With streaming, once the file downloaded enough data (known as buffering), you could hit the play button and start watching immediately.

The arch of DNP innovation shifted further when multimedia content went from being used as an afterthought to text to being used as an independent, stand-alone experience. This observation was echoed by Don Wittekind, graphics director of the *South Florida Sun Sentinel*, in the book *A Practical Guide to Graphics Reporting*: "Thanks to advances in software (Macromedia Flash) and increased bandwidth, we now incorporate every form of media into our project. This has allowed the multimedia component, which was once an accessory, to become an entire project."[59] Flash allowed all media elements to be combined into a single frame without the need for separate windows and often without the need to scroll. DNPs created at this time were finally beginning to utilize some of the unique characteristics of the new digital frontier.

Nora Paul, the inaugural director of the Institute for New Media Studies at the University of Minnesota, outlined specific ways in which DNPs were transforming modes of presentation during a 2005 keynote speech to the Korean news industry in Seoul. Paul's keynote, titled, "The Future of Storytelling in the Digital Age: Strategic Thinking for Online Journalism," encapsulated the developments in digital storytelling during this period by showing specific signs it was transforming:

- from explaining to experiencing;
- from informing to inviting opinions;
- from episodic to encyclopedic;
- from "read their stories" to "hear their stories";
- from newsprint layout to creative navigation.[60]

During an interview in 2014, Paul set up the experiential nature of DNPs emerging at this time because of Flash: "With newsprint you use text to explain to people what has happened. On TV you can show them a video. But online you can let them experience it for themselves. It's a powerful way to let people interact with a news story in a way simply not possible with other media."[61] She recalled a DNP that exemplified the shift from explanatory to experiential multimedia experiences. Paul referenced a Flash-produced

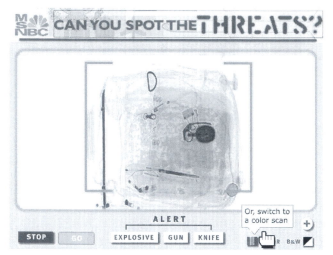

**FIGURE 2.12** "Can You Spot the Threats? Try Your Hand at Detecting Threatening Objects," "MSNBC.com"

DNP from MSNBC titled "Can You Spot the Threats? Try Your Hand at Detecting Threatening Objects," which was a baggage-screening game to illustrate the difficulties of spotting dangerous substances in luggage. After the September 11 attacks, the crackdown on airport security resulted in longer waits and baggage screening became a major part of every air traveler's experience. MSNBC helped travelers to trade places with security screeners and experience what it was like to become responsible for detecting threats.

The baggage-screening interactive is a game-like experience where the user is given two minutes to look at luggage X-ray images as they move past the screen. The player has to spot possible threats and stop the flow of bags, but if they take too long frustrated travelers would make snippy audio comments about their slow performance. This experiential package gave visitors to the website a clearer sense of air screening issues and helped to build empathy with those performing a frustrating new part of travel.

## ▶ THE EDGE

As noted earlier in the chapter, not all multimedia journalists rode the early Flash wave, due in part to its steep learning curve. But those at the forefront of this movement at the outset were the online producers at the *South Florida Sun Sentinel*. Their extensive and impressive body of Flash-based

**FIGURE 2.13** "The Edge," *South Florida Sun Sentinel*, 1999

DNPs were featured in a special section—now defunct—on the newspaper's website called "The Edge."

Over the years, Paul Grabowicz, senior lecturer of New Media at UC Berkeley, collected hundreds of interactive projects from "The Edge." Many of them were designed as simple games that people could play to better understand news events; others were just for fun, like a "South Florida Snowman," which allowed users to dress a snowman by clicking and dragging elements on the page.

In 1999, the *South Florida Sun Sentinel* described "The Edge" on their About page: "What is The Edge? The Edge is a haven for anyone who has the processing power to take advantage of Internet multimedia. Using Shockwave Director and Shockwave Flash, we bring you the news with the added benefits of sound, animation and interactivity. If you're tired of static text and images, come inside and see the site Macromedia described as having 'fully emersive [*sic*] multimedia learning experiences.'"[62]

## ▶ FLASH JOURNALISM COMES OF AGE

Until 2005, most of these DNPs were produced by large to medium-sized media operations. Limited staffing and the steep learning curve required to adopt new workflows in technologies like video, audio, and Flash left a large percentage of journalists on the sidelines, simply shoveling legacy media onto their websites. But new waves of journalists were about to flood newspaper websites across the country with audio-driven photo slideshows. They did it with the help of a software program built by photojournalist and coder Joe Weiss.

Reporter Pat Walters noted the sea change in a 2007 article for Poynter.org, saying, "Audio slideshows seem to be showing up on more and more news Web sites these days—and not just on sites produced by national news organizations. From what I can tell, much of the growth is being driven by smaller newsrooms, with many of the collections created by one program. Soundslides."[63] If any single development in the evolution of the online package is responsible for this explosion of audio-driven photo narratives, it's the creation of Soundslides, whose tagline still remains, "Ridiculously simple storytelling."

Weiss recalled the early events and motivations leading up to the creation of the rapid slideshow production tool. In a 2014 interview with the authors Weiss recounted driving away from an assignment at an orphanage for the *Durham Herald-Sun* in 1999 and being struck by the stories he heard from the kids more so than the images he made of them—a powerful statement for a photojournalist to admit. Weiss decided right then and there to go back and record audio and put together a multimedia package. Weiss purchased an inexpensive microphone and a MiniDisc audio recorder at his local electronics shop and returned. He used Flash version 4 to create his first multimedia package. Most other audio-driven photo slideshow tools at the time were tedious or difficult to use. Weiss recognized another more troubling frustration: the "ridiculously, soul crushingly time-consuming" process of working in Flash. Weiss recalled 10-hour days to create a simple 20-image audio slideshow. "Everything needed to be done by hand, I had to build all the transitions between the images, one-by-one using keyframes . . . it took a ridiculously crazy amount of time."

Weiss would spend the next five years in fits and starts, trying to find a solution to the time issue by automating the workflow. Eventually in 2004 he pieced together all of his code snippets during a multimedia workshop where the participants were creating slideshows and put them into a user interface. "It was the first time they were put together in a standalone app that someone else other than me was able to use." Weiss had an aha moment. He thought, "I'm making my life easier . . . why can't this make everyone's life better?" Weiss knew that the larger news operations could deal with the time and scale issue of producing these multimedia slideshows, but he wanted to reach the smallest of newspapers and even freelancers who were strapped for time and resources. Weiss would launch Soundslides in August 2005 for $39.95. "I did my best to pick a price that everybody could afford. It didn't take off like a rocket, but it took off pretty quickly. . . . Then in late 2006 and 2007 it was like a rocket. Everywhere I turned it was there.

I used to put a pin on a map every time a copy sold and then I couldn't even keep up with the demand. Ultimately, I didn't want to see my peers sitting in front of a computer for hours on end doing horribly redundant work[;] they should be out on the street telling stories." The small piece of inexpensive software offered a bit of promise during a time when many staffers were wondering what was going to happen to their jobs because of the economic belt tightening in the newspaper industry. Times were tough, layoffs were always on the horizon, and securing a position as a valuable contributor to the online product—while still not significantly profitable—was a safe move for job security.

"I don't know what multimedia would look like now without Soundslides. I don't know what would've happened to the profession if journalists hadn't gained some web skills via the use of Soundslides." said Weiss. Weiss's audio slideshow production program—initially dubbed "Joe's Tool" by the first workshop participants to use it—lived up to its tagline and helped a "ridicu-lous" number of journalists transition into multimedia.

Brian Storm, who hired Weiss at MSNBC, said, "I'm happy he did it because it made the whole industry move. That was just the tools becoming easier, but the introduction of Soundslides is just a key, key moment in the evolu-tion of our business."[64]

## ▶ VIDEO VIDEO VIDEO

Almost as quick as the audio slideshow revolution began, it was overshad-owed by the demand for video on the Web. Just as the industry was learning Flash and flooding the Web with audio-driven slideshows, a sudden precipi-tous fall-off would occur.

On February 14, 2005, three former PayPal employees, situated in an office above a Silicon Valley pizzeria, launched the domain YouTube.com. The video-sharing site quickly became one of the fastest growing services on the Web.[65] Users began uploading an astonishing amount of video con-tent. According to a *USA Today* article at the time, users were uploading more than 65,000 new videos and delivering 100 million video views per day in July 2006.[66] For the news industry, the growth of YouTube repre-sented a significant opportunity and challenge. Expanded bandwidth and new streaming technologies allowed video to be delivered in a smooth and seamless experience. With a sense of not wanting to miss out on the next new wave, a breed of pioneering photographer broke out of still photography into video. Accompanied by smaller, less expensive digital video cameras with high-definition quality, Pulitzer Prize–winning photojournalist David Leeson, from the *Dallas Morning News*, led the charge for video in the newsrooms.

Leeson recalled the pivotal meeting with his then director of photography, John Davidson, that would launch his video career: "As I sat down in his office, he told me that he saw someone from the web staff shooting a video in the photo studio for use on DallasNews.com. His concern was that video, a visual medium, created by someone with no background in photojournalism, could lead to an erosion of photojournalism standards on the web. So he asked me to take a closer look at video from the viewpoint of a photojournalist. The meeting ended with a succinct order I will never forget: 'Just go DO something.' "[67]

After months of producing video, Leeson discovered "a new and powerful way to tell stories. Furthermore, I saw the writing on the wall and knew that web video for news media would soon explode, and I wanted to be on the cutting edge of that innovation." As the only still photojournalist in the country shooting exclusively with a video camera, Leeson had concluded that still photojournalists transitioning to video should and could hold fast to their skills as still shooters. Video, he insisted, "is a change of cameras and little else." Leeson would spread his message and workflow to the rest of the newspaper industry—hungry for information on how to transition from still to video—at conferences and workshops across the country.

In 2005, when Leeson enthusiastically took to the podium to make his case for a wider adoption of video in newsrooms, he would explain his logic for switching from stills to video this way: "Video coverage could provide 1) still images for both the print and web editions 2) audio could be extracted from video for radio or web use 3) stills and audio could be combined to create a multimedia slide show 4) it could be used as a video or 5) all of the above."[68]

It took several years before his message was fully received. In a 2008 *American Journalism Review* article, "The Video Explosion," it was clear that the use of video as a crucial component to DNPs had grown from "a significant trend into a near stampede."[69] While commenting on a video posted to the *Washington Post* website, the article's author, Charles Layton, a former editor and reporter at the *Philadelphia Inquirer*, said, "It was not a gimmick, not an add-on, not forced or contrived, but a fully integrated piece of inter-active, multimedia journalism, as user-friendly as a spoon . . . it quickly became one of the most-viewed stories ever to appear on WashingtonPost.com." The article went on to quote *Miami Herald* photographer-turned-videographer Chuck Fadely: "We have four people on the photo staff doing video full time, and we're doing 15 to 18 [stand-alone] pieces a week." The *Herald* was also training reporters in video. "The change in the industry right now is the most dramatic I've ever seen," says Fadely. "Virtually every paper in the country is, if not diving head first, at least dipping their toes into video." Around this time a common question around newspaper photo departments was, "Can we get a video of that?"

If we rewind to 2005, we'll find that seated in the front row of Leeson's impassioned plea for video was the director of photography of the *San Jose Mercury News*, Geri Migielicz, who took heed of Leeson's message and immediately "schemed" her way into purchasing a high-definition video camera for her photography staff. After years of frustration with the lack of attention to visual storytelling on the *Merc*'s website, Migielicz saw video as the perfect opportunity to push the medium forward. Migielicz assigned two of her photographers (one of which was an author of the book, Rich-ard Koci Hernandez, the other photographer Dai Sugano) to work on pro-ducing a visual-driven website and incorporating a video workflow into the department.

After sleepless nights and plenty of energy drinks, Koci Hernandez and Sugano bootstrapped and launched MercuryNewsPhoto.com in late 2005. With the visually focused website launched, a reorganization meeting at the *Merc* threatened to create a new multimedia department, outside of the existing photo department. "I had to fight to keep what we were doing under photo supervision. . . . I made a strong case that at the heart and soul should be a photographer. It's not like they turned on the switch for the Internet and photographers were unprepared to tell stories on the Web using a computer; we had already been doing it. We were using Photoshop and had gone from film to digital, not to mention we recognized a series of images, sequentially as a slideshow from our Kodak projector days." Migielicz summed up the move to the Web this way: "it was more a seam-less, less revolutionary moment."[70]

Koci Hernandez spent more than nine months shooting exclusively with a video camera, providing content for the newspaper via a video-frame-grab process and posting short videos to the Web. With a video workflow in place at the *Merc* and more video cameras in the hands of staff photographers, Migielicz said, "We became truly, creatively free at last with the launch of the site. Suddenly restraint was a choice and going all out was possible. . . . It was freeing."[71]

Two years later, with MercuryNewsPhoto.com publishing Soundslides and Flash-based multimedia packages almost daily, they posted a break-through DNP.

The project was called "Uprooted." The ambitious project was presented as a six-part video series on the Web, with a multi-page spread published in the newspaper. The project, photographed by Sugano over a ten-month period, chronicled the displacement of a group of residents in a Sunnyvale, California, mobile home park. The Flash-based package, built by Koci Hernandez, used a traditional narrative structure for the package with a beginning, middle, and end to display the longform narrative, but divided it into chronological "chapters" or "parts" to allow the viewer to view at their own pace.

In October 2008, the *Merc* would be honored with an award unfamiliar to the newspaper industry—the DNP won a national Emmy in a new category created by the Academy of Arts and Sciences to recognize the emergence of new forms of storytelling: New Approaches to News and Documentary Programming.

Migielicz, who oversaw the launch of the website and "Uprooted," reflects, "We finally had a viable platform we could control. When I look at the projects we did with simple and often crude tools, I see the glimmering promise that is the hallmark of today's best multimedia projects. We tried to take viewers places they couldn't go and see things through the eyes and voices of the people who lived the stories we told. This powerful journalism experience has upended my career, for the better. The quality of storytelling always comes down to the quality of the idea, the story, the execution and understanding the audience. In the end, true multimedia authorship is losing yourself completely in the story, right alongside the audience."[72]

Propelled by the emergence of new tools like the hybrid DSLR (digital single-lens reflex), which are cameras able to shoot both high-definition video and stills as a single device, a solid emphasis on video-centric DNP production is still in place to this day.

## ▶ "THE INTERNET IN YOUR POCKET"

With video and multimedia production firmly in place at newspaper organizations across the country, a new innovation in the summer of 2007would upend digital news packages. No single event in the evolution of the DNP has been as disruptive to the form of online news packages as the introduction of the smartphone. On June 29, 2007, the launch of the first iPhone changed the mobile ecosystem dramatically, disrupting not only the mobile phone market itself but also the format of news people would consume on these devices. Although the impact was not readily apparent in the beginning, more than eight years later this industry is still adjusting to its reverberations.

It's important to remember that the first-generation iPhone launch wasn't about apps—in fact the App Store didn't exist then. It wouldn't open until more than a year later, when Apple truly changed the smartphone landscape. The device was squarely focused on browsing the Internet, as evident by Apple's ad campaign, "The Internet in Your Pocket." The iPhone was the first smartphone to offer a usable mobile browsing experience. Over the next few years PCs would become a decreasing share of Internet-connected devices as a result of the encroaching size of the smartphone market. This set the stage for a massively mobile connected browsing experience and a shift in content production specifically aimed at viewers whose appetite for consuming information on their mobile phones seemed insatiable. In fact, in 2014, Internet usage on mobile devices exceeded PC usage.[73] What did this shift in content consumption mean for online news producers, many of whom just became comfortable packaging content for desktop browsers? Also, there was the issue with Adobe Flash, which the iPhone didn't support. Flash had become the de facto tool for most multimedia creators. The popular industry platform Soundslides used to present slideshows on the Web used Flash as well. The mobile browsing experience would also have a considerable effect on the output of DNPs by news organizations in the years to follow.

## ▶ "THOUGHTS ON FLASH"

In a controversial move by Apple, co-founder and former CEO Steve Jobs declared that Apple would not support Adobe Flash on its devices, including the newly introduced iPad. In a post by Jobs in April 2010, called "Thoughts on Flash," Jobs asserted that "Flash was designed for PCs using mice, not for touch screens using fingers. For example, many Flash websites rely on 'rollovers,' which pop up menus or other elements when the mouse arrow hovers over a specific spot. . . . Even if iPhones, iPods and iPads ran Flash, it would not solve the problem that most Flash websites need to be rewritten to support touch-based devices."[74] While the letter drew immediate criticism in 2010, some even accusing Jobs of being misleading about the prominence of video on the Web,[75] over the years the slow evaporation of Flash as a Web technology has played out in Apple's favor and has led to an almost Flash-less mobile Internet.[76]

At the time, no one had more reason for concern than the creator of Soundslides, Joe Weiss. "If there was ever a point of crisis in my professional life as a journalist and with Soundslides, this was it. It seemed like people were told that their favorite tool didn't matter anymore. I felt enormous pressure to not screw over all the journalists that I had enabled with Soundslides."[77] Weiss spent the next six weeks re-coding Soundslides as an HTML5 technology, which meant that it would run completely in every browser, even mobile devices, and wouldn't rely on third-party plug-ins like Flash any longer. "Those six weeks were awful. I literally had people writing me everyday saying, 'I can't contribute online anymore.' No matter who you blame the fact that Flash wasn't available in a mobile world, [it] meant it was no longer a legitimate choice for the multimedia journalist toolkit."

During this period, there was a noticeable drop in the production of Flash-based interactive narratives, especially from smaller news organizations. In fact, even a cursory glance at the news industry's largest database at the time, InteractiveNarratives.org, shows a slowing of Flash-based entries into its database. "I really think that the interactive journalism world lost three years in the production of projects, just snap your fingers, 2007, iPhone, Bam! Flash is dead. No more interactive journalism. In fact we may have lost more years than that because it took a while for people to say 'we really need to stop using Flash.' It was monumental," said Weiss.[78]

The issue became worse with smaller news organizations. Seth Gitner—assistant professor of newspaper and online journalism at Newhouse School at Syracuse University and author of *Multimedia Storytelling for Digital Communicators in a Multiplatform World*—said, "I just don't see people producing interactive projects the way we were back in the early 2000s. Back then it was done on such a large scale. Everybody from large papers to small papers. Today you only see the large papers organizations producing large interactive projects. I think newspapers have stopped innovating. For them, innovation simply means a video, not interactive projects.

For one, smaller papers with very little resources can more easily monetize video. Really rich multimedia storytelling is only being done by the large organizations."[79]

Because HTML5 is more code-intensive and requires a vast amount of technical knowledge, expert producers are likely to be found in large national news organizations. Digital news packages produced in 2014 have become more sophisticated than their Flash predecessors, perhaps in part because they require so much more expertise by specialists who understand the relationships between HTML, JavaScript, CSS, and responsive design principles. While the following chapters in this book are filled with case studies of DNPs, a clear example of post-Flash innovation and a modern manifestation of our evolutionary past, the *Guardian's* "NSA Files: Decoded: What the Revelations Mean for You" bears examination.

## ▶ DECODING A MODERN DIGITAL NEWS PACKAGE

It seems fitting that the first contemporary DNP to be examined involves the work of Gabriel Dance. Dance is the managing editor for digital operations at the Marshall Project, a nonprofit, nonpartisan news organization covering the criminal justice system. Dance's background and experience have put him at the center of DNP innovation for almost a decade, starting at the *New York Times* as a multimedia producer in 2006. After the *Times*, Dance was the art director for news at the iPad-only newspaper the *Daily* and then served as the interactive editor for the *Guardian*. While at the *Guardian*, he was part of a group of journalists who won the 2014 Pulitzer Prize for Public Service for coverage of how the US government conducts surveillance. Dance and his colleagues had one of the biggest and most complex national news stories drop in their lap when Edward Snowden leaked documents to the *Guardian*, and they were given the herculean task of creating an online news package from the materials.

In an article on Knight-Mozilla's OpenNews Source publication, Dance wrote, "The goal of the NSA Decoded project was to create an interactive story that used all of the Internet's storytelling devices (video, interactives, maps, charts, text, and yes, GIFs!) to explain the story of the NSA files in an accessible and relatable way."[80] The mega-explanatory interactive, published on November 1, 2013, instantly generated a level of social media excitement not seen in online journalism since the *New York Times* published its "Snow Fall" project.

**FIGURE 2.14** "NSA Files: Decoded," *Guardian*, 2013

In trying to provide context for the story, the team at the *Guardian* managed to create a package with multimedia synergy that comes alive via video, graphic animation, and data visualizations, all triggered as you scroll down the page. During an interview with the authors, Dance explained, "I really, honestly believe that there is nothing else out there that looks anything like this ["NSA Decoded"]. Or that behaves anything like this project. And we didn't build this from a model. This is something that I saw in my head. Certainly it is influenced by many things but not a copy of anything. The team's goal was to take advantage of the tools that the web provides to help make the piece more engaging."[81]

Among the challenges for the team who worked on the project for three months was the lack of visuals inherent to the story. "We didn't have any lovely video or photos to run with it, so we knew the design would be even more important. As such we started out with a fundamentally text-first approach seen across many projects over the past few years, with annotations (video/photo/document/etc.) that would appear alongside the text as you got to a particular point in the story."[82] Then something dramatic happened. Something so secretive that Dance admits to never having revealed it to anyone before his July 2014 interview with the authors. Dance explains the secret success of the project this way: "The real reason that the project works as well as it does, and the real reason that it came together as well as it did, is that the thing that was done last, let me emphasize *last*, were the words. The [text story] to NSA decoded were the last thing we did."[83]

Dance explained that their initial approach was a traditional one with multimedia elements positioned along the side to accompany the text narrative.

> But as we continued to develop it and storyboard it, we saw that it didn't makes sense to approach it that way. If you really do think about these things holistically in terms of how much time it takes to create each element, the written words are by far the easiest and most fungible part of the project. You can rewrite a lead pretty quickly, you can write into and out of things in the blink of an eye. It's not like video where if you don't have a particular shot you're hosed—you can't use it because you don't have it! Video also takes a long time to recut and render. It's not at all like an interactive which are obviously not easy to change after they're done. So it was this real revelation that, it again speaks to the power of words in fact, that they are so flexible and so strong and so malleable that the idea of making them the last thing you do is anathema to most journalists. Most people would not be ready to hear this. Most people might ask—isn't the project primarily copy? And the answer is no. NSA Decoded is not primarily anything. There are something like 12 interactives, 18 videos and 4,000 words and none of them work without the rest of them so it's not primarily anything.

After rethinking the entire format of the project, Dance pulled all of the multimedia assets out of the sidebars and inserted them directly into the narrative. With the approval from the rest of the team, Dance said, "we decided to write into and out of the videos and graphics, essentially complementing the multimedia with copy. This was a truly liberating and infinitely flexible approach, as we were no longer beholden to any type of media to tell the story, which I think was a big part of why the project turned out to feel so cohesive."[84]

The blend of interactive elements, video, and written narrative in a thoughtfully designed package delivers something immersive and engaging. In the first four days, hundreds of thousands of readers visited the project—many of whom spent as much as 30 minutes with the project.

"NSA Files: Decoded" was created during a time when multimedia journalists were rethinking their tools and approaches. With new devices seemingly released every day and consumer habit evolving to a more mobile browsing experience, new forms like "NSA Files: Decoded" are emerging in ways not confined by the technological norms that were developed in the days of Flash-based interactives. Dance and his team built a DNP that was fluid, responsive, and interactive across devices—without Flash. The fall of Flash led to the current advancements in standards like HTML5, CSS3, and JavaScript.

The techniques and technologies employed by Dance and his team are easily labeled "innovative" if viewed through the lens of the past, but that would overlook the fluidity of the Web and its supporting technologies. New platforms and evolving Web standards seem to die almost as soon as they are born. What the "NSA Files: Decoded" team did was more valuable than innovation; it was adaptation. This is a lesson worth noting as we face all the possible future iterations of the digital news package that will be created with technologies for devices that have yet to be invented—but will most certainly appear.

Dance perfectly sums up his years of multimedia experience by saying, "The value lies in the content, and there's no template for content."

## ▶ FACING THE FUTURE

The aforementioned evolution and maturations of online news packages offer a mere glimpse of what digital storytelling has become and what might it be. In many ways multimedia journalists are still in the Morse code era of communication. The Web is still a restless teenager with a lot more growing up left.

One must ask, what works and why? The authors hope this examination of multimedia journalism in its current state will give a glimpse of what works now, as well as the potential and eventual impact that digital news packages will have on narrative structure in the future. Much of this depends on the ability to find the right balance of medium, form, and content. The early evolution proves that repurposing existing content doesn't advance storytelling as much as more adaptive attempts. Many of the digital journalists mentioned in this book had an ability to recognize the unique characteristics of any new platform and seize its unique capabilities, an element critical for success.

The future will come and story will be there to meet us.

## ▶ NOTES

1  Shapiro, Michael. "The Newspaper That Almost Seized the Future." *Columbia Journalism Review*. November 11, 2011. http://www.cjr.org/feature/the_newspa per_that_almost_seized_the_future.php?page=all

2  Ward, Mike. *Journalism Online*. Oxford: Focal Press, 2002, 122.

3  Ritchin, Fred. "Bosnia: Uncertain Paths to Peace." *After Photography: What Is Next?* May 4, 2009. Accessed January 2015. http://www.pixelpress.org/afterphotography/?p=534

4  Alpert, Jesse, and Nissan Hajaj. "We Knew the Web Was Big . . ." Official Google Blog. July 25, 2008. Accessed January 2015. http://googleblog.blogspot.com/2008/07/we-knew-web-was-big.html

5  Shafer, Jack. "On the Trail of the Question, Who First Said (or Wrote) That Journalism Is the 'First Rough Draft of History'?" Slate.com. August 30, 2010. Accessed January 2015. http://www.slate.com/articles/news_and_politics/press_box/2010/08/who_said_it_first.html

6  Storm, Brian, interview with the authors, July 2013.

7  "The Blau Monuments." The British Museum. Accessed October 22, 2014. http://www.britishmuseum.org/explore/highlights/highlight_objects/me/t/the_blau_monuments.aspx

8  Wilkinson, Richard H. *The Complete Gods and Goddesses of Ancient Egypt*. New York: Thames & Hudson, 2003, 6.

9  Campbell, Joseph. *The Hero with a Thousand Faces*, 2d ed. Princeton, NJ: Princeton University Press, 1972.

10  Miller, Carolyn Handler. *Digital Storytelling: A Creator's Guide to Interactive Entertainment*. New York: Focal Press, 2014.

11  Miller, Carolyn Handler. *Digital Storytelling: A Creator's Guide to Interactive Entertainment*. Amsterdam: Elsevier/Focal Press, 2004.

12  Salomon, David A. *An Introduction to the "Glossa Ordinaria" as Medieval Hypertext*. Cardiff: University of Wales Press, 2012.

13  Adams, Douglas. "DNA/How to Stop Worrying and Learn to Love the Internet." DNA/How to Stop Worrying and Learn to Love the Internet. Accessed January 2015. http://www.douglasadams.com/dna/19990901-00-a.html

14  Parker, Elliott S. "John Thomson, Photojournalist in Asia, 1862–1872." 1977. Paper presented at the 26th Annual Midwest Conference on Asian Affairs, Northern Illinois University, De Kalb, Illinois, October 14, 1977.

15  Newhall, Beaumont. *The History of Photography: From 1839 to the Present*. Rev. ed. New York: Museum of Modern Art, 1982.

16  King, Elliot. *Key Readings in Journalism*. New York: Routledge, 2012.

17  White, Margaret. *Portrait of Myself*. New York: Simon and Schuster, 1963.

18  Edey, Maitland A. *Great Photographic Essays from Life*. Boston: New York Graphic Society, 1978.

19  Elson, Robert T., and Curtis Prendergast. *Time Inc.: The Intimate History of a Publishing Enterprise*. New York: Atheneum, 1968.

20  McLuhan, Marshall. *Understanding Media: The Extensions of Man*. New York: McGraw-Hill, 1964.

21  *Mad Men*. "The Wheel." Season 1, Episode 13. Weiner Bros., Lionsgate Television, AMC. October 2007.

22  Migielicz, Geri, e-mail interview with the authors, August 2014.

23  Levin, Gerald M. Interview by Paul Sagan, Martin Nisenholtz, and John Huey. Riptide—Nieman Journalism Lab. February 20, 2013. http://www.niemanlab.org/riptide/person/gerald-m-levin/

24  Widman, Jake. "Lessons Learned: IT's Biggest Project Failures." *Computerworld*. October 9, 2008.

25  Finberg, Howard. "Viewtron Remembered Roundtable." Poynter.org. October 27, 2003. Accessed January 2015. http://www.poynter.org/uncategorized/17740/viewtron-remembered-roundtable/

26  Finberg, Howard. "Viewtron Remembered Roundtable." Poynter.org. Accessed January 2015. http://www.poynter.org/uncategorized/17740/viewtron-remembered-roundtable/

27  Palilonis, Jennifer. *A Practical Guide to Graphics Reporting: Information Graphics for Print, Web & Broadcast*. Burlington, MA: Focal/Elsevier, 2006.

28  Wolfe, Gary. "The (Second Phase of the) Revolution Has Begun." *Wired*. October 1994.

29  Storm, Brian, interview with the authors, August 2014.

30  Meyer, Pedro. "Some Background Thoughts." *I Photograph to Remember.* May 5, 2001. Accessed January 2015. http://www.pedromeyer.com/galleries/i-photograph/work.html

31  Stein, Bob. "From the Lightscreen - ZoneZero - Desde La Pantalla De Luz." November 29, 2011. Accessed January 2015. http://v2.zonezero.com/index. php?option=com_content&view=article&id=1351:you-could-hear-a-pin-drop& catid=5:articles&directory=9

32  Fisher, Lawrence M. "Technology; The Tools of a New Art Form." *New York Times.* September 18, 1993. Accessed January 2015. http://www.nytimes. com/1993/09/19/business/technology-the-tools-of-a-new-art-form.html

33  Williams, Charles. "Multimedia Storytelling." Dostal Project. January 1, 1997. Accessed January 2015. http://dostalproject.weebly.com/multimedia-storytelling.html

34  Storm interview, August 2014.

35  Gitner, Seth. *Multimedia Storytelling for Digital Communicators in a Multiplat-form World.* New York: Routledge, 2015.

36  Storm interview, August 2014.

37  Shapiro, "The Newspaper That Almost Seized the Future."

38  Migielicz interview, August 2014.

39  DeMuesy, Scott, interview with the authors, July 2014.

40  DeMuesy interview, July 2014.

41  Migielicz interview, August 2014.

42  "EPpy Awards—Past 1996 Winners." *Editor & Publisher.* Accessed January 2015. http://www.eppyawards.com/content/Past_1996_Winners-22-.aspx

43  Shapiro, "The Newspaper That Almost Seized the Future."

44  Harper, Christopher. *And That's the Way It Will Be: News and Information in a Digital World.* New York: New York University Press, 1998.

45  DeVigal, Andrew, interview with the authors, January 2014.

46  Shapiro, "The Newspaper That Almost Seized the Future."

47 DeVigal, Andrew. "An Interactive Graphic from May 1996." *Flickr*. November 2, 2009. Accessed January 2015. https://www.flickr.com/photos/15482523@N00/4068589784/in/photolist-7cwzZJ

48 Shapiro, "The Newspaper That Almost Seized the Future."

49 Rich, Carole. *Writing and Reporting News: A Coaching Method*, 3rd ed., Instructor's ed. Belmont, CA: Wadsworth, 2000.

50 Harper, *And That's the Way It Will Be*, 79.

51 Harper, Christopher. "Journalism in a Digital Age." MIT Communications Forum. April 23, 2008. Accessed January 2015. http://web.mit.edu/comm-forum/papers/harper.html

52 Grabowicz, Paul. "Choosing the Right Medium." Lecture, Multimedia Bootcamp from UC Berkeley Graduate School of Journalism, Berkeley, January 1, 2012.

53 Li, Xigen. *Internet Newspapers: The Making of a Mainstream Medium*. Mahwah, NJ: Lawrence Erlbaum Associates, 2006.

54 Shaw, David. "Newspapers Take Different Paths to Online Publishing." *Los Angeles Times*. January 17, 1997.

55 Boczkowski, Pablo J. *Digitizing the News: Innovation in Online Newspapers*. Cambridge, MA: MIT Press, 2004, 115.

56 Moeller, Philip. "The Digitized Newsroom." *American Journalism Review*. January/February 1995.

57 Bowden, Mark. "Narrative Journalism Goes Multimedia." *Nieman Reports* 54, no. 3 (2000): 25.

58 Bowden, Mark. "The Point: Journalism's Future Is in Global Dialogue." Philly.com. June 17, 2007. http://articles.philly.com/2007–06–17/news/24994248_1_web-site-presentation-global-dialogue

59 Palilonis, Jennifer. *A Practical Guide to Graphics Reporting: Information Graphics for Print, Web & Broadcast*. Burlington, MA: Focal/Elsevier, 2006, 44.

60 Paul, Nora. "The Future of Storytelling in the Digital Age: Strategic Thinking for Online Journalism." Lecture from Korean Press Foundation, Seoul, South Korea, 2005.

61 Paul, Nora, interview with the authors, August 2014.

62 "The Edge." *Sun Sentinel*. October 1999. Accessed 1999. http://www.sun-sentinel.com/graphics/theedge

63 Walters, Pat. "Photos, Audio and the (Glorious) Struggle to Combine Them." Poynter.org. January 9, 2009. Accessed January 2015. http://www.poynter.org/news/job-news/80101/photos-audio-and-the-glorious-struggle-to-combine-them/

64 Storm interview, July 2013.

65 O'Malley, Gavin. "YouTube Is the Fastest Growing Website: Digital—Advertising Age." Advertising Age Digital RSS. July 21, 2006. Accessed January 2015. http://adage.com/article/digital/youtube-fastest-growing-website/110632/

66 "YouTube Serves up 100 Million Videos a Day Online." Reuters. July 16, 2006. Accessed January 2015. http://usatoday30.usatoday.com/tech/news/2006-07-16-youtube-views_x.htm

67 Leeson, David. "David Leeson Essay." Backpack Journalism Project, American University School of Communication. Accessed January 2015. http://www.american.edu/soc/backpack/david-leeson-essay.cfm

68 Leeson, David. "David Leeson Essay | Backpack Journalism Project | American University School of Communication." Accessed January 23, 2015. http://www.american.edu/soc/backpack/david-leeson-essay-2.cfm

69 Layton, Charles. "The Video Explosion." *American Journalism Review*. January 2008. Accessed January 2015. http://ajrarchive.org/Article.asp?id=4428

70 Migielicz interview, August 2014.

71 Migielicz interview, August 2014.

72 Migielicz interview, August 2014.

73 Murtagh, Rebecca. "Mobile Now Exceeds PC: The Biggest Shift Since the Internet Began." *Search Engine Watch*. July 8, 2014. Accessed January 2015. http://searchenginewatch.com/sew/opinion/2353616/mobile-now-exceeds-pc-the-biggest-shift-since-the-internet-began

74 Jobs, Steve. "Thoughts on Flash." Apple.com Hot News. April 2010. Accessed January 2015. https://www.apple.com/hotnews/thoughts-on-flash/

75 Rayburn, Dan. "Steve Jobs Is Lying about Flash." *Business Insider*. April 29, 2010. Accessed January 2015. http://www.businessinsider.com/steve-jobs-is-lying-about-flash-2010-4

76 Topolsky, Joshua. "Adobe Ends Mobile Flash Development, Will Focus on HTML5." *The Verge*. August 14, 2012. Accessed January 2015. http://www.theverge.com/2011/11/9/2549196/adobe-flash-android-blackberry

77 Weiss, Joe, interview with the authors, 2014.

78 Weiss interview, 2014.

79 Gitner, Seth, interview with the authors, August 2014.

80 Dance, Gabriel, and Feilding Cage. "How We Made 'NSA Files: Decoded' - Features - Source: An OpenNews Project." November 26, 2013. Accessed January 2015. https://source.opennews.org/en-US/articles/how-we-made-nsa-files-decoded/

81 Dance, Gabriel, interview with the authors, July 2014.

82 Cage, Feilding, and Gabriel Dance. "How We Made 'NSA Files: Decoded.'" Source: An OpenNews Project. November 26, 2013. Accessed January 2015. https://source.opennews.org/en-US/articles/how-we-made-nsa-files-decoded/

83 Dance interview, July 2014.

84 Cage and Dance, "How We Made 'NSA Files: Decoded.'"

# 3

# Classification of Digital News Packages

The first step in wisdom is to know the things themselves; this notion consists in having a true idea of the objects; objects are distinguished and known by classifying them methodically and giving them appropriate names. Therefore, classification and name-giving will be the foundation of our science.

—Carolus Linnaeus, *Systema Naturae* (1735), trans. M.S.J. Engel-Ledeboer and H. Engel (1964)

On December 20, 2012, visitors to the *New York Times* website noticed something they hadn't seen before. It was a new type of article, teased on the front page, titled "Snow Fall: The Avalanche at Tunnel Creek." The story instantly became a watershed moment in the online news industry. In an entirely new way to display a story, the *New York Times* employed a mix of technological and design conventions like autoplaying background videos, embedded photos and videos, graphics that changed as the user scrolled down, and a curtain effect, in which new sections of the story seemed to cover previous parts while the user scrolled. The package redefined the notions of how a news article could be presented on the Web and focused attention to new visual and interactive multimedia embedded throughout the story. Although news stories contained complementary multimedia elements like videos, photos, and interactive graphics for many years prior, there were only sparse examples of such a tightly integrated and seamless experience where the multimedia elements were embedded into the story itself; in a way, they became the story.

In the years since, story packages like these have become increasingly popular in newsrooms. Nearly every week as of the writing of this book, we find examples of media outlets experimenting with big in-depth multimedia news packages. Journalism schools now include these dynamic displays as part of the curriculum and regularly dissect examples of these packages to better understand their nature.

It's easy to acknowledge the innovative potential of this new approach. These packages typically have slick designed interfaces, incorporate sound and visuals, and are presented in an almost cinematic-like fashion, using title pages and credits. While these sporadic examples of tightly integrated multimedia garner much attention from within the news industry, there are enormous logistical hurdles to creating these packages. Most are custom tailored, designed, and coded for specific stories—a process that is antithetical to the workflows and business practices of current newsrooms, which typically adhere to content management system (CMS) or templates.

But taking a step back, one must ask: How do these in-depth news packages best convey information? And, divorcing the glamor of new and inventive technologies found in many of these packages from the content, one also must ask whether they truly aid the end goal of imbuing readers with a story's essence and not just add visual gimmickry for its own sake.

As the publication of these news packages became more frequent, it was also clear how disparate were the approaches being taken by different organizations. Some of these stories were clearly a more linear, or narrative, experience. Others stories were divided into multiple sections with no predefined path through the story, giving users more control to decide how they wanted to consume the story. Some were cinematic-like experiences—as if you were watching a movie or playing a video game.

One person who thought a lot about online news presentation back in the 1990s was Leah Gentry, formerly with the *Orange County Register, Chicago Tribune,* and later LATimes.com. Some of her ideas were described in the

2002 book *Journalism Online* by Mike Ward,[1] and later in an interview we did with Gentry, who now works in digital marketing and social media. During several keynotes, including one in 1997, Gentry talked about the nature of Web news as a nonlinear platform and the importance of leveraging different media forms to best tell different parts of a story. Nonlinear storytelling was a crucial part of communicating on the Web back then, partially because it mimicked our natural tendencies to want to jump around a story in a lean-forward mode, such as using a computer, versus a lean-back consumption mode, such as sitting on the couch reading a book or watching a movie.

"I used to use the analogy of talking with my mother on the phone because my mother—like everyone's mother—starts stories in the middle, and then skips back to the front and then skips to the end and then come back to the middle. And that's how natural conversation works," described Gentry in a Skype interview. "But it's also how people's brain works. I thought, how would it be like if we'd organize this story that way using hypertext—and so that's how the first nonlinear storytelling project came to be and was the fertility doctor scandal at the University of California, Irvine."[2]

The fertility fraud story won the Pulitzer that year for the *Orange County Register*. Designing the online component—particularly in respect to how to organize all of the many parts of the story—was a big part of discovering the nature of the medium, described Gentry. Later, when multimedia like photos, interactive graphics, and videos were possible on the Web, Gentry formalized a process of how to think about the structure of online stories with respect to leveraging multiple mediums. She espoused a process of "deconstructing and then reconstructing" a story to better understand its components and makeup. A single story is really multiple stories, each with a component part and possibly a different medium. Separating these component parts allows for the creation of a nonlinear story where the user had complete control over how, and in which order, to consume the story.

Another person who has thought a lot about the nature of online news packages with more contemporary examples is Wes Lindamood, a senior interactive designer at National Public Radio (NPR). This was a particularly important part of working on the project "Planet Money Makes a T-shirt."[3] His team based much of their early planning of their project on analyzing other news packages and trying to categorize them along a spectrum. The

**FIGURE 3.1** Story structure diagrams that helped the *Planet Money* team developing their T-shirt project design, Knight-Mozilla OpenNews Source (reproduced via CC-BY 3.0), 2014. Credit: Wes Lindamood/ NPR.

categorization he arrived at compared the level of user interaction that was required in a project versus a lean-back-and-watch narrative experience.

Lindamood created a graphic charting the different stories along this spectrum to determine how much interaction was required from the users as they consumed the story—more specifically, how much power they had to jump around or make choices that would affect either the pacing or direction of the story. In some examples, like a news package designed by *National Geographic* called "The Serengeti Lion," the user has ultimate control to move about and decide which parts of the story they want to consume—and in whatever order they choose. In the "Serengeti" package, each section is labeled with a moniker; and the user moves about using arrow keys on the keyboard to jump from section to section (the order is randomized and different for every user), and the user can view more information about that specific part of the story. A small index link will display all of the available sections, also listing which ones the user has already visited. In his graphic, Lindamood described the "Serengeti" project as more user directed rather than discrete narrative, as the user has complete control over which sections to view and is able to carve out a path through the story as they see fit.

On the other side of Lindamood's spectrum is "Alma—A Tale of Violence,"[4] which is an example of a story package that is more of a narrative experience. The "Alma" project is a self-described Web documentary and is distributed by Arte TV, a Franco-German TV network in Europe. The online film part of Alma is a single 40-minute interview with a former Guatemalan female gang member, Alma, as she vividly describes on camera how she killed

**FIGURE 3.2** "The Serengeti Lion," *National Geographic*, 2013

another woman as part of her gang initiation. She then goes into describing her life and the gang experience, and then ends the story with how she was shot and paralyzed when she tried to leave the gang. The film is very much a confessional with gripping accounts, particularly when she describes one of her victims crying out for her children as Alma stabbed her to death.

The "Alma" story package is split into two branches: a 40-minute Web documentary, and secondarily what Lindamood describes as "information modules"—separate sections that give background information on the story if the user scrolls past the documentary. Because the main focal point of the piece is the documentary, Lindamood categorized this as a more "narrative journey" requiring less interaction from the user. While a user is watching Alma's video interview, the user has an option to move the entire video frame up, as it plays, to see some background footage (called b-roll in the broadcast world) of scenes corresponding to the narration. As Alma continues to talk and give her interview, the secondary window shows b-roll scenes of Guatemala and background footage that a video editor might have placed over the narration of Alma in a more traditional format of the film. But in this online version, the choice is given to the user either to watch Alma describe her story or to view background images while listening to the narration. Although this interactivity is available, it doesn't change the direction of the piece, nor is the user given choices that affect the path of the story. This narrative journey is akin to a documentary film, but it allows people to stay engaged with the piece in an online medium by permitting them to interact with it as they listen to the narration.

**FIGURE 3.3** "Alma—A Tale of Violence," Arte TV, 2012

This notion of a spectrum separating linear from nonlinear stories very much led our initial approaches to defining a taxonomy of story packages. The challenge in categorizing news presentations was finding clear demarcations that could separate one package from another. In many instances, there are overlapping characteristics. Was the *New York Times*'s "Snow Fall" a narrative story? Yes. Does it have videos and photos throughout the story? Yes. Does the user have control to jump around the story? Yes. But you could also say the same thing about numerous other projects, such as *National Geographic*'s "Serengeti Lions" or the *Guardian*'s "NSA Files: Decoded." However, when one views these projects, it's clear they are very different approaches to online storytelling and needed to be identified using a different set of characteristics. What were the most common themes separating one story from another?

## ▶ THE GRABOWICZ TAXONOMY

Our approach to this taxonomy of digital news packages really started with Paul Grabowicz, a senior lecturer at the UC Berkeley Graduate School of Journalism. In 2013, Grabowicz published a first attempt at classification and taxonomy of multimedia news projects on a school-related training website.[5] There were two parts to this taxonomy: The first was describing a series of approaches to packaging multiple forms of media into a cohesive experience, and the second was describing individual novel media types (e.g., interactive videos, games, graphics, etc.) that could be included within a larger news package. In the spirit of Leah Gentry's early work, Grabowicz divided stories into a linear versus nonlinear spectrum. Linear stories generally follow a directed path through the story, while other stories were nonlinear and gave the viewer lots of control to jump around the story at their own discretion and in their own order. Linear stories were more *narrative* in nature—consisting of a beginning, middle, and end—while nonlinear stories covered more of a topic and were more *informational* in nature. Nonlinear stories could also have parts embedded that could be mini-linear narratives or single-media types like a video or graphic. For example, one section of a nonlinear story package might be short profiles of characters in the story, whereas another section would be background information.

Grabowicz also came up with descriptive labels for different types of published news packages. One, called the "Christmas Tree," is a form where multimedia elements would be "hung" off to the side of a text story, similar to ornaments on a tree. The term is originally attributed to Regina McCombs, formerly of the *Minneapolis Star Tribune* and later Poynter Institute.[6] Other descriptions included terms like "embedded multimedia," used to describe the *New York Times* "Snow Fall" piece, where multimedia was embedded directly within the narrative of the story. "The Kitchen Sink" is used to describe story packages that cover a general topic rather than a single story, sometimes exhaustively, where the organization of content into a hierarchy becomes a central challenge (the kitchen sink problem). "Immersive Multimedia" was a catchall for projects that were usually interactive documentaries or video-game-like experiences, using three-dimensional representations for users to explore a space.

This approach to the taxonomy evolved over time. The shortfall with this approach was that it wasn't systematic enough and didn't give each package a common enough identity in order to compare it with others on a more granular scale (and later plot it on a graph). However, the Grabowicz taxonomy was the precursor to later versions and identified most of the structures and elements that we later included in our own work.

## ▶ FIRST ATTEMPT AT A BIOLOGICAL-LIKE TAXONOMY

While working on this book, we met a UC Berkeley visiting scholar and science writer, Caterina Visco, who was intrigued by our use of the term "taxonomy" and by applying these ideas to news. Visco had studied biology in Rome and thought it would be an interesting challenge to classify news stories in the same way biologists classify life forms.

In 1735 Swedish scientist Carolus Linnaeus published *Systema Naturae* and brought to the world its well-known Linnaean taxonomy (i.e., kingdom, phylum, class, order, family, genus, and species), which many might recall from high school biology classes. This was a rank-based system that categorized all organisms of the world into a hierarchy. At its highest level of classification, the original Linnaean taxonomy put the broadest possible form of organism at the top—the "kingdom." In 1700s, the kingdom rankings Linnaeus chose were animals, vegetables—and minerals! As discoveries of new forms of life were made over the years, the kingdoms have evolved and expanded to include microorganisms, like bacteria, and even fungi, whose cellular walls made them unlike plants in the most elementary way, so they were given an entire kingdom ranking of their own. Also, newer top-level categories above kingdom were defined: "domain," and even above that, simply "life." Interestingly, there is still much disagreement around the world regarding the precise labeling of these terms, since the sub-categories are not always pure biological descendants of top-rank descriptions. This biological ranking has been an iterative process over the centuries, changing many times, as recently as 1998.[7] As it stands now, since 1998, the current kingdoms of all life fall under these basic classifications: Bacteria, Protozoa, Chromista, Plantae, Fungi, and Animalia. There is a lot of fluidity in the precision of systematizing something as amorphous as life forms.

Much like the Linnaean classification, our process of trying to come up with a taxonomy of news packages was an iterative process. The first step we took was to define a classification of the different types of story packages, similar to a biological classification. This consisted of first identifying the characteristics of a database of more than 400 in-depth digital news packages we collected (these would be considered the very-bottom-level "species") in order to better understand their characteristics, and grouping them into a few well-defined categories. As it would be impossible to study all the species living on Earth without a system that gives them some order, so it would be difficult to study such a variety of news stories without grouping them in categories based on common characteristics. This process provided a way to understand their structure and to derive conclusions about their scope and impact on the user.

## ▶ A "LINNAEAN TAXONOMY" OF NEWS PACKAGES

**Domain** → Storytelling
**Kingdom** → Non-fictional Storytelling
**Phylum** → Non-fictional Online Storytelling

**Class** → Digital News Package
**Order** → (based on structure) → Linear, Shell, Immersive, Comprehensive
**Genus** → (based on main element) → Text, Visual, Audio, Games, Data
**Species** → Christmas Tree; Embedded Multimedia, Charticles, . . .

As shown in this chart, we attempted to identify elements of story packages in the pattern of a Linnaean taxonomy. We used the entire scope of story-telling as our "domain," non-fictional storytelling as a specific "kingdom" (to differentiate it from other types of creative fiction), non-fictional *online* storytelling as "phylum," and a news package as "class." These specific hierar-chies set up an initial framework for categorizing news stories.

The main taxonomical classification really begins in the next rung down, with the four named "orders," which are based on the structure/narrative form of the projects. We chose linear, shell, immersive, and comprehensive.

**Linear** describes more lean-back, read/watch types of stories, where the user would consume the story with little direct interaction, except perhaps scrolling. The structure is linear, with a predetermined order of how to con-sume a story—from beginning to end. These stories typically have one pri-mary medium (like text or a video), which drives the whole package, and various other media assets (like photos, graphics, or videos) are integrated throughout the narrative—directly or peripherally.

**Shell** is a term coined by Jane Stevens of the Reynolds Journalism Institute. Partly as a response to Adobe Flash projects, Stevens trained journalists to think about how a multimedia presentation could be wrapped in a packaged "shell."[8] The lesson included training in a workflow that consisted of story-boarding a project first—similar to what is done in cinema and also exhorted by Leah Gentry—by dividing the project into component parts and choos-ing the best media for each respective segment. Story shells were generally nonlinear by nature. A consumer can choose to consume the story in any order they want. Upfront, consumers are typically presented with numerous topics or sections in the form of some type of central navigation that allows them to move around the different pieces of the story. As a standard design convention, shells typically have a unified title for the entire project, which helps maintain cohesiveness to the multiple sections of a presentation. Adobe Flash shells were particularly useful at a time when users often hesitated to click links away from the story and load an entirely new web page. Flash made it easier to visit each section, was a much quicker process, and maintained continuity throughout the story. Later, this would be seen as a poor design convention as broadband proliferated and web page loading times became nonissues.

**Comprehensive** is a derivative term of the "kitchen sink" coined by Grabowicz, essentially capturing news packages, which cover topics rather than a single news story. But Comprehensive became a broader catchall term for this. Comprehensives are similar to shells in their nonlinear structure. Consumers can go through the story in any order they wish. However, instead of a Flash shell, Comprehensives were more akin to a topic page or a single-issue vertical. Some examples were the "Empty Cradles" series by the *Milwaukee Journal Sentinel.*[9] The *Journal Sentinel* published numerous multimedia pieces—charts and graphics, interactive panorama, text stories, video pieces—on a single topic. This type of package wasn't linear, although there are some narrative anecdotes within the piece. But each is designed for a specific purpose to illustrate a different part of the story.

**Immersive** is a classification that is also from Grabowicz; it aimed to describe stories that were similar to a video game or 3D environment. A number of stories, particularly ones by the National Film Board of Canada (NFB), are heavily sophisticated projects technologically and usually take up the entire screen. It gives the feel of a video game—in fact, one could even consider these a type of video game in many of the examples. These are often described as interactive documentaries, partly because NFB, who spearheaded much of this storyform, is a documentary film–focused institute. Another pioneer of Immersive stories is Nonny de la Peña, who works on immersive installations that transport users into environments. One of her early influential projects was "Gone Gitmo," in which Guantanamo Bay prison was reconstructed in the virtual world Second Life. Through the project, users could experience being a prisoner through virtual reality and thus gain empathy with prisoners' plight.[10]

The next rung of the taxonomy is the "genera," identified by individual media types: text, visual, audio, games, and data. This is designed to describe the primary medium of each of the previous packages. For the last category of the taxonomy, the "species," we used some specific examples identified by Grabowicz, such as the Christmas Tree, embedded multimedia, charticles, and others.

But as we began to deconstruct various stories into this model, it was clear these formalized patterns didn't fit into such a rigid structure. While this model was a noble attempt to classify Grabowicz's taxonomy, it didn't allow for classifications to overlap or intersect among the main categories, nor did it allow for a multiple intersections of types. Online news stories are simply too amorphous for such rigidly defined orders.

But there was a silver lining in this process. During her work in applying a biological classification, Caterina Visco did start to drill down on the four "orders" that served as the basis of further work. Despite the number of hours Visco dedicated to this process, she was especially motivated by a quote from Isaac Newton: "Truth is ever to be found in simplicity, and not in the multiplicity and confusion of things."[11]

In the next phase, we started with a large database of journalistic news packages collected by Bobbie Johnson, co-founder of *Matter* magazine. Johnson wrote a blog post on Medium highly critical of the *New York Times*'s "Snow Fall" model. At the end of the piece, Johnson created a Google spreadsheet asking the public to contribute links to examples of large immersive news packages similar to the *New York Times*'s "Snow Fall" piece (he called them "Snowfallen" stories).[12] Visco took this crowdsourced spreadsheet and appended several hundred additional story links, resulting in a list of more than 1000 news packages similar to "Snow Fall." This began a process of identifying common characteristics of each package: checking off which had videos and analyzing the various mediums that composed each story—specifically the media forms of the main element that drives each story (e.g., video, audio, photo, or text). All of this data ended up in a new spreadsheet that also noted information about each package, such as the main element driving the narrative, other complementary elements in the package, and the level of interactivity required of

|               | Text | Video | Audio | Animation | Data | Games | Map | Timeline |
|---------------|------|-------|-------|-----------|------|-------|-----|----------|
| Straight      |      |       |       |           |      |       |     |          |
| Immersive     |      |       |       |           |      |       |     |          |
| Comprehensive |      |       |       |           |      |       |     |          |
| Shell         |      |       |       |           |      |       |     |          |
| Intersections |      |       |       |           |      |       |     |          |

**FIGURE 3.4 The authors started with a simple table to deconstruct the multimedia packages into their separate elements**

the consumer to experience the piece. Visco also listed a column for "narrative form," using an expression from Grabowicz's taxonomy, but evolved the meaning to better reflect the *experience* the consumer gets. The narrative forms she settled on were Straight, Immersive, Comprehensive, Shell, and Intersections.

This grid, even if basic, helped us to understand that there were two different possible classifications that had to be examined individually: one based on the narrative structure, and the other identifying media forms that composed each package.

## ▶ CLASSIFICATION BASED ON THE NARRATIVE STRUCTURE

The text iteration of a taxonomy focused on five terms that identified the narrative structure of the packages: Straight, Immersive, Comprehensive, Shell. The fifth, Intersections, is a term that describes any stories that intersect two of the previous forms. We created a square diagram to better visualize it.

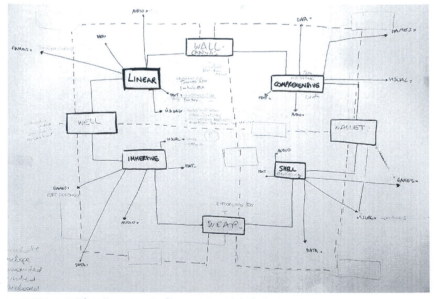

**FIGURE 3.5 The "square" diagram, with intersections**

The framework for this grid meant that stories could be placed along the lines of these spectrums. The linear designation was renamed to "Straight" with the understanding that linearity of a story was too simplistic a description; even immersive 3D games were linear, for example. Straight stories were more traditional approaches, where one primary medium led the story—text, video, or graphics—and other multimedia were complementary.

Some stories were clearly defined in these four categories: Straight, Comprehensive, Immersive, and Shell. But sometimes a story could be two of the categories. Stories that could not univocally be identified as one category would reside in one of the four Intersection segments, which were a cross between two categories. We also identified a difference in the naming of each Intersection, depending on which name came first. For example, a "Linear-Immersive" and the reverse, "Immersive-Linear," would differ in meaning depending on which form was more prominent in driving the story.

This model was a clear improvement over earlier structures. It was nimble enough to classify something as amorphous as an online story, and allowed for flexible definitions in order to draw conclusions about the nature of these stories. The key was settling on proper category names. Shell and Comprehensive were both very similar categories; their definitions differed only by the technology and presentation used to display them. Shells were presentations embedded on a page, usually with Flash or a similar technology acting as a container. Comprehensives were more akin to a topic page, with multiple stories or sections giving an exhaustive coverage of a single topic or story. We decided to merge the two in later iterations. It made sense, as Flash is a deprecated technology in online storytelling. Some packages, such as "Explore the '80s" published by *National Geographic* in 2014,[13] were among the few stories we found that exhibited an intersection of both Comprehensive and Shell. *National Geographic*'s "The '80s" is a Comprehensive-Immersive project that allowed the user to pick out various story segments in a 3D space. The project is contained within a single presentation, and each segment plays within the same frame (rather than going to a separate page). Analyzing this project proved that we didn't need to separate Comprehensive and Shell into two distinct categories.

The square diagram has many other issues as well. It prevented intersections, or mixing, all of the four categories in a simple way, as the intersections could only comprise two of any four categories. We would have had to add two more

intersection categories—Straight-Shell and Comprehensive-Immersive—
reaching a total of ten different groups. This was simply too many to serve
our original goal of a clear and simple classification. The categories also
seemed not to be clearly distinctive one from the other.

## ▶ THE TRIANGLE: CATEGORIES BASED ON NARRATIVE FORM OR EXPERIENCE

To solve the issues just described, we needed to further simplify our model.
Taking a reductive approach, we merged Shell into Comprehensive, and
what resulted was a triangle diagram. The triangle shape also allowed all
categories to intersect in a more elegant fashion. We even debated the need
for the third prong—Immersive—the elimination of which would have
resulted in a simple linear–nonlinear spectrum, similar to Wes Lindamood's
model when investigating the *Planet Money* project. However, it was clear
the third category was essential to differentiate an entire swath of projects in
our database, such as interactive documentaries that were clearly not traditional linear stories (Straight) and not Comprehensives (Shells) and yet not
a combination of the two. These immersive 3D-like interactive documentaries arguably needed a category of their own.

The triangle was an elegant solution to graphing all of the stories and discovering commonalities in story types. At the top corner of the triangle is

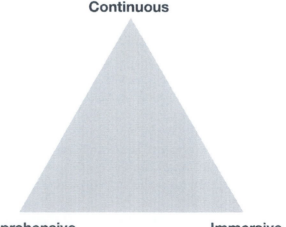

**FIGURE 3.6 The first triangle diagram**

the Continuous category, which we renamed from the older "Straight" designation. After much discussion about the specific naming of this category, we felt Continuous better represented the experience users get from these types of stories. Other names we tested were "Traditional," which felt pejorative, even when it describes some of the most powerful and compelling stories we found. "Linear" was too broad, given that many immersive stories are also linear. And "Straight" had too many other connotations in the English lexicon and could bring up a sense that the category was unadulterated or even possibly associations with a sexual orientation, which weren't our intentions at all.

On the left corner is the Comprehensive category, which is any nonlinear project that aims to be multifaceted, tackle a topic, or serve as more informational than strictly narrative. On the right corner is the Immersive category, which describes cinematic-like interactive projects that take up the whole screen and present themselves like an interactive movie or video game.

We also maintained the ability for stories to encompass multiple categories, but instead of having strict borders where elements could serve as an intersection, such as Continuous-Immersive (or vice versa), we decided that the triangle diagram would plot stories *within* the triangle. This worked especially well because it offered an enhanced level of flexibility for stories to comprise characteristics of each of the three categories at different levels of granularity.

To plot stories within this triangle diagram, we came up with a series of nine survey statements—three per category of the triangle—to test the news package against. The answers would determine where the story would be plotted in the triangle. Each survey statement tests a single characteristic of the categories, with the user giving a scaled answer of one to five, five being the most accurate description of the story being surveyed. In an early version of the triangle, we started with 12 survey statements and considered weighting each, based on how crucial it was to the category. But we later discovered discrepancies in the data because many of the original statements we came up with overlapped with multiple categories. We later reduced the number of statements to nine and tried to devise more definitive statements that would be more diametrically separated among opposing categories.

To properly gauge the efficacy of the triangle diagram, we set up several stories as our control. Through our research we knew where we believed certain

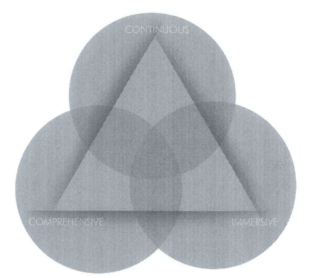

**FIGURE 3.7** The latest triangle model, with colors to show the intersections. Each dot is a package and shows where that project falls in the spectrum.

stories belonged on the triangle and the most quintessential examples of each of the three corners, as well as of the three intersections. We applied our question set to survey these stories to see if we could plot them in the proper markers around the triangle perimeter. Then, going through our database of more than 1000 stories, we had participants view a news package and answer the survey regarding the package. What resulted were markers distributed across our triangle diagram. This allowed us to view where similar story types congregated and eventually to draw conclusions as to their nature.

## ▶ CONTINUOUS STORIES

Story packages that are continuous in nature are characterized by a traditional narrative structure with a beginning, middle, and end to the story. Thus, they are also consumed in a linear fashion, meaning it is not intended for the consumer to jump around to different parts of the story out of order. Interestingly, this intention was often challenged in numerous projects that we initially thought might be Continuous, including "Snow Fall," where the story is separated into user-clickable chapters. This theoretically could encourage people to jump around the story before finishing a particular chapter, but the sequence and intention of the chapters is for them to be consumed one after another. Determining linearity can become nuanced in some story packages we found, where each chapter is separate enough from the whole narrative that it can be consumed by itself without losing context of the whole story. In these situations, the project can border on our Comprehensive category, whose chief characteristic is being able to jump around and consume segments of a story based on the user's own preferences. The benefit of answering question on a one-to-five scale allows us to determine these levels of nuance in a granular way.

Continuous stories also require one primary medium driving the story. We felt this was a necessary characteristic to describe this category, and the data we collected reaffirmed this notion. If there were too many media forms (e.g., text, video, graphics) of equal weight, the story seemed to change characteristically into a more Comprehensive or Immersive story. There were few exceptions, most commonly in stories done by the Atavist platform, where videos would be interpolated throughout the text narrative and become an integral part of the narrative. The primary media form driving the news package doesn't necessarily have to be text. We felt some projects that were video driven fit into the Continuous category. "Alma—A Tale of Violence" is an example of this. The project is a single linear interview with some interactivity and other multimedia accompaniments, but it is essentially a traditional continuous narrative.

Another characteristic we determined of Continuous stories is that they are arguably more "lean-back" in nature, meaning there was often less interactivity than Comprehensive or Immersive stories. The idea is that the story is consumed mostly by reading or watching. The more a user interacts with the content—by clicking, scrolling, or making decisions—the more the narrative form is interrupted by user choices, thus changing the nature of the story. Interactivity seemed to work better on informational stories, where the user learned about a topic, and we felt they were more antithetical to Continuous stories, which are narrative driven and in which interactivity was more of a distraction.

We did find some exceptions to this interactivity rule, particularly on stories that were linear "lean-back" experiences that required some interaction to advance the story, such as scrolling. Mike Bostock, a *New York Times* graphics editor, wrote a blog post extolling the use of scrolling as a narrative device, since it's grounded in a linear form (up being reverse, down being forward).[14] It also gave users an experience superior to clicking, because it seemed less disruptive and more natural.

Another new form of storytelling has emerged that is sometimes described as "Scrollytelling" (a term trademarked by Nick Jones of NarrowDesign.com). It uses a design convention called "parallax scrolling," where various elements on the page can move at different speeds. One example of this technique is "The Jockey" from the *New York Times*.[15] As the user scrolls, a video comes into view and becomes fixed on the page for a moment and plays. If the user continues to scroll down, the video stops and reattaches to the page and will scroll out of view. Because we felt this genre of storytelling still fit within the rubric of the Continuous category, we weighted the survey question about interactivity as a nominally important characteristic of the category.

We also included a question on our survey about the use of a CMS template in creating the news package. In a blog post, the former associate managing editor of digital at the *New York Times*, Aron Pilhofer, made the case that "Snow Fall" would not have been as effective if it appeared in the *Times*'s standard CMS template;[16] his argument was that design played a crucial role in the story. This was important in that it allowed us to realize one of the differences between traditional Continuous stories and Comprehensive or Immersive ones. In the latter two, we nearly always saw situations when the story broke the mold of the publication's CMS and was given special treatment. Yet, because the use of CMS template is not a differentiating factor of the Continuous category, it also carries relatively nominal weight on the overall plot on our triangle diagram.

As we outlined in the introduction, our goal with this taxonomy was to identify stories that were of a special nature—in-depth stories, or the digital equivalent to a longform story in print. These are packages that get some kind of special treatment to enlighten readers with analysis, anecdote, and depth, rather than simply inform the public of the day's news. As we aggregated stories for this taxonomy, we found numerous examples that were borderline in this respect, particularly in the Continuous category. We often asked ourselves if the example was a special feature "news package" by the publication or just a run-of-the-mill news story.

These are the survey statements we used for determining whether stories fall under the Continuous category, answered on a scale from one to five, with five being the most accurate statement and one being the least accurate description to the story in question.

- ▶ This project is mostly one continuous narrative.

- ▶ This story has one primary media form (e.g., text, video) driving the narrative.

- ▶ This project is more of a "lean-back" non-interactive experience.

## ▶ COMPREHENSIVE

A Comprehensive package presents an in-depth environment that contains multiple separate elements of a story under a common umbrella, like a topic page. Instead of a linear narrative that drives the users through a singular experience, the story is broken up into sections. A story package may include segments such as profiles, background information, history, or future implications—some of which can be individually narrative. But each segment is unique, and in many cases each section is told in the type of media most appropriate for the content in that segment. For example, a video is used for a segment of a story in which there is a lot of action or emotion, and graphics for a section that is informational or requires visual aids to explain complex subject matter.

The very nature of a Comprehensive story nearly demands that stories be topical and informational. One of the early examples of this is "Touching Hearts" by Joe Weiss of the *Herald-Sun* in Durham, North Carolina.[17] In 2000, Weiss went to Nicaragua as a photographer to cover a story about a group of doctors who were lending medical assistance to ailing children. When he returned, he naturally decided to construct a Comprehensive story in Flash. The story is separated into three parts: Mission, Stories, and People. The first segment, Mission, is a linear animation that explains the story and the purpose of the trip. The second section contains a series of emotionally powerful photo slideshows about the individual children, who are suffering from a range of heart conditions. The third is an informational section with more data about the doctors and the children. The choice to construct this story in segments rather than one linear piece is an almost natural approach, in part led by the capability of the technology. (Later, Weiss used his programming skills to construct the Soundslides platform.)

The main characteristics of these kinds of packages are the variability of elements as much as the absence of a predefined path—the user gets to choose how to navigate the story by selecting the segments of most interest. This gives the consumer a high level of control over the navigation of the experience. In fact, these packages are better suited for informational than narrative stories. There is no one story to tell, but a big body of information to give to the user in the most efficient way possible. This also offers the ability for users to personalize the story based on their own understanding of the subject matter, or their own interest in the topics presented, and then carve their own path through the story.

Some of the packages included in this group are more exhaustive than others (the package "Empty Cradles,"[18] published by the *Milwaukee Journal Sentinel*), while others are more restricted and framed (like "Planet Money"[19] by NPR), but all of them give the user some liberty and choice. They also usually present a medium/high level of interactivity.

The following are the survey statements tested for this category:

- ▶   This project is more about covering a topic than a single narrative story.

- ▶   This project is divided into sections or parts, intending for the user to jump around.

- ▶   This project is informational in nature.

## ▶  IMMERSIVE

Several of the subjects we spoke to during the research for this book took issue with the name "Immersive" being restricted to a single category, as all narratives aspire to be immersive in some respect. We felt this name best represented this category because the design conventions employed aim to stimulate many of the senses. Stories in the Immersive category create an environment, a space for the user to explore, and through this exploration the narrative unfolds itself. It's an environment that is very engaging, and there is a high level of interactivity between the space and the users.

Interestingly, linearity is not a prerequisite for this type of storytelling. We found numerous examples where the level of control the user had in directing the experience varied. Some Immersive news packages were like video games or choose-your-own-adventure stories, where users made choices that would determine their own experience. The experience varied from user to user based on the decisions made. Others packages were a very structured experiences with little more than a "next" button to advance the narrative through a unified path.

Narratologists have often described forms of storytelling that are non-chronological, or told out of sequence—such as those experienced in Quentin Tarantino films like *Pulp Fiction* or *Reservoir Dogs*—as "non-sequential" or "disjointed." Immersives can also be organized in this way. But when a narrative is interactive, it can be what is described as "branching," or sometimes "ergodic,"[20] where the paths through the story are decided by the consumer. Technology of the Web allows for stories to be dynamic as the user interacts with them, a complete departure from the traditional media form in journalism, such as print, television, or radio, where the delivery mechanism was static and unidirectional. We considered adding a question about the linearity of a story to describe Immersive but removed it later as we discovered such a variance in examples. This is advantageous, because the linear nature of the news package will be better determined by the Continuous–Comprehensive spectrum.

"Cinematic" is a term often associated with this category, and it makes sense. A striking commonality found in these projects was that most had some sort of initial start page displayed up front with a title, background information, and more importantly a button or link requesting action to initiate the experience—similar to a DVD/Blu-ray start menu. This analogy is interesting, because when a consumer clicks "play" on a DVD, they are initiating an experience: the start of a movie. In a similar fashion, these projects give the sense of embarking on an experience similar to a video game or movie. These start pages are less often seen in Comprehensive or Continuous stories. While this is a subtle design convention, its presence was a clear indicator of this archetype, so this is a question on the survey and it is given a moderate to high weight on its effect on the marker's position on the graph.

Immersive stories also generally contain multiple media forms, like interactive video, animation, graphics, and background music. Rarely is there ever one single media form driving the whole experience, as seen in a Continuous package, where there might be a single video or text story. The seamless integration of the multiple media forms is very natural and almost opaque to the user. Text comes up as instructions but appears as if it's a title slide in a video. This is noticeable in choose-your-own-adventure-style experiences like "Journey to the End of Coal,"[21] made by a French projection group called Honkytonk Films. The story places the user in the role of a freelance journalist exploring the crude conditions of coal mines in Datong, China. The user interacts and even interviews subjects. These are based on real interviews conducted by the filmmakers. The user chooses where to go and which questions to ask during the interviews, and text narration appears on the screen to explain the context and background of the story. The whole time, the user is presented with a combination of videos, photos, and text that are so natural to the medium, many people forget the different media types in play. Unlike a web page with a YouTube video and some type of play button to initiate the experience, Immersives offer a much more seamless continuity from section to section.

Another important characteristic of Immersives is the fullscreen layout. When these types of stories are initiated, they demand a certain presence in the browser and nearly always go edge to edge. This is a subtle design effect, which disconnects the users from their own reality to transport them into the scene of the story. Fullscreen was a convention that originally began with Adobe Flash, a browser plug-in. When the fullscreen setting was initiated, the experience seemed to pop out of the browser and display a piece of media, like a video, using the entire monitor screen, beyond the chrome of the browser application. Later, browsers would initiate their own mechanism to do this without Flash, using HTML5, as Flash became a deprecated technology.

Another role of Immersive stories is the ability to leverage numerous technological abilities that might seem awkward on more traditional stories. Such experiences as choose-your-own-adventure-style narratives would likely feel misplaced in a Continuous text story, or even a Comprehensive. But in an Immersive, the ability for the consumer to participate in the story gives a sense of role play and helps build empathy with the story's subject matter. This was seen in the first-person interactive documentary "Fearless" by Avni Nijhawan, a lecturer at the Sorbonne in Paris and a former graduate student at the UC Berkeley Graduate School of Journalism.[22] In "Fearless," the user plays the role of a woman in Mumbai, India, as she tries to commute to work using various modes of transportation. Crowded buses and trains are hotspots for women being sexually harassed in India, forcing many women to either walk or take expensive pedicab taxis to work. Nijhawan used point-of-view (POV) cameras like Google Glass to take a journey using various transportation methods. The user walks in the shoes of a woman trying to get to work and is presented with choices on how to react to situations—all in an effort to better empathize with the scenarios many women endure. Other experiences, like "Fort McMoney," are played in real time by users using interactive game elements to develop oil sand reserves in Alberta, Canada. The choices made by users, such as voting on referendums or answering surveys, affect the game for others who play.[23]

The survey statements we tested to best identify Immersive stories are as follows:

▶ This project is similar to a video game experience requiring lots of inter-activity and/or takes up the full screen of the browser.

▶ This project begins with some type of launch-like element, like a play button, to initiate the experience.

▶ This project uses audiovisual media to create an immersive environment.

## ▶ INTERSECTIONS

The beauty of the triangle diagram lies in its approach to plot stories on a graph with granular values. There were few stories that could be described entirely as Continuous, Comprehensive, or Immersive. Instead, there were nearly always varying degrees of each of these forms found in each story. The more fascinating discoveries of this graph were found in what we describe as the Intersections of two archetypes: Stories that were both Continuous and Comprehensive, Comprehensive and Immersive, or Immersive and Continuous. Unlike earlier iterations of our graph, the ordering of names doesn't matter in the triangle diagram since it's easy to plot the degree to which a marker is near a particular corner of the triangle. Partitioning our triangle into these quadrants, one can spot which stories ended up in the various quadrants of the graph.

Let's see some examples for each category:

## ▶ IMMERSIVE-CONTINUOUS

The *Guardian*'s 2013 package "Firestorm,"[24] about a bushfire in Tasmania, is an excellent example of this kind of intersection. This package tells a story

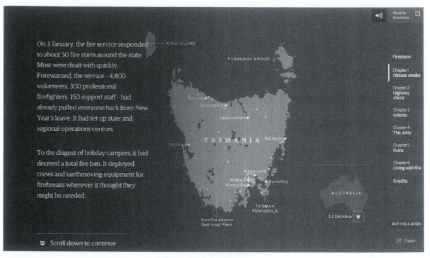

**FIGURE 3.8** "Firestorm," *Guardian*, 2013

from beginning to end of a devastating fire that nearly wiped out the town of Dunalley.

It begins with background information on the prevalence of bushfires in Tasmania, then recounts one family's near-death experience escaping the fire. The entire piece is displayed on a single web page that takes up the entire browser screen. Unique to this presentation is some special code in the background that affects the way the page scrolls, creating a friction so that as the user scrolls, there is a brief pause on certain sections. This forces the piece to be partitioned into multiple, digestible chunks. Some sections have a brief paragraph of text with background images, others play pieces of audio, and some show a short video interview. The experience from section to section is seamless, and multiple sections are grouped together in chapters. The story was published after "Snow Fall" and was compared to it in numerous blog posts[25] and industry articles.[26]

At its core, Firestorm was a linear narrative story, told from beginning to end. But its unique multimedia integration, along with the fullscreen immersion, also made it characteristic of our Immersive category. There is a start button to initiate the experience, which is rarely seen on traditional Continuous stories. This was a prototypical example of a Continuous-Immersive package.

The "Firestorm" experience is separated into chapters, which a user could theoretically use to jump around, but this is not the intention. The chapters are designed to be consumed sequentially; when clicked they do not navigate to a separate web page—rather, the page will scroll down to the section of the story where that chapter begins. It's clear the intention is to view these chapters one after another. This made the package less like a Comprehensive, which are informational pages.

## ▶ COMPREHENSIVE-CONTINUOUS

The *New York Times*'s "Snow Fall" is our prototypical Comprehensive-Continuous story—and it makes sense. The story began as a traditional text-only story, and only after most of it had been written was it decided to turn it into a multimedia story package with videos, photos, graphics, and a short documentary film. The Continuous nature of the story is apparent in the fact it's a singular 16,000-word linear narrative text story. The story is separated into six chapters, which are designed to be read one after another, but each is separate, with a title page and a unique topic of the story. The narrative is informational at parts, giving lots of background information, including about avalanches and some of the tools used by skiers to mitigate getting trapped under snow. The piece is designed with several media forms, including a shortform documentary at the end. When applied to our triangle diagram, we found "Snow Fall" fit closer to a Continuous narrative, but many qualities fell under the Comprehensive rubric.

## ▶ IMMERSIVE-COMPREHENSIVE

*National Geographic*'s "The '80s" is a story package built to complement a six-episode TV miniseries of the same name. The project displays a neon 3D wireframe, drawing inspiration from movies like *Tron*. Displayed floating in space are boxes with topics related to various 1980s nostalgia. The user can navigate from left to right to view additional modules, or click or scroll forward to go through time to different years in sort of a virtual time line. When any of the floating boxes are clicked, a window pops up and offers some multimedia—text, videos, photos—about that particular item. Some of the boxes are related to specific episodes covered in the TV miniseries.

**FIGURE 3.9** "The '80s," *National Geographic*, 2014

While the project initially presents itself as a clear Immersive-category story package, it does include the ability to navigate around different topics, rather than go through a linear narrative. We decided to define a true Immersive archetype as requiring some type of narrative experience, even in situations when the user could direct the narrative, sometimes described as a branching narrative. In "The '80s," there is no singular narrative; rather it's a Comprehensive display of information modules that the user can jump into and out of. In fact, it's unlikely most users will see every part of the project. The intention is that a user will click on only the modules that interest them most. In a project that effectively unleashes a strong sense of nostalgia, the ability for a user to create their own path through the story makes the most sense in this respect, picking out items they are most familiar with or those that pique their interest.

▶ **CONCLUSIONS**

While we were writing this book, people in newsrooms all over the world were constantly experimenting with news packages, developing new narrative forms. In the near future we will probably need to add more categories to our classification. This is a framework—a starting point for a discussion that will eventually lead to an improved and adopted classification and taxonomy of digital news packages. There is much room for change. We know these attempts are our own representation of the reality—one that is constantly changing and evolving. The community can adapt the criteria we selected. They might have to be changed or rearranged to form other categories and perhaps a new type of visualization. We welcome any discussion, any proposal, and any falsification of our model. As theoretical physicist Carlo Rovelli suggests we "keep the door open to doubt," and we ". . . will be ready to shift to a different point of view if better elements of evidence, or novel arguments emerge."[27]

## ▶ NOTES

1  Ward, Mike. *Journalism Online*. Oxford: Focal Press, 2002, 122.

2  Gentry, Leah. Skype audio interview by the authors. March 28, 2014.

3  Lindamood, Wes. "How and Why Cross-Disciplinary Collaboration Rocks—Learning." Source: An OpenNews Project. January 2, 2014. Accessed January 23, 2015. https://source.opennews.org/en-US/learning/how-and-why-cross-disciplinary-collaboration-rocks/

4  "Alma—A Tale of Violence." ARTE.TV. Accessed January 2015. http://alma.arte.tv/en/

5  Grabowicz, Paul. "Taxonomy of Digital Story Packages." KDMC Berkeley. September 29, 2013. Accessed January 2015. http://multimedia.journalism.berkeley.edu/tutorials/taxonomy-digital-story-packages/

6  McCombs, Regina. "How Far Have We Come in Creating a New, Multimedia Style for Online Journalism?" Lecture, International Symposium on Online Journalism, Austin, TX, April 19, 2003, https://online.journalism.utexas.edu/2003/transcripts/d1p3.pdf

7  Cavalier-Smith, T. "A Revised Six-Kingdom System of Life." *Biological Reviews* 73, no. 3 (1998): 203–66. doi:10.1111/j.1469-185X.1998.tb00030.x. PMID 9809012.

8  Stevens, Jane. "Multimedia Storytelling: Learn the Secrets from Experts—Digital Media Training." KDMC Berkeley. September 27, 2014. Accessed January 23, 2015. http://multimedia.journalism.berkeley.edu/tutorials/starttofinish/

9  "Empty Cradles." JSOnline. January 22, 2015. Accessed January 23, 2015. http://www.jsonline.com/news/119882229.html

10  De La Peña, Nonny. *Gone Gitmo*. Accessed January 24, 2015. http://gonegitmo. blogspot.com/

11  Powell, Corey S. *God in the Equation: How Einstein Transformed Religion*. New York: Free Press, 2003, 29.

12  Johnson, Bobbie. "Snowfallen." Medium. July 16, 2013. Accessed January 23, 2015. https://medium.com/@bobbie/snowfallen-66b9060333ad

13  "The '80s." *National Geographic*. Accessed January 2015. http://explorethe80s. com/

14  Bostock, Mike. "How To Scroll." November 3, 2014. Accessed January 23, 2015. http://bost.ocks.org/mike/scroll/

15  "The Jockey." *New York Times*. Accessed January 2015. http://www.nytimes.com/ projects/2013/the-jockey/

16  Pilhofer, Aron. "Why Design Matters: If Snow Fall Were Published in a Standard Template." Aronpilhofer.com. May 10, 2013. Accessed January 2015. http:// aronpilhofer.com/post/50087556737/why-design-matters-if-snow-fall-were-published-in

17  Weiss, Joe. "Touching Hearts." HeraldSun.com. January 1, 2000. Accessed January 16, 2015. http://media.soundslides.com/archive/2000/hearts/main.swf

18  "Empty Cradles."

19  "Planet Money Makes a T-shirt." NPR.org. Accessed January 23, 2015. http:// apps.npr.org/tshirt/#/title

20  Aarseth, Espen J. *Cybertext: Perspectives on Ergodic Literature*. Baltimore, MD: Johns Hopkins University Press, 1997.

21  "Journey to the End of Coal." Honkytonk Films. September 31, 2008. Accessed January 2015. http://www.honkytonk.fr/index.php/webdoc/

22  Nijhawan, Avni. "Fearless." Accessed January 23, 2015. http://www.fearlessidoc. com/

23  "Fort McMoney." Accessed January 23, 2015. http://www.fortmcmoney.com/#/ fortmcmoney

24  "Firestorm: The Story of the Bushfire at Dunalley." *Guardian* and *Australia News*. May 22, 2013. Accessed January 2015. http://www.theguardian.com/world/ interactive/2013/may/26/firestorm-bushfire-dunalley-holmes-family

25 Johnson, Steve. "Why the Guardian's 'Firestorm' Is Better than the Times' 'Snowfall.'" Hudson Eclectic. November 21, 2013. Accessed January 23, 2015.   http://hudsoneclectic.com/2013/11/21/why-the-guardians-firestorm-is-better-than-the-times-snowfall/

26 Quinn, Sara. "How Ongoing Teamwork Fueled the Guardian's Firestorm Interactive." Poynter. May 31, 2013. Accessed January 23, 2015.  http://www.poynter.org/how-tos/writing/214884/how-teamwork-fueled-the-guardians-firestorm-interactive/

27 Rovelli, Carlo. "2011: What Scientific Concept Would Improve Everybody's Cognitive Toolkit?" Edge.org. January 1, 2011. Accessed January 23, 2015. http://edge.org/response-detail/10314

# 4

# Continuous (Case Study: *The Verge*)

The only question to answer is: Is [longform] a valuable way to tell a story? The answer is obviously yes. And so for us longform is an integral part of what we do and [will] always be.

—Joshua Topolsky, former editor-in-chief of *The Verge*

**Publication:** *The Verge*

**Article Headline:** John Wilkes Booth Killed Lincoln . . . but Who Killed John Wilkes Booth?

**URL:** http://www.theverge.com/2013/7/31/4395960/john-wilkes-booth-killed-lincoln-but-who-killed-john-wilkes-booth

**Interview Date:** July 2014

**Interview Subjects:** Jesse Hicks, author of the case study; Joshua Topolsky, former editor-in-chief

**Taxonomy:** Continuous—The story is a longform narrative text piece with embedded video and images that are integrated into the

**FIGURE 4.1** "John Wilkes Booth Killed Lincoln . . . but Who Killed John Wilkes Booth?" *The Verge*, 2013

narrative and provide additional information about many of the events described in the story. The video gives the user a visual sense of the characters, particularly the main character, Nate Orlowek, and helps the user to better understand his personality through his mannerisms and voice. It also outlines the general story arc through a separate but similar visual narrative style.

*The Verge* is a news website that publishes technology-related articles ranging from product reviews and podcasts to longform feature stories. It was launched in late 2011 by a group of journalists from the product-review website Engadget who were fed up with its parent company, AOL, and defected to start their own website.[1] Engadget had consisted primarily of short blog-post-length articles about the latest technology devices to emerge on the marketplace. *The Verge*, on the other hand, was a publication started as a reaction to AOL's perceived disparagement of "good journalism" for the sake of increasing ad sales. Spearheaded by former Engadget editor Joshua Topolsky, *The Verge* aimed to do more in-depth reporting than Engadget was known for.

Longform story packages in *The Verge* have consistent design: they begin with a large cover image (sometimes described as a "jumbotron" in

Web-design vernacular) followed by a long text article. Embedded through-out the articles are multimedia elements. In the John Wilkes Booth piece there is a video, a map, and images from both historic and recent time periods. The article is structured in six chapters, all on a single web page, and displayed with an intentional sequence. (There is no primary naviga-tion mechanism to allow for jumping around the chapters out of order.) The interactivity doesn't go too far beyond scrolling through the article, clicking play on a video, or interacting with the map. From piece to piece, the multi-media elements may vary, but *The Verge*'s signature for these types of feature pieces is a text-driven Continuous package.

On April 15, 1865, John Wilkes Booth assassinated President Abraham Lin-coln while he was watching a play inside Ford's Theatre. Immediately after the incident, Booth fled to rural Virginia, where after few days he was located and—according to official accounts—was shot and killed by the police. But some people, like amateur historian Nate Orlowek, dispute these accounts. Orlowek has devoted his entire adult life to uncovering a different reality of Booth's demise. Over the decades he has appeared in numerous news articles and on TV shows disputing the official accounts, and believes that Booth may have managed to escape to Oklahoma, where he lived many years under the assumed identity of David E. George. Until now, they've only been theories, but Orlowek believes there is a way to definitively prove this theory using DNA from the body of Booth's brother, Edwin Booth, to verify if the body where people believe John Wilkes Booth is buried is really his. But there is a catch: a museum where vertebrae from John Wilkes Booth's autopsy are kept opposes testing for comparison on the grounds that the DNA testing would be a destructive process that would ruin some of the samples. The museum also believes any results would not be definitive in solving the mystery.

*The Verge* reporter Jesse Hicks heard about Nate Orlowek and his quest to dispute these historical accounts three or four years before the story appeared in *The Verge*. Hicks actually learned of Orlowek while attending a workshop on pitching stories. During that process, Hicks had contacted Orlowek for an initial interview in order to craft a pitch for a sample story. It was years later, when Hicks arrived at *The Verge*, that he used this pitch as one of the first stories he worked on for the publication.

"The first time . . . I probably talked to him for three hours. If I didn't follow up at the time it was just because I had too many other things to do. So, when I came to The Verge this is one of the first stories I pitched to them and we finally got it rolling," recalled Hicks.

In the *Verge* piece, Hicks carries readers through the story of Orlowek's quest using a traditional linear narrative arc, even if the piece is divided into sections. It begins with a recounting of Lincoln's 1865 assassination and then covers Orlowek's lifetime journey to discredit official historical accounts, starting with Orlowek's childhood fascinations with films like the 1936 *The Prisoner of Shark Island*, about a protagonist who gives treatment to a stranger with a broken leg not realizing it was actually John Wilkes Booth (and later being implicated as an accomplice). Orlowek would also read such conspiracy books in his teen years as *Web of Conspiracy: The Complete Story of the Men Who Murdered Abraham Lincoln*, which inspired a lifetime effort to reveal this conspiracy. In the mid-1970s, publications like *Rolling Stone* magazine did pieces on Orlowek and his theories. Later Orlowek served as a consultant for the book-turned-movie *The Lincoln Conspiracy*, both released in 1977. Orlowek was a proponent of exhuming the body of Booth for forensic analysis and even built the support of Booth family descendants, including Joanne Hulme, another character mentioned in the piece.

In the 1990s, Green Mount Cemetery, where Booth is buried, opposed exhuming the body for forensic testing based on what they describe as "flimsy evidence" to support the conspiracy. A court battle ensued, and the cemetery won the ability to keep the body buried. In 2007, as DNA testing became a more accurate method of forensic analysis, Orlowek attempted to test autopsy samples from the National Museum of Health and Medicine, in order to compare them to the body of Booth's brother. However, even that attempt failed as the museum rejected the request on grounds that the testing would destroy some of the samples. The *Verge* story ends with a defeated Nate Orlowek vowing to keep fighting for the truth.

At the time Hicks began his reporting, there were certainly plenty of media stories about Orlowek's theory. But none, says Hicks, had really looked at the "scientific" aspect of it, relying on empirical DNA evidence to give credence to conspiracy theories, and none explained the controversy of exhuming the body or how DNA testing could potentially damage specimens in the process. In the final text piece, Hicks realized there was much ground to cover.

"It needed to tell the whole story beginning with John Booth and the assassination of Lincoln," said Hicks. "It needed to tell Nate's story from his adolescence to where he is now, it needed to tell Joanne's story—the great-great-great granddaughter of Jane Booth, aunt to John Wilkes Booth, who is someone that I've found in the midst of working on it; her own perspective. It needed to cover the science aspect, which I really pitch The Verge on, as a science story as much as a human nature and history story. So there were these four or five elements that made me think OK, this has to be a medium-long form story."

## ▶ THE GENERAL DESIGN AND THE CHOICE OF A LONGFORM

The Wilkes Booth story package is contained in a single web page, using *The Verge*'s website content management system (CMS) template. There are some special design conventions employed that are not typical of everyday stories *The Verge* runs. There is an image behind the text of the Booth article that looks like parchment paper, reminiscent of old "Wanted" posters from the nineteenth century. As the user scrolls down, small pull-quotes off to the side of the article animate into view—a subtle design flourish—giving a time line of events. A 15-minute video is embedded within the body of text that duplicates much of the story, but with a very different narrative style, one that is stylistically broadcast news magazine (like a *60 Minutes* or *Dateline* type of show). The video gives a visual sense of Nate Orlowek and his character, as he is the chief subject and narrator of the piece. Other characters in the video include Joanne Hulme, a descendant of Booth, and a forensic pathologist who performs DNA testing.

Working with a team of designers and a video crew, Hicks and his editors realized from the beginning that the story would need some multimedia elements, like a time line and a map, to break up the main piece itself. To Hicks those are the kind of pieces that help keep readers engaged with the story. "We wanted to make sure that every part of this story added something to the reader experience. Each piece has to keep the reader more informed, more entertained, more persuaded by the story," Hicks said. He added that he believes multimedia elements are not always a positive force for helping readers to understand a story in a deeper way. Sometimes longform story packages are executed in a way where multimedia elements can distract rather than enhance. "What I want those interactive elements to do is give the reader something [they can't get] in the actual written story," said Hicks. "Honestly, I usually feel that there isn't a lot of stuff you can't get across in the writing in some way. . . . We have a whole bunch of new tools at our fingertips, and the question is: which of those tools make the story better for the reader and which are just the distractions?"

## ▶ THE VIDEO

It was decided early in the planning stages that a video was going to be produced and appear alongside the story. They believed (perhaps subconsciously), given the level of commitment to the piece and to establish it as a big, in-depth, longform article, that a video was a natural way to illustrate the story's weight. Joshua Topolsky, former *Verge* editor-in-chief, told us that lots of discussion with the video editor went into deciding the style of the video and into ensuring the quality would be commensurate with the considerable time and effort being afforded the piece as a whole.

In 2011, not many multimedia longform articles of this nature were being published on the Web, so they felt the process was still experimental. There was a general effort of trying to avoid duplicating the text story too much. The authors noted that much of the video was left on the cutting-room floor—shots of Ford's Theatre, John Booth's gravesite—in an effort to keep it at a minimal length for the Web. Both Hicks and Topolsky say the video is complementary to the written piece. Much of the explanatory background information that is presented in the text is lost in the video. But there is a better sense of characters' personality and some more abstract emotions that are more difficult to translate in a text piece.

"No one was doing this on the web at all in 2011. There were longer pieces, but they were not done the way we envisioned them. The same was true for the video: there was very little video of quality; there was very little video with a narrative arc that was taking seriously the techniques of great documentarians and news organizations and filmmakers," said Topolsky.

The video is 15 minutes long and unfolds as an independent mini-narrative in the piece. It is positioned just after the introductory lead of the text piece and before the initial chapter where the story really starts. But the video isn't designed with a continuity or a segue from the introduction; it's independently formatted. Yet its location does seem strategic to establish it as a complement to the text. If the video were at the top of the story, it would seem to serve as more of a lead-in to the piece.

## ▶ TIME LINE AND MAP

There is a Google map embedded in the text showing Booth's official escape route. The map appears just after the description of Booth's death from official accounts. The map is a visual way to get a sense of Booth's route without arcane descriptions of place-markers in the text. In this sense, it took weight off the text piece, says Hicks, and freed him up to assume that the map would illustrate ideas so they wouldn't need to be described in text. The map is interpolated within the text in an intentional location, and Hicks was involved in this decision. The article expects it and was designed with the Google map embed in mind. This is an essential part of story design.

There is a novel time line–like design flourish that appears to the left of most of the article. As the user scrolls down, small pull-quote-like boxes appear at various points showing a time line of events from the article. The time line serves as a visual connector through the piece, to give people a sense of scope, according to Hicks. It also aids the reader in keeping a sense of sequential continuity as they read, since portions of the story can become complex. The time line is intentionally designed to match with portions of the narrative in the written piece. In addition to the utility of a time line, the design aesthetic is that of an old "Wanted" poster from the nineteenth century. The time line enforces this choice. The time line, the special design aesthetics, and video all serve the purpose of giving the story some added weight to make it special in some sense. Visitors to the page will immediately

**FIGURE 4.2 This map in the package shows John Booth's official escape route**

the stairs. He stood in the dark, narrow passageway with a dagger clasped in his left hand, a Philadelphia Deringer in his right. He'd long planned this moment, believing Lincoln's death would rejuvenate the Confederacy. "Our cause being almost lost," he had written in his diary, "something decisive and great must be done."

He stepped forward, shot Lincoln in the back of the head, slashed his dagger across the arm of a bystander who tried to subdue him, and leaped over the railing onto the stage. He paused for a melodramatic flourish, facing the stunned crowd and yelling, *Sic semper tyrannis* — Latin for "Thus always to tyrants." He fled the theater and, amazingly, escaped the capital on horseback.

### The escaped Booth became a specter in the public mind

The killing shocked the country. Northerners feared saboteurs among them, while many Southerners believed the murder would bring harsh retribution from the post-war government. The escaped Booth became a specter in the public mind, with witness reports coming in from Chicago, Philadelphia, and Baltimore. Meanwhile, the real Booth was heading south, dodging the Union dragnet on his way to Mexico.

He didn't get far. They finally caught him in the rising dawn of April 26th, holed up in a barn in Port Royal, Virginia, with an accomplice, David Herold. Surrounded, Herold quickly gave up, but Booth refused. An officer set the barn ablaze, hoping to smoke out the

**April 14, 1865**

*John Wilkes Booth walks into Ford's Theater and shoots President Lincoln in the back of the head. He then escapes from Washington, DC, leaving the city — and the nation — in a panic. For the next 12 days, alleged Booth sightings place him virtually everywhere in the country.*

**FIGURE 4.3 The time line**

understand that this story carries a sense of weight that goes beyond other, more frequently published stories.

## ▶ THE CHOICE TO DO LONGFORM

Understanding the choice of longform is a bit like understanding *The Verge* itself. The publication was born from a desire to do more serious, higher quality journalism. Topolsky described it as a deviation from high-volume, low-quality articles, which were becoming the norm in many publications on the Web. Given the tendency of readers to check websites frequently for fresh content, and the ability to monetize those visits with ads, there was much influence from the business sides for quicker turnaround content, and for it to be done as cheaply as possible. Topolsky and a few others started *The Verge* precisely as a departure from that model and felt a compromise could be established to do both. "I'm an obsessive magazine reader and I have always been since I was a teenager and even as a kid," said Topolsky. "I think there is a tremendous value to telling a story visually, to telling a story through design, and to telling a longer story."

Topolsky also spoke a lot about the desire to replicate a magazine experience on the Web but using design conventions that were native to digital mediums. One early choice was deciding not to paginate stories, which is a method of separating a story into multiple webpages and some type of numbering system at the bottom of each page to navigate to the next section (the *New York Times* is most notable for this format on the Web). Topolsky said that scrolling seemed to be a much more natural way to consume content, and this allowed the piece to keep continuity without interruption. Also, pagination is sometimes seen as a gimmick to get additional page views for advertising purposes. "The scroll is essentially the page-turn of the Internet. Our longform pieces are continuous, they move down the page, they flow down the page, they're meant to be scrolled through," said Topolsky.

Another decision, says Topolsky, was to make these types of stories highly visual. This is seen in the look and feel of the piece—using background images and certain typefaces and in the choice to do large videos and photos interpolated throughout the piece. Such a decision was made early on during the founding of *The Verge*. During discussions with its parent company, Vox Media, *The Verge* realized that among the product sites, longform was lacking and *The Verge* was to fill that void. They worked with a company called Code and Theory to realize their design aspirations for these types of pieces.

"The only question to answer is: Is [longform] a valuable way to tell a story? The answer is obviously yes. And so for us longform is an integral part of what we do and [will] always be," said Topolsky. "I think longform [on the web] is telling stories visually, telling longer stories, and it is a part of The Verge moving forward — and I would hope part of the Web moving forward."

This story package from *The Verge*—steeped in death, mystery, and myth—driven by a longform text piece with a classic beginning, middle, and end structure clearly exemplifies the characteristics that we identity in a Continuous story package. Additionally, the focused narrative flow, subtly offering the viewer additional supporting content via embedded video and images, is presented in a linear fashion—meant to be consumed in narrative order—illustrating the package's attributes as a Continuous classification in our taxonomy.

## ▶ NOTE

1   Swisher, Kara. "Exclusive: Engadget's Top Editors Topolsky and Patel Exit from AOL's Giant Tech Site." AllThingsD. March 12, 2011. Accessed January 23, 2015. http://allthingsd.com/20110312/engadgets-top-editors-topolsky-and-patel-exit-from-aols-giant-tech-site/

**5**

# Comprehensive (Case Study: *Planet Money, NPR*)

The interface should be an expression of the editorial intention.

—Wes Lindamood[1]

**Publication:** NPR

**Article Headline:** Planet Money Makes a T-shirt

**URL:** http://apps.npr.org/tshirt/

**Interview Date:** July 24, 2014

**Interview Subject:** Wes Lindamood, senior interaction designer

**Taxonomy:** Comprehensive—A 47-second introductory trailer-like video explains the whole project on the first page the user visits. This video has to be initiated by the user by clicking a "begin" button. Once the video completes, the page auto-scrolls down to five chapter headings: Cotton, Machines, People, Boxes, and You. Each chapter takes on a different topic area of the project. For example, the "Cotton" chapter is about how cotton is still mostly grown in the United

**FIGURE 5.1** *"Planet Money* Makes a T-shirt," NPR, 2013

States, despite that much manufacturing of textiles takes place outside the United States. There is a loose sequence to the chapters in terms of chronology of the project, but they are independent enough for users to jump around and carve their own path through the story or, perhaps more specifically, skip a chapter they aren't interested in.

Leading each chapter is a short video, most around 2–5 minutes long. The video introduces the chapter as a complete news piece told with narration. After the video for each chapter completes, the web page auto-scrolls down to reveal text, photos, or GIF-like image animations, which give more background information on the topic presented in the chapter. The user also has the capability to scroll down before the video plays or to ignore the video altogether. A small callout at the bottom of the browser with arrows pointing down suggests that more content is below if the user scrolls down.

*Planet Money* is a twice-weekly NPR radio show and podcast program that covers topics related to the economy. It bills itself as being accessible to the layperson by distilling arcane economic concepts in a casual and fun manner. The "About" page on its website likens the show to a friend explaining the economy to you in a bar setting: "Imagine you could call up a friend and say, 'Meet me at the bar and tell me what's going on with the economy.' Now imagine that's actually a fun evening. That's what we're going for at Planet Money."[2]

During an episode in July 2013, show host Adam Davidson described an idea for the *Planet Money* team to make a physical T-shirt and follow the process of its creation through the world's manufacturing facilities. This journey would serve as a narrative device to explain the interconnectedness of the global economy. "Every t-shirt you own has in some way been touched by dozens of different countries; the raw material has been moved all over the world," said Davidson during an episode that launched the project. "Every t-shirt you wear tells the story of this economy that we all live in."[3]

The project was inspired by a book by Pietra Rivoli titled *The Travels of a T-Shirt in the Global Economy: An Economist Examines the Markets, Power, and Politics of World Trade*.[4] During the episode, the show's hosts described the initial difficulty they had making a T-shirt—particularly just *one* T-shirt—since the manufacturing economy relies on large volumes for any type of textile production. In order to bring this project to fruition, the show launched a Kickstarter campaign with an initial goal to raise $50,000.[5] Kickstarter is a website that allows people to solicit contributions for ideas in exchange for small rewards. Kickstarter contributors to the project received one of the T-shirts produced during the reporting project. Additional revenue collected by *Planet Money* beyond the costs of the shirts went toward reporting the story. The campaign surpassed its initial goal of $50,000, eventually raising a total of $590,807. Even the process of raising money on Kickstarter and transferring funds from their personal bank accounts became topics of later episodes.

This reporting project also saw the first collaboration between NPR's News Apps and Multimedia teams. The idea to do an in-depth Web component started early, and collaboration among different segments of the newsroom was a key component to the success of the presentation. Wes Lindamood, a senior interaction designer, wrote for Knight-Mozilla's OpenNews Source publication about the reporting process used in the *Planet Money* Web component.[6] We also spoke with Lindamood in a Skype interview for this book. "We knew we wanted to go beyond simply placing a 20-minute video inside a standard story template. The question facing us was how?" wrote Lindamood.

Planning and conceiving the final Web project had significant influence on the reporting process. In a separate Skype interview, visual managing producer Kainaz Amaria said it was important to have some preconceptions of what they were going to build before people went out into the field to report, specifically so that content from multiple journalists and from disparate locations around the world would maintain continuity stylistically.[7] These included creating a visual style guide so that the different parts of the story, shot by different journalists, would mesh together in the end. Some of the styles included holding shots on a subject's face, creative angles, and getting plenty of b-roll (background video) of various subject matter—like equipment in factories.

The last chapter of the piece, titled "You," is designed to acknowledge the sources in the story as well as the contributors to the Kickstarter campaign. It consists of a series of visual vignettes of characters who appear within the story. The video shots are held on each of the characters' faces for a few moments while music plays, and some small factoids about the character are displayed on-screen as text.

It was a way, said Amaria, to acknowledge—and humanize—all of the different people involved with creation of a T-shirt in the global economy. In essence, this was a crux of the project. According to Amaria, filming multiple pieces throughout the world by different journalists could have created a disjoined series of videos. But having a style guide before going out helped in this process. All of the video "shooters" were encouraged to include a shot of their subject's face, for a few moments, just looking into the camera. This allowed them to form this last piece as a sort of narrative climax to the

Plays pingpong and sings karaoke while at sea.

**FIGURE 5.2 One of the videos in the "You" section** *NPR*, **2013**

whole project. There was also a casualness to the videos, which is characteristic of the radio show. In one chapter, titled "Machines," a playful music video type of scene unfolds where various textile machines almost appear to be dancing because of the repetitive movements they make. The video's purpose was to illustrate the many different machines that are involved with the process of making a T-shirt.

According to the producers, without planning and conceiving the project as a Web-native presentation before the field reporting, it seems unlikely the project could have been adapted after the fact to the significant Web presentation that it ended up being. Intense planning and preconceiving went into the Web portion of the project, which in turn affected the reporting process.

The T-shirt story was also published as a standard radio show/podcast. Every week, as *Planet Money* released its usual radio shows on economic topics, some of the episodes included short mini-narratives related to the T-shirt reporting project. For example, the chapter that would later become "Cotton" in the Web presentation was one early episode in the radio show about how subsidies keep the United States as a primary provider of cotton in the global economy. Other shows—such as one titled "The Afterlife of American Clothes," about what happens to clothing after it is discarded and sent off to developing countries in Africa—never made it into the Web package. In a sense, two story structures were being manufactured in parallel: The radio show was producing episodic audio pieces, and the Web package was being organized from the ground up as a visual story-package experience. This was a different model than many story packages done by traditional newsrooms we found, which had often attempted to decorate an existing story with multimedia. Given that radio is an aural medium, additional planning for creating original content for the Web seemed more essential than simply appending videos or photos or text to an existing medium, as is often done by a print or broadcast organization.

During the planning stages for the Web component, the NPR team analyzed various longform and immersive online storytelling examples to better guide them in the direction they wanted to take on the *Planet Money* piece. They developed "mood boards" to help determine their approach. A mood board is a type of idea-generating collage, most often associated with design industries. The process is to gather many different examples that help inspire or guide decisions about how the story will be organized and presented. These can be in the form of cutouts pasted to a physical board, sticky notes with ideas written on them (as was done in the case of *Planet Money*), Photoshop-generated mockups, or even using a social media site like Pinterest to gather Web clippings as sources for inspiration.

The team also created diagrams in an exploration of how stories are presented on the Web, including one key diagram showing the spectrum they felt was a key determiner of the story structures of Web-based packages.

On the left of this diagram are examples of story packages where the user had lots of freedom to interact and direct the course of the story. On the right of this spectrum are examples where the experience is more controlled. In examples like "Firestorm" by the *Guardian*, the user has limited control to advance the story forward or backward by scrolling, but is restricted from consuming it out of order. Other examples let the user jump around at will and in any order they wish. Striking this balance was a key component of the *Planet Money* Web project. There is a give-and-take with this spectrum: The editorial voice is important to crafting a compelling narrative, one that can become emotional and create a sense of immersion or empathy. This often requires a very structured narrative presentation, and interactivity can be antithetical to those forms; the user can make unpredictable choices to interrupt the narrative. So how to do both? Lindamood believes they were able to strike this balance with the *Planet Money* project.

"There is a phrase I used with the T-shirt project: 'the interface should be an expression of the editorial intention,' and that is something I think we were trying to be very deliberate about," said Lindamood in an interview. "One way to move through the T-shirt project is when you get to the end of a video you can skip ahead to the next video. But we initiated just a simple snooze scroll down to the text at the end of the chapter, and it was kind of a signal for the user that there was a different mode of experiencing the story."

The "snooze" scroll down he refers to is a subtle design mechanism that displays additional content below once a video completes. It was a way to hint to a user additional content but left it up to users to decide whether they were interested enough in the topic to explore deeper into the subject matter.

In fact, the notion of hinting elements so the user knows what comes next played a vital design role throughout the entire project. The opening is like a trailer giving a hint of what's inside. The snooze scroll down was a way to let the user know there is additional content after the video. And the bottom of each page, called a "footer" in Web-design nomenclature, shows navigational links for each chapter along with photographs of the topic. The managing producer for the project, Brian Boyer, likens these design decisions to the design of a Frank Lloyd Wright house. During an interview he did with PBS MediaShift after the project, Boyer also said, "When you walk into a Frank Lloyd Wright house, wherever you're standing, you're always seeing a clue—a hint—of what's in the next room over. . . . When I'm in a Frank house, I always feel like I've got a chain attached to my belt and Frank is just pulling me through the house, I just can't resist moving through it. So how do you translate that to the Web? I want to keep you engaged. I want to keep showing you what's around the corner. . . . I don't want to just show you a link that says, 'hey, there's neat stuff.' [Instead] I want to give you a taste of every moment. That's why in the footer of each page is a picture of what's in the next chapter. It's not just a link that says 'next chapter.' "[8]

Lindamood also wrote in an article for Mozilla's *Source*, that it was important to develop a common vocabulary to better discuss and understand the underlying structures of many presentation types.[9] This was a common theme in many of the interviews we conducted, and a challenge in describing the nature of many of these stories. One of the clear intentions of the *Planet Money* project—reiterated by Lindamood in our interview—was the need for the design to "get out of the way of the user." The team was very cognizant of creating a story-led project where design and interactivity only existed to enhance editorial goals, rather than existing for their own sake. Some projects can start with a design convention or presentation style first and then construct the story around that. Lindamood emphasized that this wasn't the route they wanted to take, but he suggested that often logistics played a role in molding a story or limiting the possible presentational goals.

Interestingly, despite the project coming from a natively audio-centric organization, one of the primary challenges in its conception was striking a balance between text- and video-driven experiences. The videos were independent entities within each chapter that introduced the topic in a more narrative manner. The text was more informational and provided background. Both offered a benefit to the entire package, but their organization was key to providing a sense of rhythm and continuity between the chapters.

"In our exploration of other stories that combined multiple forms of media, the result often felt distracting or disjointed. Text introduced into a video-driven experience runs the risk of disrupting the rhythm of the story. And videos inserted into a text-driven experience often feel like sidebars that are an optional part of the story," wrote Lindamood.

The project ultimately consisted of a dual experience comprising both, with videos being used for the most visual elements and the background explanatory elements being told with text and graphics. Each chapter was led by a video, which also teased a viewer into the topic and motivated them to dig deeper.

"To strike this balance between a directed and interactive experience, we knew that any interactivity we added that directed the user's experience needed to be subtle. For example, the video-driven content is the emotional heart of the story and we knew we wanted direct users to experience that first," wrote Lindamood.

It is clear how design decisions of the story package influenced the meaning of the content. But Lindamood, whose chief role is as a designer, feels that design decisions are more about being subtle or minimalist and pertain more to organization of content.

"The interface shouldn't distract people from the story, it should be there to serve the story. Anytime someone starts paying attention to technique, or a certain animation, the story is suffering because people are paying attention to the interface and not the content, or it feels like ornamentation," said Lindamood in the phone interview. "The highest compliment someone can pay me as a designer, is 'I didn't even think about how it was done until afterwards. I was so enthralled by the story itself.' My personal taste is more toward minimalistic design that gets out of the way of the content: How can you present the content [in] as full and immersive way as possible?"

Lindamood's aversion to ostentatious design is understandable at a time when many in the industry celebrate the mechanics of story over the quality of the narrative. We found many experimental pieces that rely on innovative forms of interface, such as parallax scrolling, or novel forms of user-directed animation, which tend to rely on gimmick over substance. Still, Lindamood acknowledged the instrumental role design plays in affecting people's perception of the content: "I think that designers should be involved in the storytelling process from the beginning, to start to think about things like transitions or the way an audio background or the color palette can affect how someone perceives the story."

The subheading to *Planet Money*'s global narrative—"The World Behind a Simple Shirt, in Five Chapters"—is enough to explain why this story package is classified as a Comprehensive in our taxonomy. But to further expand on our methodology, the package goes beyond simply placing a singular video inside a standard story template. The team collected hundreds of hours of video, multiple gigabytes of photos, hours of audio, and a vast amount of economic data and crafted all these assets into a multi-part experience. The project's comprehensive strength lies in its in-depth environment. Journalists literally traversed the globe to present this soup-to-nuts encyclopedic report of the economics and human connection behind the complicated journey of a T-shirt. Using multiple segments and a diverse set of stories, the navigation allowed users to start the journey anywhere along the larger narrative and experience a small chunk of the overall story. It is for these reasons that "Planet Money Makes a T-shirt" is a perfect example of a Comprehensive news package.

A Comprehensive package presents an in-depth environment that contains multiple separate elements to a story under a common umbrella, like a topic page. Instead of a linear narrative that drives the users through a singular experience, the story is broken up into sections. A story package may include segments such as profiles, background information, history, or future implications—some of which individually can be narrative. But each segment is unique, and in many cases each section is told in the type of media most appropriate for the content in that segment.

## ▶ NOTES

1   Lindamood, Wes, interview with the authors, July 24, 2014.

2   "About Planet Money." NPR. April 27, 2011. Accessed January 2015. http://www.npr.org/blogs/money/2011/04/27/135599807/about-planet-money

3   Davidson, Adam, Alex Blumberg, and Zoe Chace. "Episode 455: The Planet Money T-Shirt Is Finally (Almost) Here." NPR. April 30, 2013. Accessed January 2015. http://www.npr.org/blogs/money/2013/04/30/180079862/episode-455-the-planet-money-t-shirt-is-finally-almost-here

4   Rivoli, Pietra. *The Travels of a T-shirt in the Global Economy: An Economist Examines the Markets, Power, and Politics of World Trade.* 2nd ed. Hoboken, NJ: John Wiley, 2009.

5   "Planet Money T-shirt." Kickstarter. May 14, 2013. Accessed January 2015. https://www.kickstarter.com/projects/planetmoney/planet-money-t-shirt?ref=live

6    Lindamood, Wes. "How and Why Cross-Disciplinary Collaboration Rocks." Source: An OpenNews Project. January 2, 2014. Accessed January 2015. https://source.opennews.org/en-US/learning/how-and-why-cross-disciplinary-collaboration-rocks/

7    Kainaz, Amaria, interview by the authors, January 28, 2014.

8    Lu, Denise. "Behind the Scenes of NPR Planet Money's T-Shirt Project." PBS MediaShift. January 10, 2014. Accessed January 2015. http://www.pbs.org/mediashift/2014/01/behind-the-scenes-of-npr-planet-moneys-t-shirt-project/

9    Lindamood, Wes. "How and Why Cross-Disciplinary Collaboration Rocks."

# 6

# Immersive (Case Study: National Film Board of Canada Digital Studio)

> Good stories transcend platform.
>
> —Loc Dao[1]

**Publication:** National Film Board of Canada Digital Studio

**URL:** https://www.nfb.ca/interactive/

**Interview Date:** July 26, 2014.

**Interview Subject:** Loc Dao, executive producer and creative technologist for National Film Board of Canada Digital Studio

**Taxonomy:** Immersive—Stories in the Immersive category are designed to put the user in an environment, to create a space for the user to explore. It's an environment that is engaging, and there is a high level of interactivity between the space and the users. Immersive stories are highly visual, represented by a number of characteristics such as a mix of sound, video, and interactivity. In many ways, they resemble video games. They are also represented by other more subtle characteristics, such as taking up the full screen of the browser window

**FIGURE 6.1** NFB Interactive home page, January 2015

(or even the user's monitor). Often there is some type of initiation, like a "start" button, that launches the project. These initiation devices are emblematic that the user is about to embark on an experience of depth, similar to starting a movie from a DVD player menu. Interestingly, linearity is not a prerequisite for this type of storytelling. Immersive can be either linear or nonlinear narrative experiences, or even just interactive spaces in which the user explores. This form of news package is exemplified by many of the packages created by the National Film Board of Canada Interactive Studio.

As a trailblazing organization, the National Film Board of Canada (NFB) is responsible for some of the most progressive and critically acclaimed interactive-storytelling experiments in digital media. NFB is an agency of the Government of Canada. It produces and distributes documentaries, animations, alternative dramas, and digital media productions. Since its founding in 1939, it has created over 13,000 productions and won over 5,000 awards, including 12 Oscars and more than 90 Genie Awards.

It is not surprising that NFB's interactive division, NFB Digital Studio, is leading the charge into immersive multiplatform storytelling experiences. NFB has been known for its experimentation and innovation and has a legacy of technical and creative firsts in cinema. Cinema verité—a genre where filmmakers document subjects unobtrusively—has its North American roots at the NFB, as does the technology behind IMAX. In the mid-1970s it was home to the only government-funded film studio dedicated to women filmmakers in the world (Studio D). For NFB, the evolution to digital story-telling seems like a natural progression rather than a radical leap forward.

In 2006 Tom Perlmutter, then the head of NFB's English-language program-ing division, spearheaded an early foray into mobile content with a series titled, "Shorts in Motion: The Art of Seduction." The experience integrated quizzes, advice columns, guides, and a section to create e-cards, as well as downloads of ten micro-movies, all created for mobile viewing. A year later Perlmutter would become the fifteenth NFB film commissioner and chair-person. During his tenure, he reallocated 20 percent of NFB's production budget to interactive media and started NFB's Digital Studios, focusing on interactive works. In an article in the *New Yorker*, Perlmutter recognized that multimedia storytelling required a new "narrative grammar," and he described how he wanted NFB to be "the midwife to a newborn form."[2] In an interview with the *Globe and Mail*, Perlmutter said, "We need to explore what is the language, the grammar, the aesthetics. It's something different. It's not cinema, it's not television, it's not magazines. . . . It is so rare to be at a birth of a completely new art form. . . . People will say it happened in Canada, it happened at the NFB."[3]

For more than a decade—through a series of award-winning projects—NFB has invented and continuously iterated the immersive form. Focusing on a single package from NFB would diminish the range and scope of their impact. We have decided to mention several of their groundbreaking pack-ages in chronological order.

## ▶ "FILMMAKER-IN-RESIDENCE" (2007)

Promoted as the world's first documentary experience completely online, NFB's first pilot project was created in conjunction with Canadian documen-tary filmmaker Katerina Cizek. The Immersive package titled "Filmmaker-in-Residence" chronicles life at St. Michael's Hospital in Toronto.[4] Over a period of five years, Cizek followed three organizations and their staff who were connected with the hospital at various levels in the community. The project documents a police officer and a psychiatric nurse as they work together as a crisis intervention team. Additionally, Cizek accompanies doctors to Malawi as they help with the struggle against HIV/AIDS.

Upon launching the site, the screen turns black and gives way to fading text:

*"There are Doctors. Nurses. Patients."* (fades to black)

*"Now, there's a filmmaker at the front lines of inner-city health."* (fades to black)

*"Click the arrows to follow the story."* (fade to black)

After the final piece of text, a blue sky appears along with a ground-level view of St. Michael's Hospital as the distinct ambient sounds of a bustling metropolis emanate. The package fuses fullscreen video, photos, audio, and text-based narrative in collage to create a claustrophobic-like experience. A sense of space and of immersion present themselves most powerfully at the beginning of the package. The viewer is transported inside a police car and the squawking police scanner can be heard dispatching a call. Using a mix of images and video, viewers find themselves immersed in the middle of a chaotic scene: an altercation with police and a distraught man. When the viewer clicks the "next" arrow to move on, a loud and sudden crash is heard, and there is an immediate switch to fullscreen video as the man breaks the window of the police car in a volatile moment. Purposeful editing and an expansive use of multiple forms of media lend themselves to a heightened level of immersion. The entire braided narrative takes about an hour to experience, depending on how the user skims the project.

In a 2007 review, just after the project's release, writer Ezra Winton said, "The media that will pour out of your computer screen, wrap round your head, nuzzle against you while also slapping you awake, is one of the most refreshing, engaging and political pieces I have seen on the internet."[5]

Cizek originally conceived the project as a straight documentary film but experienced an epiphany during its film, realizing that the material could be better served as a pure online experience. "At that point there wasn't yet a web-native NFB project, anything on the Web was a companion site to a film, so it was a pretty new concept. But they're risk takers and were wonderfully challenged by the idea. In terms of both the content and the approach to form, there are very few places on earth who would've done it so early and so well as the NFB."[6]

**FIGURE 6.2** "Filmmaker-in-Residence," NFB Interactive, 2007

As a backstory companion to the site is a blog where Cizek would often post. "I'm here to experiment," Cizek wrote. "With style, with form, with technology and with content. And with intent."[7] In an effort to "harness the project's momentum to effect real participation," Cizek would post a manifesto to the "Filmmaker-in-Residence" blog; a few abbreviated points are worth highlighting from her ten-item manifesto:

▶ The filmmaker's role is to experiment and adapt documentary forms to the original idea. Break stereotypes. Push the boundaries of what documentary means.

▶ Use documentary and media to "participate" rather than just to observe and to record.

▶ Use whatever medium suits—video, photography, World Wide Web, cell phones, iPods, or just pen and paper. It can all be documentary.

▶ Ask yourself every day: why are you doing this project?

▶ Always tell a good story.

Working with Web designers Subject Matter Inc., Cizek and NFB used the "Filmmaker-in-Residence package" to create a form that they could build upon for later projects. It is clear from their first foray into online interactives that a key ingredient to their success is iteration and teamwork.

The project was awarded a 2008 Webby—the Internet's version of the Oscars. In a Twitter-like restrictive fashion, winners are given only five words for their acceptance speech. Cizek succinctly summed up her philosophy of story form in these five words: "The Internet is a documentary."[8]

This early Flash-based project is a direct precursor to Cizek and NFB's next Immersive project, "Highrise: Out My Window." It would prove to be a strong continuation of their fluency across platforms and their energetic gusto for the nonlinear/Immersive interactive.

## ▶ "HIGHRISE: OUT MY WINDOW" (2009), "ONE MILLIONTH TOWER" (2011), "A SHORT HISTORY OF THE HIGHRISE" (2013)

After the success of the "Filmmaker-in-Residence" interactive, NFB asked Cizek, "How could we take some of these new ideas on how to approach form and content and take them to another level?"[9] What developed was an adaptation called "Highrise." It was inspired by the methodology she crafted with the "Filmmaker-in-Residence" (FIR) project.

**FIGURE 6.3** "Highrise: Out My Window," NFB Interactive, 2009

"Out My Window" is the first interactive in a series called "Highrise" about the towering buildings in many urban cities around the world. "Highrise" was conceived as an umbrella project that branches into independent but related immersive projects, including "One Millionth Tower" and "A Short History of the Highrise." Since its launch in 2009, the project has also had manifestations as a live presentation, a blog, installations, a mobile project, and a documentary film. Each sub-project in the series is intended to be experienced independently, but together they form an unparalleled, carefully orchestrated, rich, immersive media experience.

The project is described on the Highrise website as "a multi-year, multi-media, collaborative documentary project about the human experience in global vertical suburbs. . . . Our scale will be global, but rooted firmly in the FIR philosophy—putting people, process, creativity, collaboration, and innovation first."[10]

## Out My Window (2009)

The first project in the "Highrise" series, "Out My Window," was launched on the filmmaker's blog as "one of the world's first 360 degree documentaries, delivered entirely on the web. It's about our urban planet, told through people looking out onto the world from high-rise windows. Using some pretty cool web technology."[11]

In 2011, during a 25-minute presentation at the "Power to the Pixel" Cross-Media Forum in London, Cizek said, "Highrise is an experiment in storytelling, researching and in discovery. We were working closely with academics to develop a new body of knowledge around urbanity. . . . We did research for one year with no idea of a precise media in mind which is pretty rare for a documentary. Usually you say we are going to make a 52-minute film and then you do research for it."[12] During the pre-production phase, Cizek's team would swell to over 100 collaborators, including photographers, journalists, architects, residents, activists, digital developers, and researchers. Despite Cizek's claims of having no idea about the media type, it was clear she was aiming not for a classical documentary format, but rather a global, collaborative, immersive documentary experience.

Cizek called upon her network of researchers and visual artists to find and document stories from high-rises around the world. With teams in place in 25 countries, Cizek created a detailed 25-page brief outlining workflow, creative intent, and technical requirements for the project. "The simplicity of the concept really translated well across languages and miles," said Cizek in an article by *Point of View* magazine. "The idea is elegant enough that people get it instantly."[13] With the brief in hand, Cizek directed her team remotely from Canada. Once the narratives started flooding her office, she had an idea: "Wouldn't it be cool if we could take all these stories and put them together in one virtual high-rise, one place, online, where you click on a window and you land in an apartment in another city in the world and you learn about another life?"[14] That simple idea became the spark that would launch "Out My Window" and provide momentum for the following projects in the series.

An impressive amount of content is presented in "Out My Window." The project features hundreds of photographs and 90 minutes of video from 13 cities around the world. When the project is launched, the viewer is presented with an image of a high-rise, where they can venture in almost voyeuristically and peek inside the windows of 13 apartment spaces. The experience immediately has a game-like feel, as the elements displayed beckon to the user for interaction. It's a process of discovery as users must follow their own interests and curiosities to uncover more than 40 stories buried within the interactive experience. There are three distinct entry points into the experience: The first is a world map that appears at the top of the screen and lets users choose among the cities to explore. The second, and more intuitive, method is simply clicking apartment spaces displayed in the image on the screen. A final entry point is thumbnail portraits placed along the bottom. Together these navigation elements give the user a sense of freedom of space and choice to move around and explore in their own way.

When clicking on an apartment, viewers are transported into the living space. They are presented with a 360-degree David Hockney–style collage of photographs, and the viewer is able to spin around the room as new images appear and to reframe/redraw the perspective. Clickable objects are littered throughout the space. The types of objects vary, but they allow the user to explore the apartment and bring to life stories of the occupants. The sound design is impeccable as the subtleties and unique characteristics of each space are revealed through ambient audio that plays quiet giggles, hushed cars, background music, and a myriad of other non-signature sounds. It's the lack of recognizable sounds that one might expect—but doesn't hear—that brings a heightened level of immersion to the experience.

**FIGURE 6.4** "Highrise: Out My Window," NFB Interactive, 2009

There is no central narrative, no voice-over, and no storyteller to string the user along the story. The user navigates the story at will and makes choices about what to explore. It deviates from traditional forms of documentary films, where a narrative is tightly structured and predefined. In "Out My Window," the apartments are open and the possibilities seem endless.

The overall experience is led primarily by photography and sound. In the 2011 issue of *Point of View* magazine, Cizek said, "The Internet has really reinvigorated photography and allowed a whole new vision of how it can facilitate storytelling.... Video is a lot less interesting online than still images combined with audio. Something about the calmness of the still allows the story to come through in the sound. It changes the balance between audio and visual and creates space for the user to relate to the storytelling in a different way—it's a better environment for interactive media." Cizek would further blur the line between traditional documentary and online storytelling with the second installment of the "Highrise" project.

### "One Millionth Tower" (2011)

NFB's biggest leap forward in technology and collaboration, taking the Immersive form to new heights, started with a series of "What ifs . . .?"

For "One Millionth Tower," Cizek shifted from a global scale to a more hyper-local level. Exploring the spirit of daily life happenings presented in the "Out My Window" project, Cizek and her team regrouped with residents from Kipling Towers in Toronto—a cluster of 19 high-rises that houses 20,000 people from all over the world—with whom they'd been working since the beginning of the "Highrise" project. "We wanted to harness their knowledge and creativity to envision a better high-rise neighbourhood," said Cizek in an interview for the multimedia blog Innovative Interactivity II in 2011.[15] As she walked around the housing complexes with residents, they began to imagine ways to reinvigorate the space. *What if we made the abandoned tennis court a playground? What if we had a garden and put it over there? What if we had shared space that connected the residential buildings?*

After a brainstorming session, Cizek envisioned creating a linear animated documentary showcasing the residents' visions for improving their living space. "Together, [the residents] chose four sites around their building, and re-imagined the spaces using photography and illustration. We then thought it might be great to bring the illustrations to life, so we brought in a team of animators. So the whole project and process is very iterative and organic, merging social innovation with technological innovation," Cizek told Innovative Interactivity II.

Contrary to her plans for an animated film, the project took a dramatic turn toward the Web—as Cizek's projects tend to do—when Mike Robbins from Helios Design got involved with the project. "He said, 'This is a movie about a 3-D space, so let's make it in 3-D space,'" Cizek said in an interview with Wired.com. "Our jaws dropped open."[16]

**FIGURE 6.5** "Highrise: One Millionth Tower," NFB Interactive, 2011

The second installment of "Highrise" became the first interactive Web documentary to be built in HTML5 and Web GL (Web Graphics Library)—a JavaScript API (application programming interface) for rendering interactive 3D graphics within the Web browser without the use of plug-ins like Flash. What makes this especially remarkable is that despite being able to display an entire 3D world in the browser, the experience works seamlessly on mobile devices and desktops. This was part of a growing shift in the online world to create experiences capable of being viewed on any device. It also marks a shift for NFB away from Adobe Flash as a platform for creation and delivery.

Upon launching the interactive, the viewer is placed into an immersive environment. Graphical 3D-rendered buildings tower all around the user, which allows them to wander and explore at will using both the keyboard and the mouse, as they experience space around the high-rise that residents reimagined. One of the most groundbreaking aspects of the experience is how the video is integrated into the 3D landscape. When a user comes across an area of urban decay, a video animation shows how residents envision changing their space. For example, an animation shows where a garden might be planted instead of an empty field. The animated videos are initiated without the traditional controls of a video player, making the transition from interactive environments to video a more frictionless experience. A soundscape mixes dozens of different tracks based on the user's position and the time of day—the sound changes as the user moves. An additional layer of real-time contextual information was added by integrating time and weather information. For instance, the time of day and weather in the interactive is based on actual conditions in Toronto. If it's 10:00 p.m. and snowing in Toronto, then it is the same within the interactive.

"We've added an entire new layer to the Web and One Millionth Tower is one of the first examples of that," said Mark Surman during an interview with Wired.com. Surman is executive director of the Mozilla Foundation, the force behind one of the technologies utilized in the creation of the interactive. "In the same way we all got really excited when you could highlight a word on a page and create a hyperlink . . . that's happening now with film. I think of this as the first real web-made documentary."[15]

"What we've done with One Millionth Tower is not the future," Cizek added. "It just points to it."

## "A Short History of the Highrise" (2013)

The third installment to the "Highrise" series, "A Short History of the Highrise," is a project for which Cizek and the team at NFB were commissioned by *New York Times* editor Jason Spingarn-Koff of Op-Docs (opinionated documentaries). It was a natural collaborative union, as Spingarn-Koff is a known innovator pushing the boundaries of documentary in the digital age. In an interview with *Fast Company*, Cizek said, "For the project with the Times, I wanted a very simple idea: You could just watch the film and do nothing at all—but if you were interested, you could swipe down and find out more. I was inspired how tablets are changing the way we read. I looked at some of the more successful storytelling on tablets, and found some great examples in children's literature. I was inspired by pop-up storybooks. . . . I thought it might be an interesting juxtaposition, to tell the story of our verticalized world, using the pop-up storybook as a metaphor."[17]

In a shift from the 3D space of "One Millionth Tower," the *New York Times*'s "Highrise" story presented a more historical time line of "vertical living." The project spans the 2,500-year global history of high-rise buildings and those types of living environments. From the Tower of Babel to c. 1900 New York City tenements, narrative elements draw on the *Times*'s extraordinary visual archives—a repository of millions of photographs largely unseen for decades.

**FIGURE 6.6** "A Short History of the Highrise," NFB Interactive and *New York Times*, 2013

Each period in the evolution of high-rise buildings is highlighted as a separate chapter based on their construction: mud, concrete, glass, and home. The first three chapters are presented with a voice-over in rhyme meant to evoke a storybook experience. The fourth chapter ("Home") is composed of user-submitted images set to a musical score. Each chapter offers the option to dig deeper into the subject and explore additional archival material while viewing the film. Under the direction of Cizek, interactive elements were constructed by the *Times*'s Jacky Myint, an interactive art director and developer for the series. "With this project, we definitely took an approach of trying to do tablet first," Myint told Mashable in an interview. Myint designed the documentary experience to take advantage of touch gestures common on tablets, including dragging, pulling, and tapping to interact with the video. "That's sort of a new experience for us."[18]

The tablet-first approach is evident when you touch a building and it collapses like wooden blocks. Or when swiping, buildings will shoot up from the landscape like sprouting flowers. Each section unfolds with images brought to life with animations, videos, and games, which coalesce into a satisfying exploratory experience. In the games, the users are challenged to build condos and design a micro living space.

Exemplifying the creators' excruciating attention to detail, when the user leaves the main narrative in order to access additional content, the main narration crossfades into ambient sound, creating a seamless and natural transition while maintaining the narrative flow. In many other projects, when a viewer decides to leave the main narrative for sidebar content, the experience can feel disjointed. But in this case, after a user deviates to peripheral content, the main video narrative will rewind a few seconds, providing a soft reentry back into the documentary. It's a small fit-and-finish characteristic that better facilitates the choice to switch back and forth from a lean-forward or lean-back experience in a seamless way and lends to the overall atmosphere of cinematic immersion.

"Cinema and interactivity are influencing each other more and more," said NFB senior producer Gerry Flahive in an interview with i-docs.org. "In our Highrise project, we've always been platform-agnostic, embracing the potential of both. This collaboration with Op-Docs has given the NFB and The New York Times a chance to further advance online documentary storytelling."[19]

## ▶ "BEAR 71" (2012)

The team behind "Bear 71" created an unprecedented new form of database-driven documentary that balances an open-world immersive environment with a traditional audio-driven narrative structure. The form of "Bear 71" blurs the lines between story structure, database information, surveillance, and the complex relationship between humans and animals. The narrative initially unfolds through the voice of a grizzly bear, known as Bear 71, and is narrated by Mia Kirschner. The audio story is presented in a classic narrative structure—beginning, middle, and end—with Kirschner's powerful voice performance. But also built into the experience is ample time for the user to freely explore Alberta, Canada's Banff National Park through the use of surveillance cameras, all the while listening to Kirschner narrate the bear's life.

Filmmaker Leanne Allison, co-creator of "Bear 71," had amassed a decade of wildlife research data with her husband, a warden at Banff National Park. Using the park's substantial collection of remote trail cameras, they got to know the story of the bear known as Bear 71: all of her habits, mates, cubs, and travel routes—from the moment the three-year-old bear was collared until her death.

Allison approached NFB with the idea of a documentary film based on the surveillance footage. Jeremy Mendes, a creative technologist and interactive

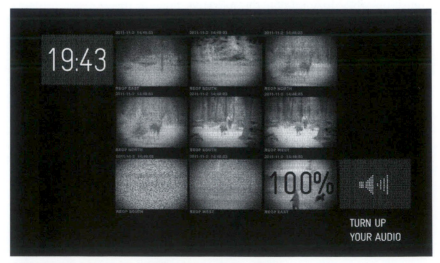

**FIGURE 6.7** "Bear 71," NFB Interactive, 2012

producer at NFB, recommended that the story be based on the database of information. NFB decided that the material had all the elements for an immersive online package, and a collaboration was set in motion.

"We decided that Bear 71 would be this sort of omniscient character that knew about technology, but she was also a bear that had evolved a million years in nature and so she knew all of that too. And I knew that we could tell this story in a very different way," said Allison in an article for *DOX: European Documentary Magazine.*[20]

Confronted with what most editors would consider an anxiety-producing amount of information, the team knew their biggest challenge would be how to allow people to experience data in a narrative form. "I think that the challenge with a project like this, is knowing how to engage an audience with a form that doesn't have a prescribed formula to follow," Mendes said in a 2012 *Fast Company* article. "Pairing a linear story with a non-linear environment was a huge challenge with a result that couldn't be fully anticipated until the whole environment was built, and at that point we knew significant change would be impossible."[21]

With the story and script in place, the team went through the typical iterations of building wireframes, prototypes, and design. Even with a solid concept on paper, there were moments where Allison felt "challenged" by the nonlinear form the package was taking. She felt that the user's ability to explore the surveillance cameras at will would "inhibit the power of the story."

In an online review of the project in *DOX*, writer Suvi Andrea Helminen initially echoed Allison's fears but felt they were unfounded. "Bear 71 gives you much more open space with all the risks that follow. That you can feel lost or overwhelmed. However, for me, when I started exploring Bear 71, the story and all the fragmented videos and pictures on the map quickly became one. When it happens, this narrative serendipity effect is very powerful. When I stumbled upon the webcam area, I was really moved. I saw the tenderness of some lady, somewhere in the world, who I couldn't speak to or interact with. Suddenly you understand this story is not 'just' about a bear, but about all of us."[22]

Ultimately the project's effective balance doesn't come from its clever use of one million photos captured with motion-detector cameras, from

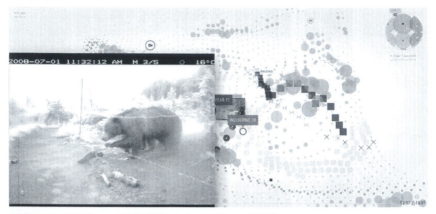

**FIGURE 6.8 "Bear 71," NFB Interactive, 2012**

the game-like open world to find caches of data, or from the powerful audio-driven narrative, but rather from the project's ability to take advantage of people's multitasking habits. It feeds users a powerful storyline while letting them explore at their own pace. The narrative is present in the opening minutes of dramatic footage of Bear 71 being trapped, tagged, and released—a lean-back and watch experience—then seconds later after the user is deposited in an abstract landscape, it becomes lean-forward.

## ▶ BREAKING THE SCRIPT

This is just a small sampling of NFB's interactive projects, of which more than 60 have been produced. They span online worlds, tablet-native experiences, real-world installations, and even live performances, all from a studio willing to break convention with an open mind toward the future.

In a 2014 interview with the authors, Loc Dao, the executive producer and creative technologist for NFB, summed up the studio's philosophy and aspirations for the future: "I see what we do as inspiration and as kind of guide to where storytelling should go or can go. . . . In all of our projects we are looking for emotional resonance, especially since technology can be so cold and removed and you're two feet away from the screen, alone. We need to convey emotion through the works, and the ones that do are the most successful." Loc added, "We are taking lessons learned from all our projects and applying them to the future. We are exploring storyworlds and social narrative stories which will involve films and interactive works combined." He hopes that the future will define NFB not as a "digital" or "documentary" studio but as a "progressive storytelling studio."[23]

NFB's passion, resources, and innovative approach to coupling technology with narrative make them exemplars of the Immersive category in our taxonomy of story packages. "FIR," "Highrise," and "Bear 71" share a genealogy—they all present a viewer with a seemingly vast and detailed world to explore and, most importantly, interact with. Their attention to the finest details submerses and envelops the user in a narrative world.

## ▶ NOTES

1  Dao, Loc, interview with the authors, July 26, 2014.

2  Kaganskiy, Julia. "Where Film Goes to Be Reinvented." *New Yorker*. April 29, 2013. Accessed January 2015. http://www.newyorker.com/tech/elements/where-film-goes-to-be-reinvented

3  Taylor, Kate. "How Tom Perlmutter Turned the NFB into a Global New-media Player." *Globe and Mail*. March 18, 2013. Accessed January 2015. http://www.theglobeandmail.com/arts/film/how-tom-perlmutter-turned-the-nfb-into-a-global-new-media-player/article11992885/?page=all

4  Cizek, Katerina. "NFB Filmmaker-in-Residence." NFB Interactive. 2006. Accessed January 2015. http://filmmakerinresidence.nfb.ca/

5  Winton, Ezra. "Review: The NFB's Filmmaker-in-Residence." Art Threat. March 2, 2007. Accessed January 2015. http://artthreat.net/2007/03/filmmaker-in-residence/

6  Beer, Jeff. "How Canada's NFB Became the World's Hippest Digital Content Hub." Co.Create. February 10, 2012. Accessed March 23, 2015. http://www.fastcocreate.com/1679850/how-canadas-nfb-became-one-of-the-worlds-hippest-digital-content-hubs

7  Cizek, Katerina. "When Media Meets Medicine It's Usually Bloody." *NFB Filmmaker-in-Residence*. November 24, 2006. Accessed January 2015. http://filmmakerinresidence.nfb.ca/blog/?p=5

8  "Documentary: Series." Webby Awards. Accessed January 2015. http://www.webbyawards.com/winners/2008/online-film-video/general-film/documentary-series/

9  Cizek, Katerina. "Case Study: HIGHRISE: Out My Window." Speech to the Cross-Media Forum in association with the BFI London Film Festival, "Power to the Pixel," London, October 11, 2011. https://vimeo.com/32321155

10  "About." *Highrise*. Accessed January 2015. http://highrise.nfb.ca/about/

11  Cizek, Katerina. "The NFB's Highrise Project Unveils Its New Interactive Web Documentary, Out My Window." NFB (blog). October 15, 2010. Accessed January 2015. http://blog.nfb.ca/blog/2010/10/15/the-nfbs-highrise-project-unveils-its-new-interactive-web-documentary-out-my-window/

12  Cizek, Katerina. "Case Study: HIGHRISE: Out My Window." Speech to the Cross-Media Forum in association with the BFI London Film Festival, "Power to the Pixel," London, October 11, 2011. https://vimeo.com/32321155

13  Jessica Duffin, Wolfe. "Crowd in the Sky: Katerina Cizek & Highrise at the NFB." *Point of View*. February 1, 2011. Accessed January 2015. http://povmagazine.com/articles/view/crowd-in-the-sky

14  Cizek, Katerina. "Case Study: HIGHRISE: Out My Window." Speech to the Cross-Media Forum in association with the BFI London Film Festival, "Power to the Pixel," London, October 11, 2011. https://vimeo.com/32321155

15  Clark, Tracy Boyer. "Behind the Scenes of NFB's One Millionth Tower." Innovative Interactivity II. November 20, 2011. Accessed January 2015. http://innovativeinteractivity.com/2011/11/22/behind-the-scenes-of-nfbs-one-millionth-tower/

16  Watercutter, Angela. "Premiere: One Millionth Tower High-Rise Documentary Takes Format to New Heights." Wired.com. May 11, 2011. Accessed January 2015 http://www.wired.com/2011/11/one-millionth-tower-2/

17  Zax, David. "How Pop-Up Books Inspired the Spectacular 'Short History of the Highrise' Series." *Fast Company*. October 11, 2013. Accessed January 2015. http://www.fastcompany.com/3019799/most-creative-people/how-pop-up-books-inspired-the-spectacular-short-history-of-the-highrise

18  Fiegerman, Seth. "'New York Times' Develops Interactive Documentary Series for Tablets." August 28, 2013. Accessed January 2015. http://mashable.com/2013/08/28/new-york-times-documentary/

19  Linington, Jess. "Op-Docs & the NFB's 'A Short History of the Highrise' to Debut at New York Film Festival." i-Docs. August 29, 2013. Accessed January 2015. http://i-docs.org/2013/08/29/a-short-history-of-the-highrise-to-debut-at-new-york-film-festival/

20  Helminen, Suvi Andrea. "Balancing Form and Content." *DOX: European Documentary Magazine*. January 2014. Accessed January 20, 2015. http://www.doxmagazine.com/balancing-form-and-content/

21 Wilson, Mark. "Bear71: A New Type of iPad Documentary Powered by Infographics." Co.Design. February 24, 2012. Accessed January 20, 2015. http://www.fastcodesign.com/1669121/bear71-a-new-type-of-ipad-documentary-powered-by-infographics

22 Andrea Helminen, Suvi. "The Interactive Dance Floor." DOX European Documentary Magazine. April 2014. Accessed January 2015. http://www.doxmagazine.com/the-interactive-dance-floor/

23 Dao interview, July 26, 2014.

# 7

# Intersections (Case Studies: *New York Times, Guardian, National Geographic*)

▶ **CASE STUDY: "SNOW FALL" (CONTINUOUS-COMPREHENSIVE)**

**Publication:** *New York Times*

**Article Headline:** Snow Fall: The Avalanche at Tunnel Creek

**URL:** http://www.nytimes.com/projects/2012/snow-fall/

**Interview Date:** July 30, 2013

**Interview Subjects:** Steve Duenes, assistant editor; Andrew Kueneman, editor of digital news design; Jacky Myint, multimedia producer

**Taxonomy:** Continuous-Comprehensive—"Snow Fall: The Avalanche at Tunnel Creek" is a multimedia narrative about an avalanche that occurred in the Tunnel Creek section of Stevens Pass, Washington, on February 19, 2012. Sixteen skiers and snowboarders were making the run together when the avalanche occurred; three died from the incident. Originally conceived as a longform text piece, "Snow Fall" was adapted to a multimedia package after reporter John Branch returned from his field reporting and editors realized the opportunity for a deeper storytelling experience.[1]

**FIGURE 7.1** "Snow Fall: The Avalanche at Tunnel Creek," *New York Times*, 2012

"Snow Fall" is structured in six chapters covering a traditional narrative arc with an anecdotal news lead. Although there is a navigation bar at the top allowing a user to jump between chapters, the story is a linear progression and the chapters are designed to be read sequentially. Multimedia elements include short video interviews, photo slideshows, short audio snippets, and animated graphics, and appear in strategic locations throughout the text narrative. In some cases, multimedia elements are tied to specific sentences or words in the text story, which are visually highlighted and when clicked will activate a media element, like a video or photo gallery. Some of the multimedia is designed as a seamless experience, embedded right between paragraphs of text. This effect is aided by various design aesthetics, such as a curtain effect where parts of the page seem to cover previous sections, or as when video animations activate only when the user scrolls to a certain point in a story. Other times, multimedia elements are placed adjacent to the text, particularly in cases when they might present an interruption from the text narrative in order to give context or additional information. The adjacent location allows these items to become optional for the reader.

Some of these media elements are in the form of short videos that illustrate concepts mentioned in text. For example, one of the early videos in the first chapter is about the allure of powdered snow that attracts skiers, despite the risks of avalanches. While this is a passing mention in the text, the video presents a sidebar story about backcountry skiing. Other times, these adjacent videos depict short interviews with a subject in the story, adding voice to a character's quote in the text. Some of the skiers wore small cameras mounted to helmets during day of the avalanche. These videos are among some of the most dramatic, and they put the reader in the moment as they watch reactions from the avalanche unfold.

Mug shots of characters in the story appear adjacent to the text. When clicked, these display a short slideshow of photos that are a mix of professional pictures by a *Times* photographer and personal photographs provided by the subject or the subject's family. These personal photos adds depth to the life of the characters; the personal photos show them with their families or in other moments.

The animated graphics in the piece come in different forms. In the first few chapters, topographic flyover videos autoplay when the user scrolls to that point in the text and provide a visual reference of Stevens Pass ski area and of Tunnel Creek. Other times a graphic illustration shows how powdered snow stacks on top of an icy crust—a dangerous recipe for avalanches. A separate topographic map in the third chapter runs alongside the text and continues to animate as the user is scrolling down the page. This shows the locations and routes of the skiers on the mountain during different points in the text article. An important component of the story is about how the groups split up during their downhill run, and this visual guide helps the reader to maintain a sense of continuity from each character's location at the various points in the narrative. The names of the characters in the text are highlighted, and a small mug shot will appear on the map next to their location in the graphic. In the fourth chapter, a video animation shows the avalanche occurring in real time, along with text descriptions that show the speed of the snow rushing down the hill. Similar to the previous embedded animations, this video autoplays when the user scrolls to this point in the story, but unlike the other videos, this one contains sound effects—the rush of the avalanche and a rapid ticking sound to give a sense of the speed of the snow. The sound shuts off immediately if the user continues scrolling.

In later chapters, small play buttons appear alongside the text for short audio snippets of 911 calls made by skiers. These are emotionally gripping elements, as they depict the voices of the characters in the moment of disaster, in some cases just as they realize the fate of their colleagues.

At the end of the article is an 11-minute video documentary that retells of the day of the avalanche using interviews shot by the *Times*. It also includes footage shot from cameras the skiers wore that day. Many of the clips in the documentary also appear throughout the text of the multimedia package.

These multimedia elements serve multiple functions in supporting the text narrative. Some multimedia elements are informational devices that help explain the science behind avalanches. Others complement the text with an emotional thrust, in a way video and audio tend to do well: hearing the voices from 911 calls, for example, watching interviews as the survivors described losing colleagues with voices cracking, or looking at photographs from the survivors' families. The text narrative alone is a gripping account of both the avalanche and its aftermath. It was keenly complemented by the multimedia to earn the high acclaim it captured.

Sports editor Joe Sexton is credited with envisioning something bigger for the story. According to Branch in a Q&A published on NYTimes.com a few days after "Snow Fall" ran, the multimedia production team was invited into the process after he returned from the reporting trip. "When I returned with their stories, and we saw how their various perspectives of the same avalanche wove together, we invited the smart people in our interactive and graphics departments to help with the telling."[2] The story took six months of production and included more than a dozen content producers to put all of the different pieces together. About a week after the story ran, the piece received close to 3 million visits and 3.5 million page views. Users spent about 12 minutes with the article according to a memo sent out by then editor-in-chief Jill Abramson.[3]

The text was highly praised, winning a Pulitzer Prize in the feature writing category for 2013. The Pulitzer committee hailed the story for its "evocative narrative about skiers killed in an avalanche and the science that explains such disasters, a project enhanced by its deft integration of multimedia elements."[4] It also spurred an entirely new category of storytelling presentation that largely integrated multimedia with text. Even the title of the story became a verb in the newsroom for a time, as in "can we 'Snow Fall' this?" Although the story wasn't initially designed for the tablet experience, many also saw it as a precursor to the types of stories that could exist on tablets. Tablets are often seen as the ideal intersection of longform and interactive media; "Snow Fall" was both.

In a paper titled "Can We 'Snowfall' This? Digital Longform and the Race for the Tablet Market," authors David Dowling and Travis Vogan surmise that projects like "Snow Fall," as well as successor projects by ESPN and *Sports Illustrated*, are a form that is conducive to the tablet experience. "The capacity to view multimedia without leaving the story presents itself as key to the immersive reading associated with the tablet. This shows that extended time spent with the text is a novel development in online reading, which has typically been associated with relatively superficial skimming."[5]

In an in-person interview with some key members of the "Snow Fall" team we conducted in July 2013,[6] it was clear the effects of the story's publication were still being felt six months later. By this time, the *New York Times* had already published several other stories in the same format as "Snow Fall": big story packages with multimedia embedded throughout. We asked assistant editor Steve Duenes, head of the graphics department that oversaw the multimedia integration of the piece, if text would always be central to such pieces. "I think you have to start by thinking about the place itself, the *New York Times*. We were a printed newspaper before we were all of these other things that we are now. The dominant stream of content on any platform is still copy—is still text—we still employ hundreds of reporters and writers and still express ourselves fully and to be articulate with language," said Duenes. "You're sort of fooling yourself if you want to completely ignore that there is a 16,000 word written article that is going to happen—because it is going to happen. And so I think it is weird to describe it as a constraint—it's obviously this huge asset. But I think embracing the idea that it is an asset has opened up a lot of possibilities for us."

Andrew Kueneman, an editor of digital news design, suggested that the text piece was vital to the overall success. "That story worked in a way keeping people moving through it. You have these visual pleasurable moments where you're like, 'oh my, what is this?' And you've never seen that before! Then you move to the bottom of the chapter and then bam [he slaps a hand on the table] there is a cliffhanger! And so you want to move to the next chapter. That story was just perfect for that because everything left you hanging."

Throughout 2013 and into the following years, the *New York Times* would do many more multimedia packages of the same ilk as "Snow Fall," but it also included ones that were led by video or graphics. In December 2013, the *New York Times* published a special end-of-the-year look at many of the big multimedia packages that had been published, calling 2013 "the year of interactive storytelling."[7] The page listed in chronological order all of the big multimedia stories of that year and further broke them down into five distinct categories: multimedia stories, data visualization, explanatory graphics, breaking news, and visual and interactive features. Some of the stories were led by mediums other than text, such as video or graphics.

The team spoke at length about the challenges of tightly editing "Snow Fall": discerning every small nuance and every graphical design accompaniment in an attempt to understand how it would affect a reader's attention to the story. In one part of our discussion, the lack of audio in many of the autoplaying videos was brought up. Jacky Myint, a multimedia producer who was central to the design of the story, said, "There was discussion about whether there should be audio. We were really trying to make those videos feel a part of that singular narrative flow, not something that stops you from the story, or takes you away from it and then tries to put you back in. The moment where you read about the Cascade Mountains, that's when you see it sort of looming out from the bottom of the page; there was a lot of work, getting that right." Duenes added that some multimedia elements needed to serve as "connective tissue" for the text and keep the pacing of the story flow intact. Deciding on the types of multimedia elements that required interruption depended on a number of factors. "I think there are different kinds of visual distractions and some of them, like a data visualization, depends on what the learning curve is for that," he said. If a graphic was too complex, it would be more interruptive to the flow of the story and probably needed to be an optional element off to the side.

In essence, "Snow Fall" is two stories: a narrative about an incident and also a broader explanatory piece about both the science that goes into avalanches and the groupthink that caused the skiers to ignore warning signs. We struggled to determine how we would quantify its taxonomical properties and where it might be placed in our triangle grid. In some ways, "Snow Fall" is a Comprehensive story about avalanches, including optional multimedia elements that the user can watch or interact with at their own discretion. In other ways "Snow Fall" feels like it belongs in our Continuous category for its linear narrative progression and because it is driven primarily by text. We placed this story as a Continuous-Comprehensive intersection. Using our survey described in chapter 3, "Snow Fall" fell closer to a Continuous, and some minor characteristics, such as its cinematic qualities and fullscreen experience, even influenced it slightly toward Immersive.

## ▶ CASE STUDY: "FIRESTORM" (IMMERSIVE-CONTINUOUS)

**Publication:** *The Guardian*

**Article Headline:** Firestorm: The Story of the Bushfire at Dunalley

**URL:**    http://www.theguardian.com/world/interactive/2013/may/26/ firestorm-bushfire-dunalley-holmes-family

**Interview Date:** July 30, 2014

**Interview Subject:** Francesca Panetta, editor

**Taxonomy:** Immersive-Continuous—"Firestorm" is a story about a series of bushfires in southeastern Tasmania that nearly wiped out the town of Dunalley in late 2012 and early 2013.[8] The package was published on May 22, 2013, in the *Guardian*'s Australian edition website, which had recently launched.

Visitors to the "Firestorm" story package are first presented with a static opening image, which displays a headline, a short description, and an "enter" button that initiates the multimedia story when clicked. Initiation buttons

**FIGURE 7.2** "Firestorm," *Guardian*, 2013

like these are subtle design characteristics of Immersive stories. They are indicative that the user is about to undergo an experience. When the button is clicked, the project expands to take up the full browser screen, and ambient audio plays the crackling sound of fire and first-responder chatter. The project is partitioned into 25 full-page sections that the user can navigate by scrolling down. As the user scrolls, a type of JavaScript mechanism sometimes called "magnetic scroll" affects how the website advances. This constricts the scroll by allowing the page to only advance by a certain amount, snapping to certain sections. This further partitions the whole experience into discrete parts.

These 25 sections, which the producers call "scenes," are spread across six chapters. A navigational element is fixed to the right side of the browser window. While it allows the user to jump between chapters, the story is designed to be consumed sequentially as a linear narrative. In each of the scenes, some form of background media is present: ambient sound, a looping background video, or a photograph with audio is displayed. These design conventions give a more immersive feel, creating an atmosphere within each section of

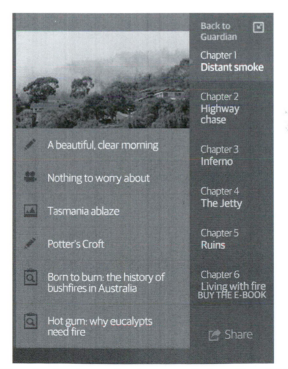

FIGURE 7.3 The six chapters of "Firestorm," *Guardian*, 2013

the project. Each of the scenes also contains short text taken from a longer text story. The text is what drives the narrative of the story, even though it's separated into smaller chunks. The text story is modular, like most news stories, and despite being presented to the viewer in smaller segments, it is able to maintain continuity from each section. Some of the sections display short videos, which are placed strategically at different locations in the text. There is often a segue from the text into each video—a dramatic pause in some cases—which then leads into a video in the next section.

Small icons on the navigation bar indicate the media types for each scene. There is an icon for short snippets of text, one for videos, one for photos or graphics (which are sometimes displayed with audio narration), and another for longer text pieces. The scenes with longer text pieces are self-contained chapters written in a more complete style and serve almost as sidebar points to the central narrative. One text section talks about the history of brush-fires; another discusses philosophical questions in the rebuilding effort, as Dunalley will inevitably face another devastating fire in the future.

The user has the ability to shut off the sound at any time by clicking an icon in the top-right corner. There are also links to "go back" to the *Guardian* and to share the story.

The impetus for doing a package of this depth began with a single photo-graph. It shows a woman, Tammy Holmes, and five children taking shelter neck-deep in water under a jetty, while an orange glow from fires on the shoreline surrounds them. The head of international news at the *Guardian* commissioned the project to "find the story behind the photograph" and to construct an interactive news package that would launch in tandem with the *Guardian*'s new Australian edition. Jon Henley, a feature writer, and Laurence Topham, a documentary filmmaker, were assigned to the story. This collabo-ration of two mediums became an essential component for this type of story. "The idea from the outset was to make it this cross-platform thing," Henley told Journalism.co.uk in an article about how the project came about. "[S]o we knew there would be an interactive. We didn't really know what form that would take but we knew there would be an interactive and we knew there would be a good piece of traditional long-form writing, kind of New Yorker essay length: 13, 14, 15 thousand words."[9] The project took three months to produce and involved multiple journalists, designers, and developers.

In an e-mail interview we conducted with project editor Francesca Panetta for this book, she described how both text and video became critical components of delivering a complete multimedia experience that covered the strengths of both mediums. "The story is visually compelling—the landscape, the archive of the fire itself, but also video is a very effective way of telling emotional stories. The text provides an opportunity to give depth and analysis in a way that can become tedious in film. By merging the two you get the best of both worlds, being able to jump from story to analysis to statics in the best medium for that part of the story."[10]

Panetta spoke in detail about how understanding the nature of each media form (video, text, or photos with audio) was important for certain scenes. The construction of "Firestorm" was an iterative process, and the team often asked what media form could be best used to explain each part of the story. Text was best used for the technical descriptions, and maps were important for understanding the geographic location of Dunalley, as well as the effects 60 mph winds had in pushing the brushfires toward the town. Probably one of the more discussed scenes in the newsroom was the jetty scene, showing the family nearly underwater as they take shelter from the quickly approaching fires. The team tried constructing the scene in multiple formats: a picture gallery, a video interview seeing Tammy and Tim talk about their story. Ultimately, they went with showing the photograph that inspired the project and added crackling sounds of fire and a short description from Tammy of being in the water. The next scenes, which only appear as the user scrolls, show subsequent photos of the children sitting on the jetty, their eyes squinting from the harsh smoke engulfing them.

Another scene that is highly regarded in the project is in the second chapter, titled "Highway Chase," which includes a video shot from a camera mounted to the front of a car. This particular point of view makes it look as if the viewer is an occupant in the car, racing down the highway. The reenactment builds suspense as Tim Holmes, who had been involved with the fire service for 25 years, describes in the audio narration how his family raced down the highway. "It was the fastest moving fire I've ever seen," he says in the video. In regards to the scene, Panetta said, "This particular shot everyone loved when they saw it. Making the audience seem like they are the protagonist is a strong storytelling method."

Panetta's role as an editor was also essential for coordinating continuity between text and video. "It was iterative. Laurence cut film material, John wrote. I then worked with the material to make it work as an interactive, working particularly with Laurence at first going through film footage and cutting b-roll, placing a-roll films in the interactive, finding what kind of cuts and lengths worked, and then later re-writing the text with John over the pictures." (B-roll is background footage, and a-roll refers to the audio track.)

In an article on the *Guardian*'s website titled "10 Things We Learned during the Making of Firestorm," developers of the project talked about requiring a new workflow in the newsroom since so many people were involved. Coordination between so many different content assets was a herculean task, and unexpectedly so when compared to more traditional newsroom workflows. Former interactive editor Jonathan Richards wrote, "The assets have different types (text / video / pictures / graphics), with different challenges on the web (compression, encoding), and they're created—and then used by—different teams (multimedia, picture desk, writers, developers). And, of course, they change all the time. ('I'm just going to upload a new version of the jetty video—is that ok?' etc.) All this can lead to a very complicated set of processes, and it's worth spending a bit of time streamlining this workflow, so that it is transparent to those who need to understand it, and robust."[11]

The narrative flow and fullscreen design of "Firestorm" give this project strong characteristics that appear in our Immersive category. It puts the viewer into an environment, aided by strong visuals and sound. But unlike many of the interactive documentaries we looked at, "Firestorm" is a fairly structured and linear experience. The story is driven by the text, even though it's not the primary medium. "We didn't want people to jump around in the story—it's linear," said Panetta. "But people want to feel they know where they are in the story. It's like knowing which chapter you're in when reading a book, how far through you are. We did user testing and everyone wanted this." Because it comprised elements of a singular narrative combined with immersive qualities, the "Firestorm" project fell almost squarely into the Continuous-Immersive category of our taxonomy. When we later quantified the project with survey data, the location on our diagram supported this supposition.

## ▶ CASE STUDY: "THE '80S—THE DECADE THAT MADE US" (IMMERSIVE-COMPREHENSIVE)

**Publication:** *National Geographic*

**Article Headline:** The '80s: The Decade That Made Us

**URL:** http://explorethe80s.com/

**FIGURE 7.4** "The '80s," *National Geographic*, 2014

> **Taxonomy:** Immersive-Comprehensive—"The '80s: The Decade That Made Us" is an interactive news package that ran as a companion piece to a six-part television documentary series on the *National Geographic Channel* on April 14, 2013.

Upon visiting the site, the user is immediate put into a 3D-like space, with neon wireframe grids reminiscent of the 1980s *Tron* movies. Floating boxes appear, each labeled with a topic related to the 1980s. Cher, Duran Duran, Ronald Reagan, cassette tapes, VCRs, even cocaine, are listed as topics iconic to the 1980s and can be explored independently. The user navigates the space by dragging. There are also navigational arrow buttons that can be clicked to explore the space. Clicking a navigational up arrow reveals that the user is actually in a time line starting in 1980 and can advance forward through the years, revealing additional boxes related to each subsequent year. There is no immediately obvious linear path through the project; it is completely left up to the users to explore on their own and pick out the items they find most interesting.

When clicked, boxes reveal a photo and description of why this topic was influential to the decade. Most also include some type of multimedia such as a found YouTube clip, sample songs from iconic musical artists, and

Wikipedia entries for additional information. When the user hovers over some of the boxes, lines appear connecting it with related topics, as well as information about which of the boxes were featured in the TV documentary.

There are some alternative methods to navigating the piece. At the top is a time line slider that provides a different method to explore through the years. A link labeled "stories" displays the topics featured in each of the six episodes of the TV series. This also presents the user with a more linear way to navigate the stories. Each of the topics in the respective episode display as a list and show a "next" button. This method allows a user to view the topics in more linear story-like order similar to the TV episode.

*National Geographic*'s six-part television miniseries was narrated by actor Rob Lowe. The show's website described the series as a "cultural program-ming event [that] is the defining biography of a generation. It's about a decade of people, decisions, and inventions that changed our future, told from the perspective of the unknowing history makers who lived these iconic moments."[12] The show covered such topics as Apple Computers, musical art-ists like Run DMC, the TV show *Dallas*, the first space shuttle launch, and political events like the Cold War, all which were part of defining the decade.

*National Geographic* commissioned marketing firm Mullen to produce the Web interactive. Mullen is known for doing a variety of marketing and advertising campaigns, in video, in print, and on the Web. Mullen described the project on their website as "a high-tech, content-rich experience that goes far beyond the limits of what TV can offer. . . . First and foremost, this is a storytelling experience. We created hundreds of explorable pieces of content, gathering facts, dates, quotes, amazing videos, and archival imag-ery. You don't just read; you watch and vote and share. We also built a 'story' layer over the content, allowing us to build larger narratives by combining many pieces of content. Get into a story about teen movies or video games to see what I mean."[13]

Mullen would later be commissioned to produce more companion sites for *National Geographic* television shows. Two of them were "Killing Lincoln" and "Killing Kennedy," named after books by Fox News political commentator Bill O'Reilly that were later adapted to films ("Killing Ken-nedy" also starred Rob Lowe). The Web interactives built by Mullen were both Immersive-style stories but told in a more linear fashion than the '80s project.

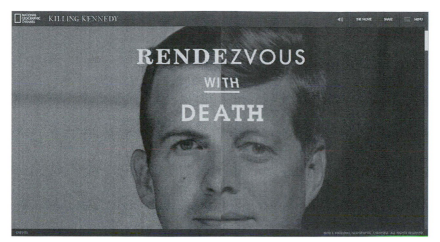

**FIGURE 7.5** "Killing Kennedy," *National Geographic*, 2013

In "Killing Kennedy," the user scrolls through multiple sections that tell a narrative of two parallel stories: the lives of both John F. Kennedy and Lee Harvey Oswald. A split-screen graphical interface aids this effect, and as the user scrolls they see a shifting effect where both sides of the screen often split, then recombine to display each section. In a video case study on their website, Mullen producers said, "We breathed new life into this American tragedy by creating an interaction mechanism that also acts as a narrative device. The split-screen site meaningfully pushes content in opposite directions leading the audience through the life stories of John F. Kennedy and Lee Harvey Oswald until they meet one fateful day in Dealey Plaza."[14]

In both the "Killing Lincoln" and "Killing Kennedy" interactive packages, the user has the power to go back and forth, but the interface is not designed to skip around at will. In "Killing Lincoln," a navigation element is fixed to the right side of the screen, more to give the user a sense how far into the story they are and a scope of how long they can expect it to be. In "Killing Kennedy," there is a hidden navigation in the upper right corner that allows a user to jump to different chapters.

These two projects—"Killing Lincoln" and "Killing Kennedy"—along with "The '80s," were all commissioned for the same group, Mullen. All three are interactive Web projects based on television shows, and all are immersive stories. Yet the '80s project takes a much more disparate route in telling the story. "The '80s" allows a user to explore all of the different topics that were presented in the documentary in a nonlinear fashion, whereas "Killing Kennedy" is a very controlled experience. The story's subject matter led the design of each of these. Both "Killing Kennedy" and "Killing Lincoln" were narrative stories, while "The '80s" was a topical subject. It is for this reason that "The '80s" shares stronger characteristics with our Comprehensive category and falls squarely in the intersection of Comprehensive and Continuous.

## ▶ NOTES

1   "How We Made Snow Fall." Source: An OpenNews Project. January 1, 2013. Accessed January 2015. https://source.opennews.org/en-US/articles/how-we-made-snow-fall/

2   "Q. and A.: The Avalanche at Tunnel Creek." *New York Times*. December 21, 2012. Accessed January 2015. http://www.nytimes.com/2012/12/22/sports/q-a-the-avalanche-at-tunnel-creek.html

3   Romenesko, Jim. "More than 3.5 Million Page Views for New York Times' 'Snow Fall' Feature." JimRomenesko.com. December 27, 2012. Accessed January 2015. http://jimromenesko.com/2012/12/27/more-than-3-5-million-page-views-for-nyts-snow-fall/

4   "Feature Writing Archives." The Pulitzer Prizes. Accessed January 2015. http://www.pulitzer.org/bycat/Feature-Writing

5   Dowling, David, and Travis Vogan. "Can We 'Snowfall' This?" *Digital Journalism* 3, no. 2 (2014): 209–24.

6   Duenes, Steve, Andrew Kueneman, and Jacky Myint, interview with the authors, July 30, 2013.

7   "2013: The Year in Interactive Storytelling." *New York Times*. December 30, 2013. Accessed January 2015. http://www.nytimes.com/newsgraphics/2013/12/30/year-in-interactive-storytelling/

8   "Firestorm: The Story of the Bushfire at Dunalley." *Guardian*. May 22, 2013. Accessed January 2015. http://www.theguardian.com/world/interactive/2013/may/26/firestorm-bushfire-dunalley-holmes-family

9   Reid, Alastair. "How the Guardian Built Multimedia Interactive Firestorm." Journalism.co.uk. May 29, 2013. Accessed January 2015. https://www.journalism.co.uk/news/how-the-guardian-built-multimedia-interactive-firestorm/s2/a553101/

10 Panetta, Francesca, interview with the authors, July 30, 2014.

11 Richards, Jonathan. "10 Things We Learned during the Making of Firestorm." *Guardian, Developer Blog.* June 7, 2013. Accessed January 2015. http://www.theguardian.com/info/developer-blog/2013/jun/07/10-things-we-learned-making-firestorm

12 "The '80s: The Decade That Made Us." *National Geographic Channel.* April 14, 2014. Accessed January 2015. http://channel.nationalgeographic.com/channel/the-80s-the-decade-that-made-us/

13 "Like, Explore the 80's." Mullen. April 9, 2013. Accessed January 2015. http://www.mullen.com/like-explore-the-80s/

14 "National Geographic Channel—Killing Kennedy." Mullen. November 7, 2013. Accessed January 2015. http://www.mullen.com/work/national-geographic-channel-killing-kennedy/

# Lean-Back,
# Lean-Forward,
# Stand-Up

Existence is no more than the precarious attainment of relevance in an intensely mobile flux of past, present, and future.

—Susan Sontag

This chapter discusses the interplay between content and device. Research on this topic shows that people consume content differently on smartphones, tablets, laptop computers, iPods, and wearable devices like glasses or watches in terms of time spent, attention span, level of engagement, and level of distraction. In many cases this also affects content and the way it is presented—not only from a design perspective, but even at the editorial level. Consumption patterns can influence the length of a story, the media form used (e.g., video, text, audio), the narrative structure of a story, or even the subject matter. Consumption patterns already affect the way stories are told in mediums of traditional journalism. For example, two forms of print media—news magazines and newspapers—typically tackle different story subjects at varying degrees of depth based partly on the way they are consumed, magazines traditionally covering longer stories with deeper analysis, and often consumed less frequently and in different settings than a daily newspaper.

New interfaces also present entirely new ways people can interact with content. A touch screen provides new experiences that may not be possible on a laptop computer. Mobile devices typically contain external sensors that can incorporate surrounding information as part of the story: location information, visual information from a camera, and the orientation of the physical device. Wearable devices such as Google Glass are completely driven by audiovisual information and have different set of constraints and possibilities. Smart watches are designed with different information delivery modes than their smartphone counterparts, and they stimulate a different set of senses. Many watches utilize haptic feedback, a small motor that vibrates to alert a wearer with notifications. Some have earphone jacks to allow a wearer to listen to content, and others have small screens for displaying limited text. When we consider that one of the essential roles of journalism is information conveyance, finding the most effective methods to express news becomes instrumental.

## ▶ LEAN-FORWARD MODE

We know from decades of research that "lean-forward" devices—such as desktop computers—correlate with shorter attention spans, especially when compared to modes where a user is in a more comfortable setting, such as watching television or reading a book on a couch in the living room. The typical television show lengths are set in half-hour increments, whereas most Web videos are only a couple minutes long. Usability experts like Jakob Nielsen of the Nielsen Norman Group have been studying consumption habits since the 1990s. For years, Nielsen has conducted eye-tracking studies where participants wear small cameras on their head to track their eye movements and understand how people read content in different settings and on different platforms—both digital and print. Through years of empirical testing, they've discovered that users view web pages in a frenetic manner in what Nielsen describes as "scanning" mode: users quickly peruse content, picking out only pieces of information. A 1997 seminal report titled "How Users Read on the Web" explained results of one such study with a declarative summary: "They don't." Instead, it says, "People rarely read Web pages word by word; instead, they scan the page, picking out individual words and sentences. In research on how people read websites we found that 79 percent of our test users always scanned any new page they came across; only 16 percent read word-by-word."[1] The report detailed lessons for writers on how to write effectively for computer screens using a combination of active prose, special formatting (like bulleted lists and highlighted words), and concise text for an audience that largely glosses over most text in web pages.

Later, a 2008 study by a German group titled "Not Quite the Average: An Empirical Study of Web Use" reaffirmed many of Nielsen's findings, giving additional quantitative proof of how quickly people gloss over content on the Web. It was different from previous Web usability studies in that it was a naturalistic survey where browser activities of participants were observed over several months without any special instructions. Based on the time spent per web page, participants had—at most—enough time to read 28 percent of the words during an average visit. The study also found habits of Web users were quickly evolving in terms of their sophistication; more importantly, Web browsing was largely an interactive experience with rapid activity. "Users do not navigate on these sites searching for information, but rather interact with an online application to complete certain tasks. . . . We found that Web browsing is a rapid activity even for pages with substantial content, which calls for page designs that allow for cursory reading."[2] A key point in this summary is the application to "complete certain tasks," demonstrating just how active Web browsing is compared to more consumption-like activities, like reading in print.

Books like Maggie Jackson's *Distracted: The Erosion of Attention and the Coming Dark Age* talk about the intense cognitive load required to focus in a digital era while juggling multiple competing platforms of content.[3] Multitasking is detrimental to focus and concentration, she found, and a proliferation of digital devices in our lives erodes the ability for society as a whole to consume content of depth. Nicholas Carr takes this further in his book, *The Shallows: What the Internet Is Doing to Our Brains*, suggesting that not only were such distractions causing us a loss of focus, but that digital media was changing the very physiology of the neural synapses in our brains and our ability to concentrate in other parts of our daily lives. "Given our brain's plasticity, we know that our online habits continue to reverberate in the workings of our synapses when we're not online. We can assume that the neural circuits devoted to scanning, skimming and multitasking are expanding and strengthening, while those used for reading and thinking deeply, with sustained concentration, are weakening or eroding."[4]

Both Carr's and Jackson's books may be pessimistic, perhaps even fatalistic, outlooks on digital media as a whole. Still, we can appreciate the revelations they inform about specific modes of consumption. Both of these books tend to lump all digital media into these distracting forms when compared to print. We can, however, parse this further into specific device modes and posit that certain design conventions can actually lend themselves to different consumption patterns. For example, the iOS mobile operating system found on iPads varies considerably from its PC cousin. The one-app-open-at-a-time mode on mobile is constraining but also liberating from the multiple windows and workspaces that clutter desktop experiences.

The term "lean-forward" is not only about the physical nature of consumption; it describes a cognitive mode as well. Through the 1980s and 1990s, desktop computers largely became the linchpin of office workspaces. They were devices of interaction, work, and creation. Slowly, as personal computers became popularized and made their way into homes, they evolved into devices of leisure, but their central function as a device to accomplish a task remained. Banking, travel, shopping, and communicating are all activities closely associated with computers. The term "lean-forward" describes a method of consuming content on a device that is multifunctional, work oriented, composed of distractions. It is frenetic and bombards users with multiple streams of content. On a Web browser, this can be multiple tabs, or multiple programs open, always running in the background. Alerts, e-mails, and notifications from Facebook or e-mail are constantly vying for attention. The average time spent on a particular website is abysmally low when compared to print and broadcast mediums. And it makes sense when one considers the nature of the medium, both its function and design.

## ▶ LEAN-BACK MODES

Conversely, a lean-back device is one where the user is in a consumption mode. Often this requires little direct interaction with the device, and the attention span is greatly increased. Such lean-back forms originally described print media, and by relatively newer definitions, television and movies. The highly stimulating characteristics of television and film might seem antithetical to the passivity of lean-back. But in this sense, the definition of lean-back has evolved to specifically describe a posture designed around consumption versus interaction, rather than describing a level of visual stimulation.

In *The Digital Media Handbook*, Andrew Dewdney writes, "Television is characteristically a 'lean-back' media while the computer and Internet is a 'lean-forward' media. As a way of characterizing the typical difference between the viewer of television and the user of the computer lean-back and lean-forward is a highly successful contrast and conveys the dominant way in which the viewer or user is 'positioned' or, structured, by particular media. Lean-back carries that sense of passivity involved in a common cultural habit of watching television, while lean-forward accurately indicates a work ethic associated with using a computer."[5]

In lean-back mediums, the physical posture of the consumer is generally one of comfort and usually without much distraction; a living room couch or the bed, where a person would curl up with a book, might be prime examples. (These are generalizations, of course, as any parent might suspect the living room is anything but free of distractions.) Other locations often connoted with lean-back mediums would include places where people read: a doctor's office waiting room or an airplane ride. Sunday mornings have special meanings in the media industry. Since the nineteenth century, Sunday magazines rose to prominence with publications like the *San Francisco Chronicle*'s Sunday magazine, launched in 1869, or the *New York Times Magazine*—published on Sundays—which launched on September 6, 1896.[6] Sunday, being a day of rest, was an opportunity for longer articles, for more in-depth analysis, and to experience the leisure of reading. The place, day, and time people consumed media influenced decisions of content for these publications.

In lean-back modes, media tends to be more immersive, in-depth, and narrative. In some forms, it can also potentially be sedative and less interactive. But neither term, lean-forward or lean-back, is intended to be pejorative, instead simply describing a form of consumption, and contained within each are pros and cons. In fact, despite the lack of interactivity and visual stimulation of lean-back print mediums, MRI scans by researchers at Emory University have shown that reading a novel actually had many positive physical effects on the brain. In a 2013 medical study, 21 participants were given MRI scans on 19 consecutive days, on 9 of which they read part of a novel. The results showed, during the days they read the novel, new neurological connections being formed in their brain that improve comprehension, and these connections even persisted five days after the reading was completed.[7]

▶ TABLETS: LEAN-FORWARD OR LEAN-BACK?

Tablets have divorced the computer from a workstation environment, moving deeper into people's personal living spaces. People use tablets on couches, in beds, and on car or plane rides at a much greater frequency than desktop/laptop computers, according to Forrester Research.[8] In a 2011 study, 88 percent of respondents used tablets in a living room and 79 percent in the bedroom, compared to a paltry 35 percent who used them in places like the workplace or a home office. The study was aimed at marketers, trying to discover implications for delivering advertisements to the device. The survey results were a part of a larger report by Forrester titled "The Tablet-TV Connection," which found that video ads might be better suited to tablets because of the leisurely modes in which they were used.[9]

But mode of consumption is not only about where these devices are used; it also pertains to the types of content associated with using them. Which of these devices are primarily used for work and which for play? It matters when certain types of content are designed for leisure rather than utility.

In April 2010, Steve Jobs introduced the Apple iPad to the world at a large public event in San Francisco. During a portion of the demo, he conspicuously sat on a small black couch on stage while demonstrating the tablet's capabilities projected on a screen behind him. The couch was an unusual prop, not seen in numerous product demos he had performed in decades prior.

**FIGURE 8.1** Steve Jobs presenting the iPad in San Francisco on January 27, 2010. Photo by Matt Buchanan, CC-BY 2.0 license via Wikimedia Commons

It is unknown if this was an intentional move by Apple—a company known for enormously detailed choreography in its presentations. Regardless, the couch is symbolic of the type of consumption this device respects. It's a casual device, one on which you want to lean-back and consume content, rather than create content. The consumption/creation debate isn't definitive, however. Even Apple has fought against this declaration in subsequent years, with Steve Jobs saying during one interview with former *Wall Street Journal* reporter Walt Mossberg at a yearly D8 conference in 2010 that content creation was a central benefit of the iPad.[10] (It should be noted that at the time, Jobs was advocating for a suite of iWork productivity software for the iPad.) During the same interview, Jobs famously likened PCs to trucks. "When we were an agrarian nation, all cars were trucks, because that's what you needed on the farm," Jobs said. "But as vehicles started to be used in the urban centers, cars got more popular. . . . PCs are going to be like trucks. They're still going to be around, they're still going to have a lot of value, but they're going to be used by one out of 'x' people."

Data also show people using iPads in the evening hours after they've left work, which suggested it is used more for leisure and consumption. In 2011, marketing research firm ComScore released a white paper titled "Digital Omnivores: How Tablets, Smartphones and Connected Devices Are Changing U.S. Digital Media Consumption Habits." The paper made lots of headlines at the time because of its timing as one of the first major studies about tablets just over a year after the iPad's release. One of the more notable revelations in the study was a clear spike in evening traffic by tablet users.

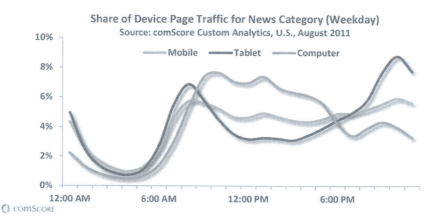

**FIGURE 8.2 Device use through the day for news consumption, ComScore, 2011**

"On a weekday morning, news sees an equal spike in consumption across computer, mobile, and tablet devices. Throughout the course of the day, however, a higher share of news is consumed over computers, due to high workplace computer activity. Tablets had the highest relative usage during the nighttime hours, peaking between the hours of 9:00 PM and midnight, which suggests that people probably favor tablet usage as they retire to the couch or bed at the end of the day."[11] Another paper by Google titled "Understanding Tablet Use: A Multi-Method Exploration"—which studied 33 participants and was released at a conference about human-computer interaction—showed that the top places people use tablets were the couch, bed, home, table, kitchen and office, and in that order.[12]

This was much different than how people consumed content on computers. Analytics data throughout the 2000–2010 decade—before tablets became mainstream—showed that people often checked news websites at their place of employment and typically on a work computer. Many working journalists at the time will familiarly recall the new digital primetime. There was an industry-wide surge in traffic to news websites around noontime—presumably when employees were on lunch break. This trend began to dictate the publishing cycle of Web content; lunch was a time for a quick news fix. Now, with more recent data showing people using tablet devices primarily during evening hours, the calculus changes about the types of content that might be most conducive for the lean-back format.

In its 2012 annual report, the Economist Group differentiated lean-forward and lean-back with the addition of a sub-category called "Lean-back Digital"[13] (or in some interviews lean-back 2.0),[14] which dealt with the disparity of the lean-back modes of traditional media and new interactive digital devices that were consumption-oriented. "The web provides a completely different experience from print. Yes, visitors to Economist.com do read content there, but the web offers an interactive, snacking, lean-forward and, increasingly, a social and shared experience," wrote Oscar Grut, managing director of *Economist* digital in their 2012 annual report. "Many of our readers tell us that this experience [on tablets] is, in fact, even better than print, because as well as being lean-back, digital editions are delivered immediately and reliably (much more so than via the postal service); the backlit screens display images, maps and charts beautifully; and the devices offer opportunities to innovate and deliver more functionality—so, for example, our tablet and smartphone apps also deliver the full newspaper in audio each week."

Other news organizations are experimenting with iPads in a more interactive way. The National Film Board of Canada (NFB) Interactive team is known for its extraordinarily immersive documentary films. For years now they have been producing rich interactive documentary-like experiences on PCs using technologies such as Flash and more recently HTML5. During a 2013 Tribeca Film Institute yearly Interactive conference, Loc Dao, head of NFB Digital Studio, spoke about some their latest projects and how they were being adapted for the iPad. "People will be experiencing our work on computers for years to come, but they'll be experiencing it more and more on buses, on smartphones, in bed on the couch on their iPads," said Dao.[15]

Dao followed with demonstrations of graphic novels and other longform projects that were largely touch-activated, and the user would need to interact with the device in order to push the narrative forward, a departure from lean-back-and-watch documentary films.

So are tablets truly lean-back devices? Certainly, people engage with the device through touch and interaction, which typically are characteristics of lean-forward mediums. They can become participatory and much more elaborate than non-digital print mediums and even harness external sensors not commonly found on laptops. In other cases, tablets are more akin to books, where people use them to consume media at the end of the day. The jury may still be out on whether tablets are lean-back or lean-forward, and it may not ever be definitive, as different use-cases segment tablet usage into different categories. Whether tablets are definitively lean-forward or lean-back may not matter as much as maintaining a critical eye toward a user's consumption when developing content for these devices. People read books on tablets. They also play video games. The usage intention and capabilities is an important characteristic of any device, whether it be a smartphone, television, or newspaper. How people react as they are reading/watching, the cognitive load on their thinking, the level of distraction—these are all important questions to ask of any medium. More importantly, designing content effectively within a medium with respect to these characteristics is instrumental.

## ▶ SMARTPHONES AND THE STAND-UP MODE OF CONSUMPTION

There is a third, less-defined category that has emerged relatively recently. During numerous journalism conferences academics were trying to determine the consumption mode of smartphones and wearable devices. Smartphones are used with great utility and are with consumers nearly every moment of the day. Numerous surveys and studies released yearly reinforce this. A 2013 IDC survey sponsored by Facebook, titled "Always Connected: How Smartphones and Social Keep Us Engaged,"[16] showed that nearly 80 percent of respondents used their smartphone within the first 15 minutes of waking up in the morning (it goes up to 90 percent among 18- to 24-year-olds). In addition, phone usage patterns continue evenly throughout the entire day. People use their phones constantly from the moment they wake until the evening, when usage first begins to drop. Another digital marketing company called Compete conducted a 2010 survey trying to quantify specific locations people are most often using smartphones. Locations surveyed included using smartphones at home, waiting in line, while shopping, at work, while watching TV, during a commute, or in the bathroom.[17] Other surveys looked at habits and activities of smartphone users. A 2012 InsightsNow survey commissioned by AOL and BBDO titled "Seven Shades of Mobile" tried to dissect the "true" consumption habits of smartphone users by averaging interactions that excluded the more typical e-mail, SMS, and voice call uses. It grouped usage into a hierarchy of seven categories: 46 percent "me time," which is relaxation or entertainment, such as watching videos or playing games; 19 percent time spent socializing; 12 percent shopping; 11 percent "accomplishing," like managing finances or using a productivity app; 7 percent "preparation," which defines an activity like booking travel; 4 percent "discovery"; and 1 percent for hobbies or self-interest.[18] This wide spread shows that about half of the time is spent for passive leisure and half for actively engaging with content. Smartphones are a truly multifunctional, multipurpose device when it comes to consumption habits. There are dozens of surveys and studies showing similar statistics, almost too many to count. It's no mystery that smartphones have invaded nearly every part of our lives and are always available, always with us. Usage only begins to wane—but only barely—in the evening hours, at a time when tablet usage begins to rise. This might suggest that smartphones aren't used with the same intention as a lean-back medium; many people don't make plans around their smartphone usage in the same way they might plan for an evening of reading or watching a movie. Still, it's clear these are devices of both leisure and utility. One thing is clear, however: they are used constantly.

While no single term has universally taken hold to describe this form of consumption (as of the writing of this book), we have begun using the term "stand-up" mode to describe devices that are with us throughout the day. They are used for snacking on content in bits and pieces, but also for leisure. They are multifunctional, but also constrained. The smaller screens of smartphones are limiting in what they can display, and force content designers to readjust their presentation and design-thinking for a new form of consumption. In other stand-up mediums, like Google Glass or smart watches, the constraints are even more pronounced. Some devices are limiting visually, others can only reliably deliver content through notifications, like the buzz of a watch. One of the authors of this book was an early beta tester for Google Glass, part of the Google Glass Explorer program, and had personal experience with an early version of the *New York Times* Google Glass app, which displayed text on tiny cards. It became clear that despite Google advocating its head-up display (HUD) as a technological innovation, the device clearly isn't suited for longer text. Content needs to fit the medium in which it is told.

## ▶ GOING AGAINST THE GRAIN

While devices can be thought of as lean-forward, lean-back, or stand-up, what about content? Though story design can be adjusted for a specific platform, does certain content become conducive to specific devices? If a PC is such a frenetic experience, why are there so many websites with long articles? Longform.org, LongReads.com, Instapaper, Atavist, innumerable magazine websites, even *The Verge* and Buzzfeed—all have longform text articles that would seem antithetical to PCs' lean-forward consumption patterns. A Digitalsmiths 2013 report showed that longer video was surging on smartphones, including comedy sitcoms and former TV shows. Other sites like Netflix, Hulu, and Amazon Instant Video are seeing record growth among digital devices like laptops and smartphones.[19] Publications like the *New York Times* are posting text articles to Google Glass, an arguably audiovisual device. During interviews for this book, we found many cases in which media designed for different modes of consumption were being posted online—a podcast episode posted on a web page for example. Some of these are cases of technology simply outpacing customs and familiarity. Other times, it had to do with institutionalized workflows within certain organizations that made adaptations difficult or undesirable, particularly in cases when a legacy medium is preferred by the organization. A phone may not be the greatest experience to watch a two-hour movie, nor would a laptop be the most comfortable device to read a 10,000-word article, but invariably some people still will. Content adaptation is a slow process—and has been for a number of years—and it often wins out despite the logistical hurdles. Much of these cases can be attributed to peripheral effects, like the economic business models of an organization, or workflow issues.

## ▶ FRAGMENTATION OF CONTENT

Most news package content we found for mobile had been adapted from other models, like the desktop Web or even a legacy medium. In these cases, a news package would be designed first for the PC Web experience, then secondarily would be refactored for mobile screens. In response to the influx of mobile usage, a new term is taking hold in the industry: "mobile first." But how this strategy plays out in more tangible terms is anything but clear. Some news organizations like AJ Plus (AJ+)—an extension of Al Jazeera's emerging news network in the US market—don't have a desktop website (at the time of this book), only a mobile app. This is intentional. In interviews with the editors of AJ+, we learned there was much discussion within the organization about living up to the reality of a mobile-first mantra and having a mobile app be the centerpiece of the organization. Other experiments in utilizing the mobile space include the book *The Silent History*, an interactive multimedia novel that is only available on the iPad. When visiting the website www.thesilenthistory.com, a title page directs users to download the app; there is no desktop content by which to consume the novel. It's not an adaptation but a solely native iPad experience. Another type of service called Appumentary allows content creators to create an interactive documentary-like experience as a native iPad app. "Appumentaries are digital applications that build upon storytelling presented in books and films to deliver interactive experiences. We can leverage technology to convert isolated groups of individuals into communities. We can transform passive experiences into interactive ones that present content in myriad ways. We can provide ways for audiences to respond, for teachers to enlighten, and for students to explore."[20] But only users with iPads can see this content.

What results with these native-mobile forms is a fragmentation of content. And in this is a dilemma: How does a news organization convey a single story on multiple platforms? The easy way is design adaptation. "Responsive design" is a Web term that refers to the ability of a website to adjust to multiple screen sizes and display content in a way that is conducive to large-screen PCs, tablets, and mobile devices, but the content remains the same. For content to become native to a specific type of device—particularly when leveraging characteristics like touch or external sensors—the story needs to be constructed from the ground up, resulting in a fragmentation. Nowhere is this clearer than radio news organizations like NPR, whose Web story packages are entirely new forms of content that are formulated from the ground up, many times due to the disparity of aural mediums and the Web. This fragmentation creates logistical hurdles for many news organizations wanting to build multiplatform native experiences.

In his 1964 book *Understanding Media: The Extensions of Man*, Marshall McLuhan coined the phrase "The Medium is the Message." McLuhan surmised that a medium influences how a message is perceived and there was a deeper relationship between medium and message than simply being a conveyance of information. McLuhan's philosophical research extended beyond the unit of story content to the overall effect of a medium on society and the causality of news through mediums like television, whose proliferation through the 1950s and 1960s was having dramatic effects on society and its perception of world events. The focus of *Understanding Media* was more about the medium's effect on society than the adaptation of content specifically. Still, these ideas acknowledge the symbiotic relationship between medium and message. "A new medium is never an addition to an old one, nor does it leave the old one in peace. It never ceases to oppress the older media until it finds new shapes and positions for them."[21] What's interesting is that McLuhan's notions began to lose fashion through much of his later years—in the 1970s and 1980s—and were only recently reinvigorated through the advent of the Internet, which many feel is a manifestation of both his "Global Village" ideas and his writings about how mediums influence messages.[22] Today, McLuhan is largely seen as a thinker before his time.

Lean-back, lean-forward, and stand-up are notions that pertain to today's devices. But whole new categories of technological platforms will be emerging in the coming years. Smart watches, wearable tech like glasses, appliances in the home, and virtual reality headsets will undoubtedly change the news consumption habits of many consumers. As in-depth content remains a desideratum of the news industry, understanding how each of these platforms affects consumption becomes essential—not just identifying their characteristics, but uncovering design formulas for how to effectively communicate on them. Understanding a medium allows us to create better messages.

## ▶ NOTES

1 Nielsen, Jakob. "How Users Read on the Web." Nielsen Norman Group. October 1, 1997. Accessed January 2015. http://www.nngroup.com/articles/how-users-read-on-the-web/

2 Weinreich, Harald, Hartmut Obendorf, Eelco Herder, and Matthias Mayer. "Not Quite the Average: An Empirical Study of Web Use." *ACM Transactions on the Web*, 2008: 1–31.

3 Jackson, Maggie. *Distracted: The Erosion of Attention and the Coming Dark Age.* Amherst, NY: Prometheus Books, 2008.

4 Carr, Nicholas G. *The Shallows: What the Internet Is Doing to Our Brains.* New York: W. W. Norton, 2010.

5 Dewdney, Andrew, and Peter Ride. *The Digital Media Handbook.* New York: Routledge, 2006, p. 363.

6 Woodward, Calvin. "Rough Seas: Say a Prayer for the Sunday Magazine, a Meandering Journey for the Mind That's Sailed into Some Dangerous Waters." *American Society of News Editors: The American Editor*, October–November 1999.

7 Berns, Gregory S., Kristina Blaine, Michael J. Prietula, and Brandon E. Pye. "Short- and Long-Term Effects of a Novel on Connectivity in the Brain." *Brain Connectivity* 3, no. 6 (2013): 590–600.

8 "North American Technographics Telecom And Devices Online Recontact Survey, Q3 2011" Forrester Research. September 2011. https://www.forrester.com/North+American+Technographics+Telecom+And+Devices+Online+Recontact+Survey+Q3+2011+US/-/E-SUS867

9 Epps, Sara Rotman. "The Tablet-TV Connection." Forrester Research Report, p. 8. April 11, 2012.

10 Swisher, Kara. "Full D8 Interview Video: Apple CEO Steve Jobs." AllThingsD. June 7, 2010. Accessed January 23, 2015. http://allthingsd.com/20100607/full-d8-video-apple-ceo-steve-jobs/

11 "Digital Omnivores: How Tablets, Smartphones and Connected Devices Are Changing U.S. Digital Media Consumption Habits." ComScore. October 2011.

12 Müller, Hendrik, Jennifer L. Gove, and John S. Webb. "Understanding Tablet Use: A Multi-Method Exploration." *Proceedings of the 14th Conference on Human-Computer Interaction with Mobile Devices and Services Mobile HCI 2012*. September 24, 2012. Accessed January 23, 2015. http://research.google.com/pubs/pub38135.html

13  Grut, Oscar. "The Economist Group Annual Report 2012." Economist Group. January 1, 2012. Accessed January 23, 2015. http://www.economistgroup.com/pdfs/annual_report_2012_final_for_web.pdf

14  Greenslade, Roy. "Andrew Rashbass: 'The Biggest Reason We're Successful Is That We Are Lucky.'" *Guardian*. November 27, 2011. Accessed January 23, 2015. http://www.theguardian.com/media/2011/nov/27/andrew-rashbass-economist-group-interview

15  Dao, Loc. "NFB Interactive Since Bear 71." Talk, TFI Interactive from Tribeca Film Institute, New York City, April 20, 2013.

16  "Always Connected: How Smartphones and Social Keep Us Engaged 2013." IDC Research Report. This was a survey of 1,000+ 18- to 44-year-old iOS and Android smartphone owners in the United States each day for one week (Friday–Thursday) in March 2013, for a total number of respondents of 7,446.

17  Kim, Bohyun. *The Library Mobile Experience: Practices and User Expectations.* Chicago: ALA TechSource, 2013; Compete Quarterly Smartphone Intelligence, January–February 2010, n=1246.

18  "Seven Shades of Mobile." InsightsNow survey for AOL and BBDO. 2012 (n=1051).

19  "Digitalsmiths' Q1 2013 Video Discovery Trends Report: Consumer Behavior Across Pay-TV, VOD, OTT, Connected Devices and Next-Gen Features." Digitalsmiths. January 1, 2013. Accessed January 23, 2015. http://www.digitalsmiths.com/digitalsmiths'-q1–2013-video-discovery-trends-report-consumer-behavior-across-pay-tv-vod-ott-connected-devices-and-next-gen-features/

20  Zeff, Joe. "Spies of Mississippi: The Appumentary." Joe Zeff Design. April 11, 2014. Accessed January 23, 2015. http://www.joezeffdesign.com/jzdblog/spies-of-mississippi

21  McLuhan, Marshall. *Understanding Media: The Extensions of Man*, critical ed., ed. W. Terrence Gordon. Corte Madera, CA: Gingko, 2003, 237.

22  Stille, Alexander. "Marshall McLuhan Is Back from the Dustbin of History; With the Internet, His Ideas Again Seem Ahead of Their Time." *New York Times*. October 13, 2000. Accessed January 23, 2015. http://www.nytimes.com/2000/10/14/arts/marshall-mcluhan-back-dustbin-history-with-internet-his-ideas-again-seem-ahead.html

# 9

# A Major Shift in Approach

In the late 1990s when a news organization decided to do a special report, they already had rigid workflows in place based on years of tradition. Journalists and editors already knew the media forms that the package would take—even before a story idea was pitched. In the case of a newspaper organization, there would certainly be photos, possibly several graphics, and of course text. Space dedicated for the project would be determined on factors like the number of photos chosen and the length of the edited text. The newspaper was a well-oiled machine, and most of this process was automatic. This news creation process was similarly formulaic in broadcast and radio mediums.

Entirely new workflows would come with the emergence of the Web. As newsrooms embraced new technologies like Flash and recognized the power of the Web to reshape presentation, a special feature might now include digital-centric interactive elements. These new and emerging story-forms birthed new approaches to content-gathering practices.

In the early days of the Web, before dedicated online producers, Web-based packages were a hodgepodge self-initiated by the "geekier" individuals from various departments. It wasn't uncommon to have a photographer, graphic designer, or a technology reporter take an interest in creating the online version of the project. Drunk with the power of unlimited space, these newbie Web producers were using material that normally would be left on the cutting-room floor in legacy mediums. More photographs, more graphic elements for animations, maybe a Q&A backstory from the reporter would result in a sidebar of extras. "Storyboards," "wireframes," and "pre-visualization"—terms normally reserved for Hollywood or Silicon Valley start-ups—were making their way into the lexicon of the newsroom. An evolution was under way. Not only was the role of the journalist changing, so was the process of gathering and presenting a story.

Fifteen years after newsroom story production started its metamorphosis in the late 1990s, a new workflow for online packages is taking hold today. In both newsrooms and journalism school classrooms, it is common to see a group of writers, photographers, editors, designers, animators, coders, and social media editors gathered around a single workspace—brainstorming, white-boarding, and wireframing. You'll hear terms like "agile," "UI," "UX," "user feedback," and "minimal viable product" being tossed around. Additionally, you'll hear questions like, "What's the right media for the story? What's our social media plan? Who's our audience? What platform are we developing for? Is the project going be responsive? What about an app? How are we going to measure engagement and success?"

Imagine a cohort of story-builders congregating around an Arthurian round table discussing the various approaches to the story package. The circle implies that everyone who has a place at the table has equal status. This idea can be applied to media types on the Web. In a Web-first approach, all media have equal status and potential to be the lead element driving the story. On the Web, stories no longer need to default to text, video, or audio; if the story calls for it the experience could be driven exclusively by another media form, like animated graphics. This metaphor can be extended to exemplify how the overall workflow has moved from a top-down hierarchical system to a circular one.

In traditional models, the story is constructed from the top down, where initial meetings were attended by only the highest ranking editors, then it trickled down as the media elements are passed from one department to another with little back-and-forth movement. Some journalists in the chain typically had little opportunity to provide input on changes that were being made to the story. However, the new digital-centric workflows are more circular in nature, and all stakeholders meet from idea inception to project deployment. They discuss story construction without hierarchical barriers. This workflow is not unlike the physical reorganization that happened in newsrooms like the *Wall Street Journal, Telegraph*, and Italian newspaper *La Stampa*, which were made to facilitate multiplatform publications. *La Stampa*, for example, was determined to lose the demarcation between print and digital. They relocated parts of the newsroom in order to close a physical gap that existed between the managing editor and the Web editor. They built a new newsroom based on concentric circles. At the center of the circle now sit the news executives, art directors, photo editors, and Web editors, who assign stories and direct operations. They are free to exchange information and requests among themselves. In the second circle sit the editors responsible for the fastest moving news categories: politics, crime, business, etc. In the outer circle are the technical and typographic staff responsible for preparing content for its online and offline publication. There is a high degree of visibility around and between the circles.[1]

Amid these changes, digital editor Marco Bardazzi commented that the impact of bringing new people into the circle was the "contamination" of existing staff with ideas and approaches from developers and designers:

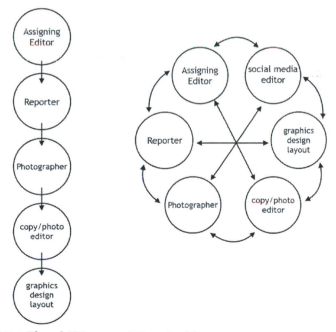

**FIGURE 9.1 The shifting workflow inside newsrooms**

"Contamination comes from the new figures we have introduced: developers, designers and a few digital gurus we have picked. [It's a] positive contamination, the contamination of ideas."[2]

While no single approach is best for every story or organization, we draw conclusions about some of the practicalities in executing digital news packages—in terms of workflow, planning, production, and the level of expertise needed to produce them. We also describe the mindset needed to approach online stories with a digital-first mentality. As news consumption through digital mediums surpasses traditional products of newspapers, terrestrial radio, or television, journalists of all disciplines need to rethink their approach to storytelling.

Surprising as it may sound, the workflow we outline in the following pages isn't merely intended for large projects and teams, but for all projects types, despite the size of the team or the deadline. We've seen success in the classroom with groups a small as two and as large as six. For instance, a project with a three-day deadline uses the same workflow as a project with a six-month deadline—only in a more rapid fashion.

## ▶ CREATING DIGITAL NEWS PACKAGES, A WORKFLOW

In these next few pages, we present a sample workflow for creating digital news package content. It's important to understand that the workflow presented here is only a starting point and deliberately leaves adequate space for adaptation and modification. The workflow principles are based on our professional experience in the field and in the classroom and on information from interviews.

The framework that makes up workflow in digital news package development borrows heavily from filmmaking and is based on the three "Ps." It starts with pre-production—sometimes referred to as the planning phase—then shifts to the production phase, where story content is gathered. The final phase is post-production, where content editing and final platform design take place. Typically, post-production takes longer than the actual gathering of content; therefore, it's important to leave adequate time to edit the multimedia elements and put the fit and finish on your designs. To accelerate this process, some larger organizations have created story templates in order for content to be packaged and published in a more timely fashion, but they still follow the general three Ps workflow. There are more possible iterations for digital storytelling workflow; this is a starting framework.

## Basic Workflow Outline

### *Pre-production—Planning Phase*

- ▶ Initial Q&A/Planning      Is this a multimedia package?

- ▶ Brainstorming Session      What interactive approach is appropriate?

- ▶ Choosing the Tool(s)      What's the right medium?

- ▶ Creative Inspiration      Where will I find inspiration?

- ▶ Audience      Who is my audience?

- ▶ Platform      What platform am I focusing on?

### *Production—Content Gathering Phase*

- ▶ Fieldwork

- ▶ Regroup, Evaluate, Revise

### *Post-Production—Editing, Final Design*

- ▶ Script

- ▶ Design

- ▶ Prototype

- ▶ Test, Evaluate, Revise

- ▶ Launch and Update

**Before You Start**   Crafting a digital story is a creative enterprise. The first step is simple: collecting and organizing everything relevant to the project in one place. Once the decision to produce a multilayered interactive story is made, every fleeting idea becomes a potential asset.

It's important to capture as many ideas as possible. A paper notebook or a digital tool like Pinterest comes in handy. Analog or digital doesn't matter—but being disciplined about this practice does. From an inspirational webpage (keeping track of the URL) to the elegant font in a magazine, it's all fair game.

All digital news packages require a complex set of steps before completion. Their success depends on the amount of purposeful preparation. A clear vision and a strong narrative rarely emerge without disciplined attention to the planning phase. The plan's details aren't often as crucial as the mere fact there is a plan.

Not all stories lend themselves to a larger multimedia package. As exemplified by many of the case studies throughout this book, successful multimedia packages are multidimensional. They can include media elements such as a strong emotional situation captured on video, a process that can be animated with motion graphics, information designed as a data visualization, or perhaps a photograph that can be coupled with a strong soundscape. Although not all projects require such a vast array of possibilities to qualify as multimedia, there must be enough depth and discrete layers to merit creation and be labeled a digital news package.

These are some rules, which we use in the classroom and can be equally applied in the field, that make up a multimedia development checklist:

- ▶ **In one complete sentence, or in less than 30 seconds, explain the essence of the story as a multimedia package.** Sometimes described as an elevator pitch, this approach forces clarity and provides you with confidence to win over an editor and gather other potential team members to rally around your project.

- ▶ **Who or what are the central characters?** Knowing the answer to this question will keep focus and prevent the story from deviating off course, as most layered stories are complex.

- ▶ **Why should one be interested in this story? What's at stake? Are the stakes high enough to keep people interested?** If these critical questions can't be answered confidently—it's an indication that the idea may not merit an audience's attention.

- ▶ **How many different scenes or situations can one capture in photos, video, or audio to make people connect with the central character or subject matter?** Rich media experiences may require more than just talking heads, they require subjects in motion. This question forces creators to fill their content inventory with potential points of interest and decide which situations are critical to document. The more recorded situations one can capture, the more options there are during post-production.

- ▶ **Is there relevant data or statistical information that can be presented?** Using charts and other graphic elements aids the viewer in understanding complex information at a glance while adding another layer to the package.

The purpose of answering this set of questions during the pre-production phase is to find the essence of the project and to provide a goal. You can use the analogy of planning a cross-country journey: pre-production is the part of the process where a person decides their destination and where they might stop along the way—it's a road map. As with all road trips, even a planned route leaves room for side trips and veering off course due to bad weather.

Once a rough outline of the project is achieved, one of the toughest questions in the workflow process is, "What interactive approach is appropriate?"

Based on the taxonomy presented in chapter 3, here are some guidelines gleaned from the characteristics of previously produced news packages. Let's examine three distinct models of digital storytelling to determine the characteristics of a project. Our goal is to use these models to help inform producers of how the elements of both *story* and *design* are interconnected.

Regardless if the project is solo or being produced in a team, it's important to have a roundtable discussion with collaborators to discuss as many aspects of the project as possible. An effective brainstorming session is based on the technical diversity of the group at the table. Programmers, designers, visual journalists, researchers, writers, and editors are all vital to the process.

*Comprehensive Package Characteristics*   Is the story based on a broad topic rather than a single narrative story? Then it may need to be modeled after packages listed in our Comprehensive category. These are the general characteristics:

▶   The project explores a large topic.

▶   The project has multiple narrative threads, usually no central character, but many diverse stories.

▶   It is a nonlinear presentation—the user can start the experience anywhere and end up anywhere.

▶   The user has more navigational control over the experience.

▶   There are many diverse elements—data visualizations, videos, slideshows, text, audio.

▶   An example of this type of story is NPR's "Planet Money Makes a T-shirt."

▶   The ideal team size is small to medium.

▶   The technical skill level required varies depending on the scope and sophistication of the project.

*Immersive Package Characteristics*    If the project will place a viewer in an environment built to evoke empathy, or will need to provide a freedom of exploration, then an Immersive approach might be ideal. These are the general characteristics:

▶   The experience is initiated with some type of "start" button—prompting the user to commit time and attention.

▶   These types of stories are usually presented in a fullscreen mode.

▶   They invite a rich environment with a high level of interactivity.

▶   They can be presented in both a linear and a nonlinear style.

▶   One example is National Film Board of Canada's "Bear 71."

▶   The ideal team size is a large organization.

▶   The technical skill level required is generally high, as these tend to be very sophisticated and complex projects.

*Continuous Packages Characteristics*   If the story revolves around a central character or subject and there is a strong narrative structure, then a Continuous package is most ideal. These are the general characteristics:

▶   Contains a traditional narrative structure—beginning, middle, and end.

▶   The story or presentation style is linear.

▶   One dominant medium drives the experience.

▶   The user has minimal control over the experience.

▶   There is minimal interactivity with the user throughout.

▶   An example would be the longform packages from *The Verge*, like "John Wilkes Booth Killed Lincoln . . . but Who Killed John Wilkes Booth?"

▶   The ideal team size is small, or even an individual.

▶   The technical skill level required is basic understanding of multimedia tools.

## A Sample Deconstruction

During the mid-1990s, it became clear that a new workflow was needed for online story construction. Leah Gentry, then at the *Chicago Tribune*, introduced a unique approach during this pre-production phase called "deconstruct, reconstruct, storyboard"—which endures today and merits incorporation.[3] With a hypothetical story as an example, the concept might unfold this way: let's say the organization wants to do an in-depth news package about an outbreak of a deadly virus, such as Ebola. The first step is to deconstruct or divide the story into its component pieces—looking for similarities and relationships—then group those that are similar.

*Example*

**Package headline idea: Deadly Outbreak**

*Possible Components:*

▶  Explain the virus; how is it transmitted?

▶  Travel restrictions

▶  Human toll

▶  Hospital preparations

▶  Government response

▶  Previous outbreaks

Once the initial concept is divided into different parts, the next step is to decide what to cover and what media form to use. The key is using a media type that will present that segment of the story in the most compelling and informative way—where medium is complementary to that part of the story.

Choosing the media form that best communicates each part of the story can be one of the more difficult decisions. What should be shot in video? What should remain as still photos? Is this just a text story? Could something be an animated motion graphic? Understanding the strengths and weaknesses of these different types of media, and how to match those up with different kinds of stories, helps sort this out. The following list goes through the different types of media—video, photos, audio, graphics/maps, and text—and the kinds of stories or characteristics of stories that lend themselves to those forms.[4] These aren't hard-and-fast rules—just general guides to help you make intelligent choices about when to take a video camera, a photo camera, and so forth on a story.

VIDEO    One quality of good video is depicting action, particularly any time a text description would not fully convey the significance of the story. Video is also good for conveying a central place in a story visually, with its power to transport the viewer to a scene and get a better sense of place. Video is good for identifying with—or getting a sense of—a central character in a story. Other characteristics include drama, humor, and stories about crime or crime scenes, generally because video has the power to take the viewer to the scene.

- ▶ **Action**—natural disasters, sporting events, dance performances, etc.

- ▶ **Central place in a story**—a video transports the viewer to a location and gives a sense of what a place is like.

- ▶ **Central characters in a story**—video lets people see and hear subjects and how they behave. Video is especially useful if the subject in a story is interesting or animated.

- ▶ **Drama**—an emotional climactic moment.

- ▶ **Humor**—think about the most popular videos on YouTube.

- ▶ **Crimes and crime scenes**—it almost doesn't matter how boring the crime scene is or how bad the video is, many people will still want to watch it.

- ▶ **How things work or how to do something**—video is good for showing simple processes, such as things with moving parts. These are often called "explainers."

- ▶ **Raw video**—people really like raw video that provides an unfiltered look of what happened, especially on a breaking news story.

PHOTOS   Images tend to be more emotive in nature. Some of its characteristics include causing reflection or contemplation, evoking strong emotion, and getting a sense of a central character or a central place in a story. One only needs to consider the purpose of a mug shot, a common tradition in newspapers, to see the power of a photograph to convey a person's essence. Photography demonstrates key differences from video. The frozen nature of the moment allows viewers to contemplate peak action, expressions, and body language. Henri Cartier-Bresson, founder of Magnum Photos and often billed as the "father of photojournalism," described this peak action as the "decisive moment" and published a book by the same name in 1952.[5]

- ▶ **Reflection**—a part of a story that is contemplative, or a moment you want people to ponder. The frozen image does this better than video, which is always in motion.

► **Emotion**—images are very emotive in nature and can evoke strong feelings.

► **Central characters in a story**—a photograph gives the viewer a sense of a person, to reflect on who the person is rather than seeing how they behave.

► **Central place in a story**—a photograph can also transport a viewer to a location, but with the opportunity to reflect on it. It's more intimate than using video. For example, if there was a story about a natural disaster, a video might take the viewer there while it's happening, but photos may be used to take the viewer to the scene in the aftermath, so the viewer can reflect on what happened. Panoramas are sometimes a very effective ways of taking the viewer to a place and immersing them in it.

AUDIO    At times audio appears as a stand-alone form, such as when a user clicks "play" to hear a clip, or as a podcast one would download onto a device like an iPod, car radio, or smartphone. Other times audio appears in the form of narration or background for a photo slideshow. Regardless of the context, the key characteristics of audio generally include emotion, especially since the human voice evokes emotional reactions; reflection when a listener ponders or thinks, a process more conducive when audio lacks visual stimuli; getting a sense of a person, when hearing a voice gives you an emotional connection with a subject; and taking someone to a central place in a story, usually through the use of familiar ambient sounds.

► **Emotion**—audio is good for stories that are particularly emotional. The human voice especially evokes emotion.

► **Creating a mood**—ambient sounds or the cadence of a voice can set a tone or create a mood for a story.

► **Reflection**—audio is good for reflection, to think about and ponder by listening, rather than watching a video as things go by.

► **Sense of a person**—a person's voice gives a sense of who they are and creates an emotional attachment to them.

► **Central place in a story**—audio can transport listeners to a place in their head. Ambient sound such as common, easily recognizable sounds can take someone to a place.

If you compare the kinds of stories that lend themselves to audio with those that are good for photos, you'll see a lot of similarities. That's one reason why photo slideshows with audio can be very effective—the two types of media complement each other.

DATABASES, GRAPHICS, AND MAPS   Graphics are best suited for presenting statistical information or data; for explaining how things work or describing a complex process; for demonstrating environments where humans can't go, such as a story about space, microbiology, or the innards of a machine; when using time lines to visualize historical events in a spatial context or to better understand chronology; and for using maps to better understand location of events or places or providing context with quantitative data, such as the case in the notorious red state versus blue state US election maps.

▶ **Statistics and data**—displaying data in graphics or on maps makes it easier for readers to digest complex subject matter in a more visual way.

▶ **How things work or how to do something**—graphics are especially good for describing complex processes or things that aren't easily described with text.

▶ **Taking people to places they can't go**—graphics are good for illustrating places humans can't easily go. For example, a story might include graphics of microorganisms or planets in deep space.

▶ **History**—time lines are especially effective ways of showing a spatial continuity of historical events.

▶ **Geo-locational events and stories**—these can be plotted on a map so the viewer immediately has a sense of where something happened or can obtain information for a particular place.

TEXT   Text is an essential medium on the Web. Text tends to be the primary form of communication for many digital devices—computers, smartphones, and tablets. Interestingly, early anecdotal evidence suggests an exception to this rule with wearable devices, like Google Glass or smart watches. The *New York Times* Google Glass app reads stories for you, despite the fact that a user could theoretically read them in the tiny head-up display. Key strengths for text as a medium include background information on a story; analysis and explanation; history or understanding through additional context; summaries; and breaking news, which seems to work better in text form on the Web due to its efficiency of delivering content in a more immediate fashion. Because the Web is so conducive to text, many of the lessons of multimedia storytelling extol the use of text as an accompaniment to all forms of multimedia. Users generally want some type of text description explaining what a video will show them before they commit to press play. Caption-writing has always been a crucial part of the photojournalism craft, to explain a photograph in more detail or offer additional background information.

▶ **Background information**—text is one of the most efficient ways to give people background information.

▶ **Analysis and explanation**—text can often be better at analysis than other mediums because of its efficient density on the page. Video is always moving, so depth is more difficult.

▶ **Historical context**—although a graphical time line can be more effective.

▶ **Summaries**—these are especially important with a multimedia package. Most other media forms need to have accompanying text to give people context, in the case of a photo or graphic, or to give information before a person commits to playing a video.

▶ **Breaking news**—the quickest way to get information out, and the most efficient way for people to scan it for what's happening now.

With these rules about the strengths of each media type in mind, we can identify which media types might best be used to communicate parts of the fictitious "Deadly Outbreak" package. The first story topic listed from the deconstruction exercise was an explanation of the virus. An interactive graphic would likely be the best way to visually communicate how a virus is transmitted. The next topic covers the travel restrictions set in place by various countries. Using the previous list we can determine that text is most effective for explanatory parts of a story. Journalistic instincts tell us that the human toll would make for a compelling video because of its emotional nature. Text is best used to analyze and explain how hospitals and the government are responding to the outbreak. Finally an interactive map and time line would be best to explain previous viral outbreaks throughout history.

Now that the story is broken down into its elements—both in terms of content and media types—it's time to reconstruct it into a rough storyboard.

New media educator, Jane Stevens, notes that a storyboard helps to:

▶ Define the parameters of a story within available resources and time;

▶ Organize and focus a story;

▶ Figure out what medium to use for each part of the story.[6]

A storyboard doesn't have to be high art—just an outline, something resembling a list or several sticky notes. It's not written in stone, it's just a guide. Typically, the storyboard will evolve and change after the field reporting. The storyboard process is one that can be described as fluid—adapting to new content and revising accordingly.

In its most simple form, our storyboard might look like this:

**Package title: Deadly Outbreak**

| *Possible sections* | *Media type* |
|---|---|
| Explain the virus; how is it transmitted? | Animated graphic |
| Travel restrictions | Text |
| Human toll | Video |
| Hospital preparations | Text |
| Government response | Text |
| Previous outbreaks | Map and time line |

The storyboard now begins to identify the need for specific resources (time, equipment, technical assistance) in order to execute the story.

Once a content plan is sketched out, it's time to tackle the form the story might take online. Based on the taxonomy characteristics, this package resembles a Comprehensive approach. There are several factors that could alter this approach. For example, if one finds a strong character-driven narrative that tells the story through the eyes of a central character and contains a classic narrative structure, then this package might change to a more Continuous model, where the narrative drives the story and the multimedia supports parts of it. This package could ultimately resemble both a Comprehensive and Continuous hybrid of characteristics and thus be considered an inter-section. One important factor in determining approach is time. A tight dead-line might force a Continuous approach. Additional time might allow for a more Comprehensive approach. With a generous allotment like six months to produce the package, one might explore the idea of creating an Immersive news package that helps put viewers in the shoes of a virus victim, seeing the world through their eyes as they navigate a complex medical system for treatment. While sensitivity must be taken when deciding the approach, it's not as far-fetched an idea as it sounds. These brainstorming sessions should be an open forum for even the most ambitious blue-sky thoughts. Creative ideas should not be limited by current thinking or tradition.

When the team at the *Wall Street Journal* was brainstorming ideas on how to cover the rollout of the Affordable Care Act (ACA) or "Obamacare" in 2013, their biggest editorial challenge was how to make this complex story personal. They decided they would film an interactive POV video of some-one waking up the morning Obamacare was implemented, to explain the effects they would feel once the law took place. The film was staged and shot with helmet cameras. Jarrard Cole, producer and senior video journal-ist for the *Journal*, described a brainstorming session with his colleagues: "We asked ourselves, what if we told this story from a first-person perspec-tive, which is kind of a crazy idea for news, since usually we deal with real environments. But we thought it might make for an interesting avenue to explain the story. . . . We realized that there was a lot to cover . . . through one character's eyes and for time purposes there was going to be too much content to fit into a reasonable video for someone to experience."[7] Using the POV video as a starting point, the team went back to the drawing board and came up with an experimental idea. They thought about adding an interac-tive layer on top of the video, to give the viewer the choice to explore more informational details by clicking on links that appeared while it was playing. Their pre-planning paid off, and many of the potential hurdles in story con-struction were avoided with extensive and detailed planning.

*Creative Inspiration*   Producing digital new packages is a creative en-deavor, and taking time to explore the landscape is a transformative and necessary step in the process—one that shouldn't be skipped. In her book *The Creative Habit*, Twyla Tharp said, "In order to be creative, you have to know how to prepare to be creative." There is no mystery to cre-ativity; it's a simple process of "preparation and effort," says Tharp.[8] This is another opportunity to break out a notebook or journal or to create a

Pinterest account and collect inspiration. See everything as usable fuel to power production. Many of the producers interviewed for this book immediately pointed to sources of influence in their "genealogy of ideas."[9]

When asked by the authors in a 2013 interview, "Do you have a secret cachet of inspiration?" *New York Times* multimedia producer Jacky Myint said, "I keep both social bookmarking account like delicious[.com] within a new project. You just do a general assessment of what's out there already. When I was working on Snow Fall, I was looking at the Dock Ellis ESPN stuff, Pitchfork and The Verge had been doing some interesting scroll-based narrative presentations. . . . There's definitely a lot of inspiration just seeing what worked well when those sites and how we could improve upon that the same thing. With my new project I'm working on, I'm looking at what the National Film Board of Canada has done in the past and what other different interactive documentaries have done. What other people are doing in the space is really important."[10] We all build on the work, knowledge, and accomplishments of others.

*Audience/Platform*   Failing to consider the potential audience and the platform that is used to interact with content can be fatal. While there is no catchall approach to determining every audience, a few best practices are applicable. It's clear—in broad strokes—today's audience is a cross-platform multitasking junkie. A sharper picture of their habits emerge when we examine site analytics. Also helpful at this stage is to move beyond the concept of seeing audience as only gender or age, but rather consider one that encompasses their experience when interacting with the project. This is commonly referred to as User Experience (UX) and involves a person's behaviors, attitudes, and emotions when interacting with online content. This can also translate into the question, "Who is this story for? Who is your audience?" In some instances, audience surveys might be appropriate. It's commonplace these days to create an online questionnaire to gauge the audience for a story. Learning about the audience might influence the way a news package is constructed.

At this stage another valuable question to consider is what platform(s) the news package is being developed for: tablets, smartphones, desktops, or wearables? Make a list of the unique capabilities and limitations of the chosen medium and how your content might take advantage of the strengths of the chosen medium or overcome its limitations. Using as much analytical information as possible to paint a picture of the audience will help craft a more viable project with genuine appeal.

## ▶ A CASE STUDY IN WORKFLOW: "YOUR HOSPITAL MAY BE HAZARDOUS TO YOUR HEALTH"

It's hard to imagine that a choose-your-own-adventure-style news package about malpractice lawsuits could be built in a week, but that's exactly what a team of collaborators from PBS Frontline, ProPublica, and the design agency Ocupop did at the Tribeca Hacks Storytelling Innovation Lab in 2013.

The team, comprising documentarians, Web developers, and designers, used ProPublica's ongoing research on patient safety as a starting point for their idea. Their goals were ambitious: take what would have otherwise been an hour-long news show and instead make a three-minute video with interactive annotations overlaid on top. (See Figure 9.2.) "One can see the whole story in a glance, but closer examination reveals layers upon layers of finer detail," wrote developer and designer Justin Falcone in Knight-Mozilla's OpenNews Source publication. Falcone wrote about the rapid creation process used to create the online feature, titled "Your Hospital May Be Hazardous to Your Health."[11]

Falcone described the team as a "single organism; every step necessarily involved each part of the team: the reporters fact-checked the producers, who storyboarded the animations with the designers, who sketched out

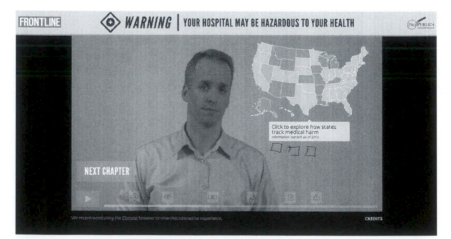

**FIGURE 9.2** "Your Hospital May Be Hazardous to Your Health," PBS Frontline, ProPublica, and Ocupop, 2013

the interactive segments with the developers, and so on. Artists and coders collaborated."

The weeklong deadline left the team with very little time and put considerable constraints on the project. "We just didn't have time for Big Design Up Front," said Falcone. The pre-production process of Big Design Up Front (BDUF, sometimes pronounced B-duff) is a workflow where the project's design is well thought out and is completed before the creation of content. Falcone described a frenetic vibe of scripting and re-scripting the idea for the main video right up to its filming, contributing to the lack of pre-production focus on design. "These tight quarters were the secret to the success of this project . . . this was the first time I really got to experience the power of real-time collaboration. Being able to size-up features as soon as they were proposed and explain alternative methods of conveying the same information . . . freed us to create features that might not have even been considered otherwise."

The project's shortcomings are particularly visible with the relationship between content and design. An effective news package is one where the design reinforces the editorial mission, rather than existing for some ancillary reason or to provide some visual attraction. "One of the greatest ways this project suffers is that the design and the content are so dependent on each other . . . we have not yet trained ourselves to design from the inside-out," Falcone wrote.

Falcone sees a future digital storytelling environment where these kinds of packages are not merely stories but represent an entirely new way of information delivery. "To borrow the parlance of 1998, this could be a 'portal' into an ever-expanding network of interactives, with continuous updates and additions. The tools we have now, however, are built for self-contained articles and hierarchical structures; the frameworks we need to build will draw as much from Wikipedia as they do WordPress."

Falcone hopes that digital content producers can shift the current conversation away from gimmickry and "high production values," which he considers superficial, and instead focus their attention on recognizing the value of reduction. Falcone closes the article with this hope: "We'll instead realize that these are where journalistic storytelling finally embraced the nature of the web and replaced the flat with the fractal."

## ▶ NOTES

1  "EidosMedia—Redesigning the Newsroom." EidosMedia.com. October 10, 2014. Accessed January 23, 2015. http://www.eidosmedia.com/2014/10/02/customers/redesigning-the-newsroom_vsdT7SvkUvmolIbZcE2BiM.html

2  Jackson, Jasper. "Changing Newsroom Culture at the FT, La Stampa, Trinity Mirror, Le Soi." The Media Briefing. October 13, 2014. Accessed January 23, 2015. http://www.themediabriefing.com/article/the-ft-la-stampa-trinity-mirror-and-le-soir-on-changing-newsroom-culture

3  Ward, Mike. "Online Story Construction." In Ward, *Journalism Online*, 123. Oxford: Focal Press, 2002.

4  Grabowicz, Paul. "Picking the Right Media for a Story." KDMC Berkeley. September 2012. Accessed January 2015. http://multimedia.journalism.berkeley.edu/tutorials/picking-right-media-reporting-story/

5  Cartier-Bresson, Henri, and Henri Matisse. *The Decisive Moment*. New York: Simon and Schuster and Éditions Verve of Paris, 1952.

6  Stevens, Jane. "Multimedia Storytelling: Learn the Secrets from Experts - Digital Media Training." Digital Media Training. September 27, 2014. Accessed March 23, 2015. http://multimedia.journalism.berkeley.edu/tutorials/starttofinish/

7  Cole, Jarrard, interview with the authors, July 2014.

8  Tharp, Twyla, and Mark Reiter. *The Creative Habit: Learn It and Use It for Life: A Practical Guide*. New York: Simon & Schuster, 2003.

9  Kleon, Austin. *Steal Like an Artist: 10 Things Nobody Told You about Being Creative*. New York: Workman, 2012.

10  Jacky Myint, interview with the authors, July 30, 2013.

11  Falcone, Justin. "How We Made It: Your Hospital May Be Hazardous to Your Health." Source: An OpenNews Project. June 13, 2013. Accessed January 2015. https://source.opennews.org/en-US/articles/how-we-made-hazardous-hospitals/

# 10

# Stepping Back, Moving Forward

After more than a year of study, dozens of interviews, and analysis of hundreds of online news packages, we share some conclusions about how technology has shaped news. This book gave us an opportunity to examine the evolution of digital news packages, from the advent of personal computers in the 1980s to today's more modern browsers and mobile devices.

Looking at the early days of digital news, it's hard to not agree that journalism industry was more innovative than it is often given credit for. Failed experiments like Mercury Center, Knight Ridder's Viewtron, Nando.net, the *Sun Sentinel*'s "Edge," and other early R&D efforts to put news on tablets proved that much of the innovation happening in the news industry was simply before its time. These suffered from what Harvard business professor Clayton Christensen calls the "innovator's dilemma" in a 1997 book of the same name.[1] Without a large user base and a solid economic business model, early forays into digital news were losing efforts economically. As Christensen points out, large business firms often fare poorly in the face of disruptive technology—and this has been happening for hundreds of years. Early adopters are often the biggest risk takers in any new technology, as strategies for implementing new business models are untested. Typically, new technologies begin with small markets far before they appear to warrant significant investment. Those organizations that do invest often create divisions within their legacy organization, and sometimes even compete with themselves. The early efforts to go digital in the news industry were also exacerbated by the dot-com bust of the late 1990s.

These failures were not without a silver lining. Despite the economic losses of digital initiatives of the 1990s, the early forays were enormously informative for the evolution and development of online storytelling, a form that after nearly 30 years is still in many ways in its nascent stages. Nowhere is this clearer than how news packages evolved from the early crude web pages of the mid-1990s, to the dynamic display of interactive stories with the advent of Adobe Flash, and then to the immersive fullscreen multifaceted stories using a mix of HTML5 and JavaScript seen today. Changes in technology over the last two decades have had dramatic effects on the presentation of news. The rise of smartphones and tablets resulted in a complete depreciation of Flash as a technology for producing news and likewise changed the way multimedia stories were packaged on the Web. Many multimedia journalists who had invested heavily in learning Flash had to migrate their knowledge base. It wasn't just about learning a new tool but about creating an entirely new set of design rules for telling stories.

Every time a new technology platform emerges, the formulas for telling stories in that particular medium resets, and a whole new language needs to be invented. This happened recently with the proliferation of mobile devices. Mobile devices had a number of characteristics that affected the presentation of news, including a smaller screen size, a touch-screen interface, geo-locational awareness, and other sensors such as those detecting its orientation. These elements had deep impacts on story design and created new dilemmas for content designers, who had to completely rewrite the rules of content display.

What can be even more concerning is that these types of disruptions are likely to happen again. The technological evolution is unstoppable. While many journalists are busy catching up to current mobile platforms, an entirely new breed of devices are starting to emerge, such as "wearables," which include devices like glasses and watches. In March 2014, Facebook spent $2 billion to buy a company called Oculus Rift, which makes virtual reality technology. In a statement on the purchase, Facebook CEO Mark Zuckerberg said, "This is really a new communication platform. By feeling truly present, you can share unbounded spaces and experiences with the people in your life. Imagine sharing not just moments with your friends online, but entire experiences and adventures."[2]

Throughout 2015, a growing number of Internet-connected devices in the home, dubbed "The Internet of Things," are offering additional platforms for delivering news.[3] A new product announced at the time of writing this book called the Amazon Echo presents a new category of device.[4] It's a small cylindrical product that is placed in the home and is always listening for voice commands. It is able to respond to virtually any query, answering questions relating to the weather and unit conversions, or it can be commanded to perform tasks like playing music. Similar listening devices are showing up in cars, on phones, and in other home appliances. Everything from a wall clock to a toaster oven may present opportunities for news delivery. It will be necessary to understand the characteristics of emerging technologies and how consumers interface with them: What is their level of attention? What media forms can be presented on these devices? What are the opportunities for interaction or even contributions from consumers? Each of these questions can influence story design within a device. It's easy to jump headfirst into repurposing existing stories for new platforms without giving ample consideration of how best to adapt them.

Changes in technology also mean new roles for journalists in newsrooms. Web developers, back-end programmers, social media outreach editors, graphic designers, and other visual journalists have become central to story production. Existing roles are also changing. In newspaper environments, photojournalists' work—which often resulted in only a few pictures being run complementary to a text article—began to be reshaped in the form of online slideshows with audio narration or Web videos. In some newsrooms, this rebranding resulted in titles like "multimedia reporter" or the more contemporary "visual journalist." At the *San Jose Mercury News*, Dai Sugano once held the title photojournalist, but he is now senior multimedia editor, and his role encompasses shooting photos as well as producing videos, slideshows, and other interactive presentations. Jennifer Daniel of the *New York Times* designs graphic illustrations, data visualizations, and interactive features and uses the title visual journalist, which she prefers. Before joining the *Times*, she was a graphics director for *Bloomberg Businessweek*, designing page layouts and other graphics. The transition of her title, she says, better reflects her role in the newsroom, which often requires her to create interactive graphics, research data-intensive stories, or design news packages.[5] News production workflows, particularly on in-depth packages, are more team efforts now.

## ▶ CONCLUDING THE TAXONOMY OF NEWS PACKAGES

The idea for this book was fueled by a series of events that really began with the publication of "Snow Fall" by the *New York Times*. During this time, numerous news outlets began publishing large in-depth multimedia news packages with varying approaches to story design. It was our colleague, senior lecturer Paul Grabowicz, who took on the task to categorize these news packages in a systematic way in order to better understand their nature. He described these early efforts as a "taxonomy"—a fortuitous description, as it eventually steered our research to the very foundations of narrative storytelling and helped us to construct a model for how stories could be classified. This allowed us to quantify and chart stories on a triangle diagram. This process revealed how different news organizations approach online stories, as well as the types of subject matter that best lend themselves to different models of storytelling.

Some news organizations had stories congregate on specific areas of our diagram, partly as a result of their core medium. For example, online news packages from the National Film Board of Canada (NFB) fall almost entirely in our Immersive category because of the nature of the documentary film medium from which the organization descends. NFB stories are typically fullscreen audiovisual experiences that are cinematic and have characteristics that align with our Immersive category. Other news organizations had projects falling in every area of our grid. In these cases, storyforms were based more on the nature of the individual subject of a story rather than the type of news organization that developed it.

We found that story packages with a more linear narrative—a beginning, middle, and end—were most often placed in our Continuous category. These are packages that told a narrative story, usually about a person or an event. In these types of stories, multimedia tended to be integrated within the narrative, or if it was distracting, it often was presented as an optional element off to the side. This judgment is made based on the subject matter of the multimedia element—whether it fit within the context of the narrative—but it is also based on the cognitive load the multimedia presents. A still photograph or a simple graphic might serve the story well to break up the text and maintain a continuity through the story. *New York Times* assistant editor Steven Duenes described these multimedia elements as "connective tissue," elements that keep the narrative flowing from too much interruption. But if the learning curve of a particular graphic was too steep, or a video or photo required significant attention, it might be best left off to the side, where it becomes an optional element.

Topical stories, or informational stories, fell into our Comprehensive category, which tended to tackle broader subjects rather than single linear narratives. The nonlinear nature of Comprehensive stories allows a user to jump around and consume a story package in any order they wish. These are advantageous forms because they allow users to pick out the pieces that are most interesting to them. In many cases, the path through the story is also based on the knowledge the consumer already has on the subject matter. A Comprehensive package on global climate change, for example, might contain many facets that a consumer is already familiar with. Presenting these in a linear form constricts the user from bypassing elements they already know. Comprehensives also present opportunities for different media forms to fit together without the fear of distraction. A small quiz or game might make a good accompaniment to a larger narrative. The challenge with Comprehensive news packages is getting the users to consume as much as possible and to make sure no elements get lost in the collection. Organization and design of the story becomes a key aspect. In the case of "Planet Money Makes a T-shirt," subtle design conventions were used throughout the piece to hint to the user that additional media was right around the corner.

In Immersive packages, the user is put into an environment where they can explore. These types of packages are great for building empathy, since they transport a user into a space. Some of the challenges to this type of storytelling are that it still requires a specialized skill set and typically a larger team of producers. There are some software tools that are lowering the barrier to entry for creating certain types of experiences. The Klynt software tool allows people to create choose-your-own-adventure-style films, where people can make choices about what to see next. This is done relatively easily using a user-friendly software interface instead of writing code.

Another challenge with Immersive projects is keeping users stimulated throughout the experience. Because of the depth of many of these projects, it's easy for users to quickly get frustrated or bored if the pace is too slow.

Plenty of interactivity can help, allowing the user to participate as much as possible. Also, the learning curve of some Immersive projects can be steep, and users lose patience quickly while wading through lists of instructors or complex tasks. The projects that were most successful were intuitive and had more natural interfaces.

Our goal is that these ideas help inform producers about how the elements of both *story* and *design* are interconnected, specifically how visual layout, presentation, and structural display of a story package influences the meaning of the content. Still, the foundations of storytelling are eternal. A good news story informs, interests, and engages the audience. It adds value to their lives. In some cases it's in the form of a narrative that helps the consumer connect with the story through anecdote. Other times, a good story is informative and helps the consumer better understand the relevance or significance of a topic. In some cases, a good story helps to build empathy through a complete immersion of media, using sound, visuals, and interaction in meaningful ways. This taxonomy is a starting framework for classifying elements of storytelling. It's clear they will have to be extended and adapted to emerging technology platforms. A device like the Oculus Rift virtual reality headset may lend itself to a more Immersive experience, borrowing on techniques developed from interactive documentary filmmakers. Audio devices like Amazon Echo, Siri, and other listening technologies could offer narrative audio experiences similar to podcasts—or even interact with other devices like smartphones to create inventive new ways of telling stories. Smart watches may resemble the lean-forward interactions of PCs, creating an environment where users skim, picking out pieces of content. Alerts and breaking news might be most conducive to these forms. Because each of these devices—virtual reality headsets, wearables, and home audio devices—changes the way users interact with technology, it's difficult to predict their full implications or whether any of these will truly take off. At the Tribeca Film Interactive festival in 2013, Loc Dao, head of NFB Digital, said, "Computing has followed the interface. First the keyboard, then the mouse, then touch, and next is the real world."[6]

Although the foundations of storytelling persist through the ages, the format in which it is presented changes. The medium through which it is consumed changes. Just as mediums like cinema had to adapt in early days to new tools and sensory effects like lighting, acting, sound, and music, so the devices of the Internet are constantly changing and causing the mediums to adapt. Interaction, graphical design, and the physical interface all play critical parts of the storytelling process. Through all of our research, we found that one thing is clear: Story design matters.

## ▶ NOTES

1   Christensen, Clayton M. *The Innovator's Dilemma: When New Technologies Cause Great Firms to Fail.* Boston, MA: Harvard Business School Press, 1997.

2   Zuckerberg, Mark. "Announcement on Oculus VR." Facebook. March 25, 2014. Accessed January 2015. https://www.facebook.com/zuck/posts/10101319050523971

3   Ashton, Kevin. "That 'Internet of Things' Thing." *RFID Journal.* June 22, 2009. Accessed January 2015. http://www.rfidjournal.com/articles/view?4986

4   "Explore Amazon Echo." Amazon.com. Accessed January 21, 2015. http://www.amazon.com/oc/echo/

5   Daniel, Jennifer. "Creating Art for News." UC Berkeley New Media Lecture Series, October 16, 2014.

6   Dao, Loc. "NFB Interactive Since Bear 71." Talk, TFI Interactive from Tribeca Film Institute, New York City, April 20, 2013.

# Note on the Authors

Authors Jeremy Rue and Richard Koci Hernandez have been at the forefront of the visual storytelling revolution for the past decade. The authors' work and approaches were born from the test of real-world experience. Both have taken their talents and moved into higher education, where they continue to collaborate in developing visual storytelling for multiple platforms and share their expertise with the future generation of storytellers at the UC Berkeley Graduate School of Journalism.

# Index

*Note*: Page numbers with *f* indicate figures.